DATE DUE

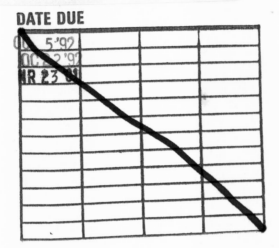

CRASHES AND PANICS:
THE LESSONS FROM HISTORY

Edited by
Eugene N. White
Rutgers University

Salomon Brothers Center
for the Study of
Financial Institutions

Leonard N. Stern
School of Business
New York University

DOW JONES-IRWIN
Homewood, Illinois 60430

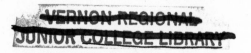

Project editor: Jean Roberts
Production manager: Ann Cassady
Jacket design: Sam Concialdi
Typeface: 11/13 Times Roman
Printer: The Maple-Vail Book Manufacturing Group

Library of Congress Cataloging–in–Publication Data

Crashes and panics : the lessons from history / edited by Eugene N.
White.
    p.   cm.
  Papers of a conference held at the Salomon Brothers Center for the
Study of Financial Institutions at New York University's Stern
School of Business in Oct., 1988.
  ISBN 1–55623–361–2
  1. Depressions—History—Congresses. 2. Business Cycles—History—
Congresses. I. White, Eugene Nelson, 1952– . II. Salomon
Brothers Center for the Study of Financial Institutions.
HB3716.C7 1990
338.5'42—dc20   90–31807
                                             CIP

1 2 3 4 5 6 7 8 9 0 M P 6 5 4 3 2 1 0 9

CONTENTS

PREFACE

The stock market crash of October 1987 was quite an unpredicted event. Shocked by the loss of over $1 trillion in financial assets, many observers falsely predicted a recession or depression would follow. Both our inability to anticipate the market crash and our wrong prediction of an economic downturn were depressing to financial economists in business, government and academia.

This large "event" seemed to me to involve a set of issues and unresolved problems that the Research Center I direct ought to investigate promptly with the aim to stimulate fresh research. The Salomon Brothers Center for the Study of Financial Institutions at New York University's Stern School of Business is dedicated to "support objective analysis of the ongoing revolution in financial institutions and markets and to serve as a primary locus of critical discussion in the public policy issues surrounding the rapid evolution of our financial system."

Accordingly I decided that the Center should commission a set of research papers from academia for presentation to a conference for critical discussion by business and government officers as well as academics, and, if all went well, publication in our series of Proceedings volumes. Things did go well as this book evidences.

But in the very beginning, there was a problem. I thought the best way to initiate the research was to revisit financial historical analysis of crashes to see if there were some lessons for understanding and handling the current variant. The conference was scheduled for the first anniversary of the Crash, October 19, 1988.

But the Stern School of Business, like most schools of business, lacked a resident financial-economic historian. Fortunately, we were able to borrow the services of Professor Eugene White, an economic historian from Rutgers University, to organize and coordinate the papers and proceedings, as well as to edit this volume.

A. W. Sametz, Director
Salomon Brothers Center for the
Study of Financial Institutions

INTRODUCTION

In the wake of the stock market crash of October 19, 1987, the public demanded an explanation. The breathtaking plunge in stock prices had brought huge losses to investors and left all Americans fearful for the economy's future. Protected by the New Deal's guardian institutions and regulations, the public had felt assured that the 1929 crash could not re-occur. When it did happen, the media, analysts, and a presidential commission found new trading strategies and financial instruments to be principally responsible. While these explanations met the need for readily identifiable culprits, they are far from satisfactory. These specific elements did not exist in 1929 and yet the collapse of 1987 seems to have followed a parallel course. Furthermore, 1929 and 1987 were not the only times asset markets experienced a dizzying boom followed by a resounding bust. In search of the underlying causes for the 1987 crash, historical evidence can play a very useful role by identifying asset bubbles' common characteristics.

The study of earlier crashes is also important because our investigation of the events of 1987 is strongly influenced by how the past has been interpreted. Simply mentioning the Tulipmania, the Mississippi Bubbles and the South Sea Bubble conjures up images of a public easily given to surges of irrational, overenthusiastic investment. However, this view of the seventeenth and eighteenth century bubbles is not the product of careful scholarly studies. It is, instead, derived primarily from Charles Mackay's 1841 book, *Extraordinary Popular Delusions and the Madness of Crowds*. Although it had been reprinted before, this book received a new lease on life when it appeared in print again in 1932 with an adulatory forward by Bernard Baruch who drew parallels to 1929.

The image of a volatile stock market accompanied by financial panics in the nineteenth century is as much a part of popular American lore as are the industrial Robber Barons. After the panic of 1907, Congress felt obliged to rein in banks and financial markets and passed the Federal Reserve Act, which aimed to stabilize the economy and financial markets. The crash of 1929 and the ensuing Great Depression revealed the ineffectiveness of this remedy and forcefully suggested the penalty for failing to control the "madness of crowds." Public anger, fueled by sensational congressional hearings produced the New Deal legislation, which imposed new regulations and reshaped financial markets and institutions. These changes seemed to solve the problem of the stock market. The consensus interpretation of 1929, emphasizing the gullibility and folly of the investing public, was provided by John Kenneth Galbraith's *The Great Crash 1929* (1954). The long respite between 1929 and 1987 suggested that a crash could never occur again, and a few scholars ventured to study these phenomena.

The conference held by the Salomon Brothers Center for the Study of Financial Institutions at New York University one year after the 1987 crash was aimed at correcting this deficiency. The studies produced for this conference by economists and economic historians provide valuable new evidence on the nature of these bubbles that challenge the orthodox interpretations. The discussants and conference participants had a unique opportunity to compare the case studies, identify the common characteristics, and consider the policy implications of these new interpretations.

Peter M. Garber's chapter on the tulipmania reveals that there is little, if any, evidence for the "madness of crowds" in the seventeenth century Netherlands. Employing newly discovered data, he shows that the outrageous prices recorded for tulip bulbs were for recently discovered rare varieties. The subsequent price decline was merely a consequence of the successful propagation of these bulbs. Like a good detective, he traces the origin of the story of the tulip "mania" back to a few contemporary pamphlets sponsored by the ruling elite. This group sought to quash the new financial markets that had developed around the tulip trade in favor of the established ones that they dominated.

Larry D. Neal unravels the extraordinarily complex financial deals surrounding the South Sea Bubble, using an array of new data that he has collected. According to Neal, the bubble arose out of the government's assignment of a debt conversion to the South Sea Company. The proposed conversion intended to exchange heterogeneous and difficult to trade annuities for more uniform modern securities. The increased liquidity created by this transaction provided a gain that was to be shared by the government, the debt-holding public, and the South Sea Company. However, under government pressure, the company promised more than it could deliver. Its machinations to carry out the conversion under this condition produced the bubble. Far from being the consequence of a foolish and overly optimistic public madly buying securities, the bubble arose because of the real, if imprecisely known, opportunities for gain.

Americans have always tended to see crashes as purely domestic events. Charles P. Kindleberger provides a corrective view of events in 1873, emphasizing the international scope of the boom and bust. He notes that it was not simply the securities markets which were affected but also other assets, notably land. This perspective suggests that the peculiarities of American institutions and markets that have been blamed for bubbles are not the key factors.

In the wake of 1987, there was extraordinary concern about the increased volatility of securities markets. Fearful of its effects, policy makers have considered many suggestions to limit price movements. These recommendations were made with little historical perspective on the problem. By collecting data on stocks, bonds, commercial paper, and interest rates back to 1834, Jack W. Wilson, Richard E. Sylla, and Charles P. Jones provide a much needed historical examination of the issue. Focusing on the period before the establishment of the Federal Reserve, when financial markets were unregulated and there was no central bank, they find rises in volatility did not regularly precede either stock market crashes or banking panics. Furthermore, the periods of greatest volatility, for the different financial assets they investigated, are far apart in time. Volatility seems to be much more of a consequence than a cause of upheavals in financial markets.

Eugene N. White examines the various explanations for the boom and bust of 1929 and finds many of them wanting. He links the steady rise in stock prices in the late 1920s to the changes in financial markets and the evolution of American industry. Nevertheless, in early 1928, the stock market began to rise more rapidly than can apparently be justified by dividend or earnings growth. Attempts by the Federal Reserve to slow the stock market did finally succeed but only at a cost of pushing the economy into a sharp recession. The parallels between 1929 and 1987 suggest that changes in the economy at large drove the market up, while the differences in Federal Reserve policy reveal why a depression did not immediately follow the second crash.

Statistical testing for bubbles in financial markets has largely ignored the great bull market of the 1920s. Gary J. Santoni and Gerald P. Dwyer, Jr., correct this omission by employing the econometric methods to determine whether fundamental changes in earnings and dividends or some mania-driven bubbles produced the bull markets of the 1920s and 1980s. They find no evidence to support the contention that the exuberant stock markets were the result of anything but fundamentals.

Mark Rubinstein and Leland Hayne survey the 1987 collapse and find that the explanations proposed by official investigations fail to be supported by the evidence. Their analysis of how the market panic unfolded offers new challenges to the standard models of financial markets and has important implications for regulation.

Taken together these essays provide a much needed historical background for interpreting the stock market crash of 1987. As our perceptions of the crash are strongly colored by the conventional views of earlier panics and crashes, any assessment of 1987 requires a careful reevaluation of these episodes. The research presented in this volume finds that past wisdom about the nature of these phenomena is based on scant evidence and often biased accounts that do not stand up to close scrutiny. Combining new data and analytical methods, these studies forge new interpretations that reshape our view of the past and provide a fresh perspective on 1987.

Eugene N. White

CONTRIBUTORS

Michael D. Bordo is Professor of Economics at Rutgers University. He is a leading authority on monetary history and has recently co-authored two books, *A Retrospective on the Classical Gold Standard* and *The Long-Run Behavior of the Velocity of Circulation.*

Forrest Capie is Professor of Economic History at the City University (London). He is author of many articles on British economic history and co-author of *A Monetary History of the U.K.*

Gerald P. Dwyer is Professor of Economics at the University of Houston. His research and publications focus on the banking system and its regulatory problems.

Frank Edwards is Professor at the Graduate School of Business at Columbia University. He is one of the leading authorities on financial regulation and has been at the Comptroller of the Currency and the Federal Reserve Board.

Barry J. Eichengreen is Professor of Economics at the University of California, Berkeley. He is the author of many articles on the economic history of the 1920s and the Great Depression in the United States and Europe.

Peter M. Garber is Professor of Economics at Brown University. He is a specialist in monetary and financial theory and has written extensively on speculative bubbles.

Gary Gorton is Assistant Professor of Finance at The Wharton School at the University of Pennsylvania. He has written numerous articles on the problems of the American banking system in the late nineteenth and early twentieth centuries.

Charles P. Jones is Professor of Finance at North Carolina State University. His writings include many articles on portfolio management and corporate finance and three textbooks.

Charles P. Kindleberger is Emeritus Professor of Economics at the Massachusetts Institute of Technology. His numerous books include *Manias, Panics and Crashes, The World in Depression,* and *A Financial History of Western Europe.*

Hayne Leland is Professor of Finance at the Haas School of Business at the University of California, Berkeley. He has written widely on issues of financial economics.

Merton H. Miller is a Professor at the Graduate School of Business at the University of Chicago. He is one of the founders of the field of modern corporate finance.

Frederic S. Mishkin is Professor at the Graduate School of Business Administration at Columbia University. He has written many influential theoretical and empirical articles on monetary economics.

Larry D. Neal is Professor of Economics at the University of Illinois-Urbana and editor of *Explorations in Economic History*. He is currently writing a history of early eighteenth century European finance.

Mark Rubinstein is Professor of Finance at the Haas School of Business at the University of California, Berkeley. He has written the seminal book on financial options and many articles on the current state and problems of financial markets.

Gary J. Santoni is Professor of Economics at Ball State University and recently was at the Federal Reserve Bank of St. Louis. His specialty is banking and financial markets.

Robert J. Shiller is Professor of Economics at Yale University. He is one of the leading specialists on volatility and the behavior of financial markets.

William Silber is Professor of Economics and Finance at the Stern School of Business, New York University. His many articles and books have investigated the structure of markets and financial innovation. He is a member of the New York Mercantile and Commodity Exchanges.

Richard D. Sylla is Professor of Economics at North Carolina State University. He is an authority on the history and development of American banking and capital markets.

Peter C. Warman is an economist at AT&T.

Eugene N. White is Associate Professor of Economics at Rutgers University. He has written numerous articles on the history of American banking and financial markets and a book, *The Regulation and Reform of American Banking 1900–1929*.

Jack W. Wilson is Head of the Division of University Studies and Associate Professor of Economics at North Carolina State University. He has written many articles in economics and finance and is currently re-searching the development of the stock and bond markets of the nineteenth century.

PART 1

BEFORE THE MODERN AGE: FLOWER BULBS AND LIFE ANNUITIES

CHAPTER 1

WHO PUT THE MANIA IN THE TULIPMANIA?

Peter M. Garber

Suppose that the Directors of the New York Stock Exchange and the Commissioners of the SEC possessed the power to write the only history of the Crash of 1987. Suppose also that in 2338 A.D. a conference is held to assess the previous year's financial collapse in the light of history. What lessons would its participants draw from the received historical record of the infamous Crash of 1987?

First, they would learn that a major cause of the Crash was the rapid growth of securities futures and options markets and the unsafe behavior of the participants in them. Such markets required relatively low margin levels and permitted extensive short selling, that is, the sale for future delivery of an item not currently in the hands of the seller. They would conclude that such conditions led to a channelling of speculative activity that overwhelmed the bounds of safety and propriety.

The participants in the conference of 2338 would readily adopt these conclusions as points of departure for understanding their own recent financial crisis because none of the numerous scholarly accounts of the Crash of 1987, written over the preceding 350 years, would have dissented from the definitive story. Although apparently independently researched, each study would refer, as good scholarly studies do, back along a chain of publications whose ultimate, unique source was the NYSE's history of the Crash.

No hint would arise that the promulgators of the received history might have had a self-serving interest in stifling speculative activity in futures markets and other markets in derivative securities nor in re-channelling speculation into the market that they controlled. The NYSE would claim that customers and traders of futures and options *gamble* in Chicago, while its participants *invest* in New York.[1]

The Dutch tulipmania of 1634-37 is the analogous event for our own historical retrospective on the Crash of 1987. Modern references to the episode depend on the brief description in Mackay (1852).[2] Beginning in 1634, non-professionals entered the tulip trade in such large numbers that prices of individual bulbs reached astounding levels. For example, a single Semper Augustus bulb was sold at the height of the speculation for 5500 guilders, a weight of gold now equal to $50,000 at $450/oz. In the final stage of the mania in 1636–7, large amounts of foreign funds entered the country, and people from all classes liquidated other assets to participate in the tulip market. The frenzy suddenly terminated in February 1637. Overnight, even rare bulbs could find no buyers at 10 percent of their previous prices, creating a long-term economic distress.[3]

The speculative excesses of the tulipmania have provided a ready historical benchmark to the financial press as an explanation of the 1987 Crash.[4] In addition, similar to our hypothetical NYSE history, our tradi-tional perceptions of the activities and follies of the tulipmania are traceable through a long chain of references to a few anonymous pamphlets published in 1637. The economic forces behind the pamphlets' publication were the members of the Dutch oligarchy who had conducted a long struggle to eliminate futures and options trading in order to channel capital into the "safer" markets which they controlled.

In this paper, I will demonstrate that the most famous features of the tulipmania are explainable as market fundamentals in the bulb markets. I will show that the tulipmania has, nevertheless, been used by modern students of financial markets and economics to motivate a non-market fundamentals approach to asset pricing. I will then trace the traditional version of the tulipmania back to its original sources and argue that the promulgators of these sources were indeed groups self-interested in stifling the development of innovative securities markets.

TULIP MARKET FUNDAMENTALS

As a bulb flower, the tulip can propagate either through seeds or through outgrowths or buds on the mother bulb. The flowers appear in April or May and last for about a week. In June, bulbs can be removed from their beds but must be replanted by September. To verify the delivery of a specific variety, spot trading in bulbs had to occur immediately after the flowering period, usually in June.

Tulips are subject to invasion by a mosaic virus whose effect, called "breaking," is to produce remarkable patterns on the flower. The pattern imposed on a particular flower cannot be reproduced through seed propagation; seeds will produce bulbs which yield a common flower, since they are unaffected by the virus. These bulbs may themselves eventually "break" at some unknown date but into a pattern which may not be remarkable. A specific pattern can be reproduced by cultivating the buds into new bulbs. The high market prices for tulips to which the traditional version of the tulip mania refers were prices for particularly admired broken bulbs.

The Bulb Market, 1634-37[5]

Market participants could make many types of deals. The rare, prized flowers were called "piece" goods, and particular bulbs were sold by their weight.[6] The weight standard was the "aas," about 1/20 of a gram. For example, if a Gouda of 57 azen (plural of aas) were sold for a given price, the sale contract would refer to a particular bulb planted at a given location. Once markets developed in common bulbs, they were sold in standardized units of 1,000 azen or by the pound (9,728 azen in Haarlem, 10,240 azen in Amsterdam). Purchase contracts for "pound" goods would not refer to particular bulbs.[7]

Formal futures markets developed in 1636 and were the primary focus of trading before February 1637. Earlier deals had employed written contracts entered into before a notary. Trading became extensive enough in the summer of 1636 that traders began meeting in numerous taverns in groups called "colleges" where trades were privately regulated by a few rules governing the method of bidding and fees.[8]

Typically, the buyer did not currently possess the cash to be delivered on the settlement date and the seller did not currently possess the bulb.

Neither party intended a delivery on the settlement date; only a payment of the difference between the contract and settlement price was expected. Thus, as a bet on the price of the bulbs on the settlement date, this market was not different in function from currently operating futures markets.[9] The operational differences were that the contracts were not continuously marked to market, required no margin deposits to guarantee compliance, and consisted of commitments of individuals rather than of an exchange so that a collapse would require the untangling of gross, rather than net, positions.[10]

Serious tulip fanciers who traded regularly in rare varieties refused to participate in the new speculative markets. Even after the collapse of the speculation, they continued to trade rare bulbs for "large amounts."[11]

During most of the period of the tulip speculation, high prices and recorded trading occurred only for the rare bulbs. Common bulbs (pound goods) were not objects of speculation until November, 1636.

THE PRICE EVIDENCE

In Figures 1 through 8, I depict the price data through February 1637 in guilders per bulb or guilders per aas that I have been able to reconstruct for various bulbs.[12] The last observations for each series (except for the Switsers) were recorded on February 5, 1637. For that date there are usually several price observations for each flower. The price lines connect to the weighted average of prices for February 5.

Posthumus claims a class difference existed between those who traded in piece goods and those trading in pound goods, even in the colleges. Members of the middle classes and capitalized workers such as the weavers disdained the pound goods and traded only in the rarer bulbs. Some bulbs that can be included among "piece" goods are Semper Augustus, Admirael Liefkens, Admirael van der Eyck, and Gouda. The common bulbs that were traded in pound lots or "pound" goods were Gheele ende Roote van Leyden, Groote Geplumiceerde, Oudenaerden, and Switsers.[13]

The pound goods were always less costly than the piece goods. In the last month of the speculation, however, their prices increased much more rapidly than did those of the piece goods, rising up to twenty-five-fold. Over a much longer period, the prices of the piece goods doubled or perhaps tripled.

FIGURE 1
Semper Augustus

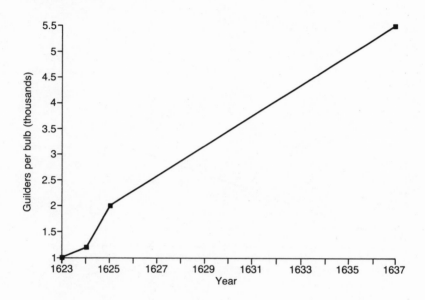

FIGURE 2
Admirael Van Der Eyck

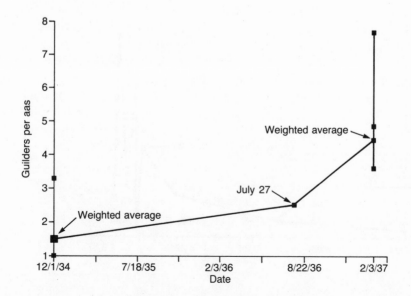

FIGURE 3
Admirael Liefkens

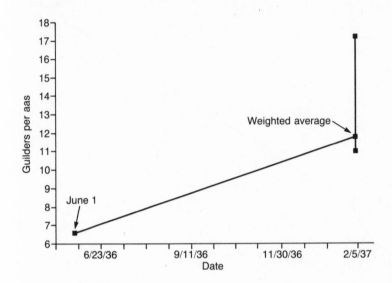

FIGURE 4
Gouda

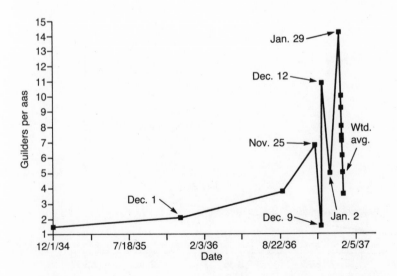

FIGURE 5
Switsers

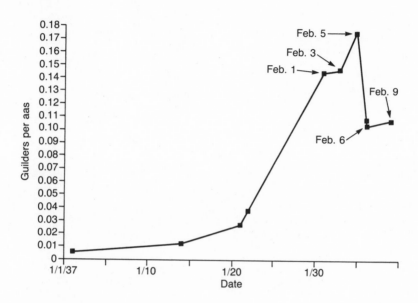

FIGURE 6
Groote Geplumiceerde

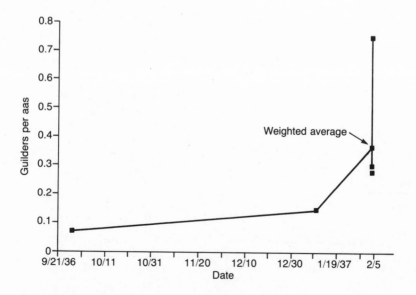

FIGURE 7
Gheele Ende Roote Van Leyden

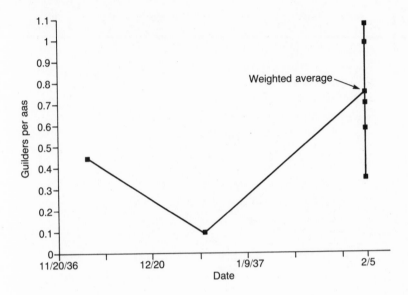

FIGURE 8
Oudenaerden

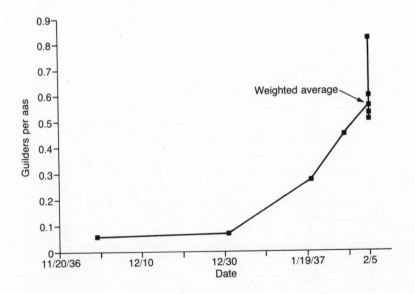

Post-Collapse Tulip Prices

The tulip speculation ended after the first week of February 1637 for unknown reasons. A general suspension of settlement occurred on contracts coming due. The disposition of contract settlement is murky, though Posthumus (pp. 446–447) states that many cities followed the example of Haarlem where in May 1638, the city council passed a regulation permitting buyers to terminate a contract on payment of 3.5 percent of the contract price. It is not clear whether many contracts were settled even at this price.[14]

With the end of large-scale bulb trading after February 1637, records of transaction prices virtually disappeared. Prices no longer were publicly recorded and only an occasional estate auction of an important florist would reveal the magnitude of prices.[15] Fortunately, van Damme (1976, pp. 109–113) reports prices from a post-collapse estate auction in 1643. In the estate auction of the bulb dealer J. van Damme (no relation), 42,013 guilders were raised through the sale of bulbs.[16] This amount reflects a bulb value comparable to the 68,553 guilders derived from the February 1637 estate auction from which we have received most of the tulipmania peak price data.

Individual bulbs could still command high prices six years after the collapse. Four bulbs whose prices were listed individually also appear among the bulbs traded in 1636–7: Witte Croonen, English Admiral, Admirael van Eyck, and General Rotgans (Rotgansen). Witte Croonen were pound goods and the others were piece goods. Table 1 presents a comparison of 1636, 1637, and 1642 or 1643 prices.

Eighteenth Century Tulip Prices

Though a few prices are available from the years immediately after the collapse, a gap of about 70 years arises in detailed tulip price data. High prices are available only for much later periods, and these are an order of magnitude lower than those quoted during the speculation. We shall see, however, that the pattern of price depreciation for the 18th century bulbs is similar to that for rare bulbs starting from the peak of the speculation.

In Table 2, I report prices for bulbs from January 2, 1637, February 5, 1637, 1722, and 1739. Even starting in January 1637, before the peak of the speculation, the price decline is remarkable. Prices fall to levels of 1, 0.5,

TABLE 1
Guilder prices of bulbs, 1637, 1642, and 1643[a]

Bulb	January 2, 1637	February 5, 1637	1642 or 1643	Annual Depreciation[b]
1. Witte Croonen (one-half pound)	64	1668	37.5	76%
2. English Admiral (bulb)		700	210	24%
3. Admirael van Eyck (bulb)		1345	220[c]	36%
4. General Rotgans (bulb)		805	138	35%

[a]Before the crash the prices were given by weight. Afterwards, prices were for a standard bulb. Prices have been adjusted, but they may not be exactly comparable.

[b]From February 1637 peak to 1642 or 1643.

[c]Adjusted downward 5 guilders to account for the English Admiral outgrowth.

0.1, or 0.005 percent of their January 1637 values in a century. Also noteworthy is the convergence of prices of all individually sold bulbs to a common value, regardless of the initial bulb values.

In Table 3, I have compiled the prices of bulbs common to the 1707 auction and either the 1722 or the 1739 price lists. While this was not a period known for a tulip speculation or crash, prices display the same pattern of decline. Bulbs appearing on an auction list were for recently developed rare varieties which commanded relatively high prices. By the time they appeared on a general catalogue, they had diffused sufficiently to become relatively common. Again, price declines repeat the pattern of the tulipmania bulbs. Indeed, the valuable bulbs of 1707 even converged approximately to the same prices as the valuable bulbs of 1637.

In the evolution of prices of newly developed, fashionable tulip bulbs, a pattern emerges. The first bulbs, unique or in small supply, carry high prices. With time, the price declines rapidly either because of rapid reproduction of the new variety or because of the increasing introduction of new varieties.

To apply this pattern to the post-collapse period, we treat as rare all 18th century bulbs selling for at least 100 guilders (Premier Noble, Aigle Noir, Roi de Fleurs, and Superintendant).[17] Prices for these bulbs declined at an average annual percentage rate of 28.5 percent. From Table 1, the

TABLE 2
Guilder prices of tulip bulbs, 1637, 1722, and 1739[a]

Bulb	January 2, 1637	February 5, 1637	1722	1739
1. Admirael de Man	18.0	209.0		.1
2. Gheele Croonen	0.41	20.5		.025[b]
3. Witte Croonen	2.2	57.0		.02[b]
4. Gheele ende Roote van Leyden	17.5	136.5	.1	.2
5. Switsers	1.0	30.0	.05	
6. Semper Augustus (7/1/25)	2000.0	6290.0		.1
7. Zomerschoon		480.0	.15	.15
8. Admirael van Enchuysen		4900.0	.2	
9. Fama		776.0	.03[b]	
10. Admirael van Hoorn		65.5	.1	
11. Admirael Liefkens		2968.0	.2	

[a]To construct this table I have assumed a standard bulb size of 175 azen. All sales by the bulb are assumed to be in the standard weight, and prices are adjusted proportionally from reported prices. When more than one bulb price is available on a given day, I report the average of adjusted prices.

[b]Sold in lots of 100 bulbs.

prices of the three costly bulbs of February 1637 (English Admiral, Admirael van Eyck, and General Rotgans) declined at an average annual rate of 32 percent from the peak of the speculation through 1642. Using the 18th century price depreciation rate as a benchmark also followed by expensive bulbs after the mania, observed prices were 16 percent lower in 1642 than they should have been. Even if the entire discrepancy occurred in February 1637, the crash for rare bulbs was not of extraordinary magnitude and did not greatly affect the normal time series pattern of rare bulb prices.

WHY WOULD BULB PRICES RISE?

If rare bulb prices normally tend to decline, why do the charts depict price increases prior to February 1637? Let us consider how a newly developed variety would be priced. Although it was unique, the new variety might not

TABLE 3
Guilder prices of tulip bulbs, 1707, 1722, and 1739

Bulb	1707	1722	1739	Annual Depreciation 1707-22	1722-39
1. Triomphe d'Europe	6.75	0.3	0.2		
2. Premier Noble	409.0		1.0	19%[a]	
3. Aigle Noir	110.0	0.75	0.3	33%	
4. Roi de Fleurs	251.0	10.0	0.1	22%	27%
5. Diamant	71.0	2.5	2.0	22%	
6. Superintendent		100.0	0.12		40%
7. Keyzer Kazel de VI		40.0	0.5		26%
8. Goude Zon, bontlof		15.0	10.0		2%
9. Roy de Mouritaine		15.0	2.0		12%
10. Triomphe Royal		10.0	1.0		14%

[a]1707–1739.

Sources: Krelage (1946) and Bradley (1728).

immediately be prized; and most new varieties were not considered particularly beautiful. Only with the passage of time would the status of a variety become clear; and as its renown increased, so would its price. This would explain the steady increase in the price of Semper Augustus. Similarly, a shift in fashion toward the appreciation of tulips in general over a shorter period would generate the rising prices of all the rare bulbs observed in the rest of the charts.

Pound Goods

The one-month price surge for common bulbs in January 1637, when prices rose up to twenty-five-fold, does appear bizarre. After February 9, 1637, the first price observation for a common bulb, the Witte Croonen, is available only in 1642. Table 1 presents the prices for one-half pound of this bulb. From February 1637 to 1642, the price depreciated at an annual rate of 76 percent. As an 18th century benchmark rate, I have used 17 percent per year, the average rate of depreciation of all bulbs priced between 10 and 71 guilders in Table 3. If Witte Croonen depreciated at this benchmark rate and the discrepancy occurred entirely in February 1637, the price must have collapsed in the crash to 5 percent of its peak price to have attained a 1642 price of 37.5 guilders. Witte Croonen prices rose by about 26 times in January 1637 and fell to one-twentieth of their peak value in early February. The 18th century benchmark pattern of price depreciation, however, would have justified a peak price of 84 guilders; so the January price is not out of line.

A precipitous price decline for common bulbs is confirmed by observations on Switsers in Figure 5. The peak price for this bulb of 0.17 guilders/aas was attained on February 5, the apparent peak of the market. Data from notarized contracts on February 6 and 9 indicate a sudden decline to 0.11 guilders/aas. This represents a substantial decline from prices in the first five days of February, but it still exceeds the prices attained on January 23 and is not of the same order of magnitude as the collapse indicated above for Witte Croonen. Thus, the bizarre behavior of cheap bulb prices seems a phenomenon of the last two weeks of the speculation. Price increases through mid-January, while rapid, were not as great as in the final two weeks, and there is no evidence that they were out of line.

The Bubonic Plague

External to the bulb market, one important event in the period 1634–37 may have driven the speculation. From 1635–37, the bubonic plague ravaged the Netherlands, killing 17,193 people in Amsterdam alone in 1636 (one-seventh of the population). It also caused 14,502 deaths in Leiden in 1635 (33 percent of the 1622 population); and it killed 14 percent of the population of Haarlem, the center of the tulip speculation, from August to November 1636.[18]

Van Damme (pp. 129–30) quotes C. de Koning, who states that the plague began in 1635 and forced the city authorities to take drastic health measures:

> These and other precautions could not prevent the progress of the outbreak that caused 5723 to die during August, September, October and November, 1636, so many that the number of graveyards was too small. So great was the misery and sorrow of citizens and inhabitants that the best description would only be a weak image of the great misery of those unhappy days, which is why we will end the story by thanking the almighty God for saving us from this great terror from which our forefathers suffered so much. In the midst of all this misery that made our city suffer, people were caught by a special fever,

by a particular anxiety to get rich in a very short period of time. The means to this were thought to be found in the tulip trade. This trade, so well known in the history of our country, and so well developed in our city should be taught to our fellow citizens as a proof of forefatherly folly.

Of the plague in Haarlem, van Damme notes that "one can presume that the tulip futures speculation reached its peak when the plague was worst." De Vries (1976, p. 226) claims that the plague outbreak of 1635–6 "perhaps by spreading a certain fatalism among the population kicked off the most frenzied episode of the mania."

The population of the Netherlands faced a high probability of imminent death from 1635–37, coincident with the tulip speculation, which declined thereafter. Although the plague outbreak may be a false clue, it is conceivable that a gambling binge tied to a drinking game and general carousing may have materialized as a response to the death threat. Lacking is an explanation of why this loss of morale took the form of a game centered around tulip speculation and why it did not recur in later plague outbreaks. Furthermore, other descriptions of the episode fail to mention the plague.

MODERN INVOCATIONS OF THE TULIPMANIA

Mackay's tulipmania description has strongly influenced the attitude of participants and observers of the financial markets. In an introduction to Mackay's book whose reprinting he had encouraged, Bernard Baruch emphasizes the importance of crowd psychology in all economic movements. Dreman (1977) stresses psychological forces in asset price determination, using the tulipmania as a prototype of market mania. Dreman constantly invokes the tulipmania as a reference point in discussions of succeeding major speculative collapses. He states (p. 52):

> If, for example, my neighbor tried to sell me a tulip bulb for $5,000, I'd simply laugh at him…. The tulip craze, like the manias we shall see shortly, created its own reality as it went along. It is ludicrous to pay as much for a flower as one pays for a house….[19]

Malkiel (1985) extensively cites Mackay in his chapter "The Madness of Crowds." In reference to other speculative episodes, he asks:

Why do such speculative crazes seem so isolated from the lessons of history? I have no apt answer to offer, but I am convinced that Bernard Baruch was correct in suggesting that a study of these events can help equip investors for survival. The consistent losers in the market, from my personal experience, are those who are unable to resist being swept up in some kind of tulip-bulb craze. (pp. 44–45)

The tulipmania made its first appearance in serious economics articles with the development of capital theory in the 1950s and the discovery of the potential existence of multiple, dynamically unstable asset price paths.[20] Samuelson (1957, 1967) presents the tulipmania metaphor and associates it with "the purely financial dream world of indefinite group self-fulfillment." (1967, p. 230) Students of Samuelson, in a flurry of research activity concerning the "Hahn problem," employ the tulipmania as an empirical motivation. Shell and Stiglitz (1967) state, "The instability of the Hahn model is suggestive of the economic forces operating during 'speculative booms' like the Tulip Bulb mania."[21]

The "sunspot" literature has revived references to tulips as a motivation for the line of research. For example, Azariadis (1981, p. 380) claims that, "The evidence on the influence of subjective factors is ample and dates back several centuries; the Dutch 'tulip mania,' the South Sea bubble in England, and the collapse of the Mississippi Company in France are three well-documented cases of speculative price movements which historians consider unwarranted by 'objective' conditions."[22]

In his presidential address to the American Finance Association, van Horne (1985), influenced by a series of anomalies that have cropped up in recent research on returns in financial markets, embraces the possibility of bubbles and manias. As an example, he refers explicitly to the tulipmania, where a "single bulb sold for many years' salary."

Shiller (1984, 1986) and Shiller and Pound (1986), also motivated by empirical anomalies, have promoted crowd behavior or fads as an explanation of asset price movements. Shiller (1986) argues that the standard and accurate view, until the last few decades, has been that asset markets are driven by capricious investors acting on the basis of fads and bubbles. As one example, he provides a quotation of one of Mackay's descriptions of the high prices paid for tulips during the mania.

BACKTRACKING THE LEGEND

It is useful to investigate from which sources Mackay constructed our traditional version of the speculation. Mackay provides few references, but at one point, he cites Beckmann (1846), from whom he actually plagiarized most of his description. Beckmann carefully cited his sources of information about the functioning of the markets and bulb sales prices. Beckmann read the dialogues between Gaergoedt and Waermondt (anonymous, 1637; hereafter denoted "G&W") and Munting's (1672, 1696) discussions of this episode. G&W is a series of three pamphlets in dialogue form providing details about the markets and numerous prices of various bulbs, taken mostly from the final day of the speculation. All the price data described in Munting can be found in the G&W dialogues, so Munting must have used G&W as a primary source. Thus, the current version of the tulipmania follows a chain of references originating in the G&W dialogues.

ESTABLISHMENT ATTITUDES TOWARD FUTURES MARKETS AND SHORT SELLING: THE SOURCE OF THE PAMPHLETS[23]

Schama (1987), in his history of the Dutch Golden Age, discusses the forces that led to the successful development of the Dutch economy in the 17th century. He structures his description around a perceived tension in the ruling oligarchy between "speculation" and safe "investment." The oligarchy and its magistrates sought a balance between "safe" and "unsafe" areas of economic activity, knowing that sustained economic well-being depended on secure enterprises while growth depended on a willingness to undertake risky new ventures.

Safe areas of economic and financial activity were those regulated by public authorities such as the City Chamber of Marine Insurance, the Wisselbank, and the trade in commodities through the Baltic Sea, which the Dutch effectively monopolized. Riskier though still vital areas of economic activity were the more distant trades in the hands of the Dutch East India Company and the Dutch West India Company. The East India Company was enormously successful, earning large profits for its shareholders. The West India Company, more an instrument in the military contest with Spain and Portugal, performed poorly.

Trading activity in company shares on the bourse was yet a riskier financial activity. Such trades involved spot transactions, stock options, and futures trades. Soon after active trading in East India Company shares was initiated in 1606, organized bear raids were conducted on share prices under the direction of the noted speculator Isaac Le Maire. These involved short sales of stock and the spreading of negative rumors about the affairs of the company.

Reaction to these practices led to an edict in 1610 which prohibited such manipulative activities. Most notably for our purposes, the edict banned "windhandel" or "trading in the wind," trading in shares not currently possessed by the seller. Sales for future delivery were permitted to people who actually owned shares. Future sales which were not obviously for such hedging purposes were prohibited. The authorities continually regarded futures trading as immoral gambling, and the edict was reiterated and extended with the renewal of war with Spain in 1621 and again in 1630 and most notably in 1636.

The authorities did not prosecute people for participating in proscribed futures contracts. They simply refused legal enforcement of such contracts. In a process known as "an appeal to Frederick" (the Stadholder or Prince), a buyer of a prohibited futures contract could repudiate it with the backing of the courts. Thus, the futures trades and short sales frowned upon by the authorities could continue as long as contracts could be privately enforced. A repudiation might lead to the exclusion of an established trader from the bourse and a consequent loss of trading profits in the future, so a buyer would not likely repudiate a moderate loss on a futures contract. If the loss were sufficient to bankrupt and impoverish a trader, he would be likely to repudiate.

To the authorities, the tulipmania represented an obviously unsafe financial speculation in which a legitimate business had suddenly degenerated into a bizarre form of gambling. The futures trading, the center of the activity, was clearly banned by the edicts; and in the end, the courts did not enforce deals made in the colleges, all of which were repudiated. It is incomprehensible that anyone involved in the fluctuating associations of the taverns would have entered such unenforceable agreements in the first place unless they were merely part of a game.

According to Schama, the speculation frightened the Dutch elite with a demonstration of how quickly a seemingly safe activity could convert itself into undisciplined gambling.

It was, in their view, money run amok, a kind of anarchy in which all the conventions and rules for virtuous and sober commercial conduct had been thrown to the wind. (p. 359)

The ruling elite implemented a propaganda drive against such behavior.

...the magistrates of the Dutch towns saw niceties of equity as less pressing than the need to de-intoxicate the tulip craze. ... But they still felt impelled to launch a didactic campaign in tracts, sermons, and prints against the folly, since its special wickedness had been leading the common people astray. To the humanist oligarchs, the tulip mania had violated all their most sacred tenets: moderation, prudence, discretion, right reason and reciprocity between effort and reward. (pp. 361–62)

The objectives of this campaign were to channel speculative proclivities into the safe areas of economic activity. By chance, the safe areas coincided with those controlled by the ruling elite. Among the numerous anti-speculative pamphlets launched during this reaction were the G&W dialogues.[24]

CONCLUSION

We have shown that the unexplainable part of the tulipmania was confined to a 2–3 week period in 1637 and to trades in the futures markets for common bulbs which established themselves in taverns in the winter of 1636–7. The bizarre activity was confined to common people who had little net worth but who, nevertheless, made the analog of "million dollar bets" with each other. Such bets were unenforceable in the courts. The image that we have of this event originates exclusively from groups opposed to it whose objective was to channel economic activity into zones which they controlled.

Since the now existing organized futures markets and their customers have their own protectors with equal access to public opinion, the image that we have of the Crash of 1987 is more equivocal. Yet, those organizations associated with the "safer" spot market in stocks pin much of the blame on the more "speculative" futures markets. Thus, the SEC (1988, p. xiii) report claims that the existence of particular trading strategies involving the futures markets accelerated and exacerbated the declines in prices.[25] Such strategies generate "negative market psychology," causing high spreads and price volatility and increased velocity and concentration of stock trading. This leads to greater "risks incurred by stock specialists" (p. xiv).

The SEC (1988) report proposes to equalize margins in futures markets to those in stock markets since "low margins contribute to increased speculative trading, in normal market conditions, [and] contributes to the illusion of almost unlimited liquidity" (p. xv). It recommends providing for physical settlement of stock in futures contracts to increase the risk that a participant must liquidate his position. It also proposes price limits and trading halts. Finally, it proposes short sale restrictions since "The absence of short sale restrictions in the derivative markets, coupled with the greater leverage of futures, presents the potential for greater speculative selling than could occur in the stock market." (p. xvi) From the historical perspective of the tulipmania, we are not surprised that all these restrictions would have the effect of channeling speculative activity into the "safer area" of the stock market.

APPENDIX
The 17th Century Tulip Price Data

Table 4 contains price data for various tulips. For each type of bulb, the observations are ordered by date; and they include the price paid, the weight in aas of the bulb, the price per aas, and the data source. I have gathered the data from different sources of uneven reliability.

Some sources are marked with numbers to indicate the numbering of notarized contracts reported by Posthumus in *Economisch-Historisch Jaarboek* (1927, 1934). These were carefully drawn contracts sworn before notaries; and they probably are the most reliable data, representing serious transactions which did not occur in the colleges. Also, many are dated before the peak of the speculation in January-February 1637. The delivery dates for the contracts are unclear. A few contract prices reported in Krelage (1946) are labelled as "Krelage-46-p482."

Next in order of reliability are the bulbs labelled "Children," which I have taken from *Economisch-Historisch Jaarboek* (1927). These bulbs are taken from a price list labelled "List of some tulips sold to the highest bidder on February 5, 1637, in the city of Alkmaar. These tulips were sold to the benefit of the children of Mr. Wouter Bartelmiesz at a total amount of Fl. 68,553." A facsimile of this list is also reproduced in Krelage (1946), p. 488. Again, the delivery date and terms of payment are not clear from the available information. Also, the February 5 date seems at odds with the collapse date, which G&W claim occurred on February 3. As recorded auction prices, however, the list represents some actual transactions.

Lower in order of reliability are the numerous prices reported in G&W. The third dialogue "Prijsen der Bloemen" presents a list of about 250 bulb prices and weights, but it does not report the dates of the sales. Fortunately, since a great deal of overlap appears between the G&W prices and the "Children" prices, the author of G&W must have had access to the "Children" list in constructing the G&W list. Thus, I used the February 5 date of the "Children" list to date the reported prices in the G&W list, including those G&W flowers not reported in the "Children" list. Also, finding many of the G&W flowers listed among verifiable transactions generates some confidence that the G&W author did not simply make up the prices reported in the third dialogue.

In discussing the rapidity of price movement during the speculation, G&W present the prices of twenty bulbs observed at two different times in the speculation, claiming the earlier prices were taken from 4 to 6 weeks prior to the later prices for each bulb. However, they do not indicate the dates on which the later transactions occurred. Fortunately, most of the later transactions for these bulbs are among the bulbs in the "Children" list or in the extensive G&W list described above. Since these bulbs are the only "time series" reported in G&W, it is important to include them. Thus, I have presumed that the later transaction for each bulb occurred on

February 5, 1637, and that the earlier transaction occurred on January 2, 1637, five weeks earlier. This explains why so many January 2-February 5 pairs appear in the list in Table 4 and in the Figures.

Finally, the list contains several transactions listed in Munting and in Krelage (1942) which I could not find among the above sources. Unfortunately, Krelage reports the price per aas involved in particular transactions and not the price and weight of the transacted bulb.

Eighteenth century prices come from several sources. Krelage (1946) reproduces tulip lists from auctions on May 17, 1707, in the Hague (p. 542) and on May 16, 1708, in Rotterdam (p. 541), on which a participant fortuitously annotated the final sales prices. While the 1707 auction list contains 84 different bulb names and that of 1708 contains 12, no bulb name of the hundreds commonly traded in 1637 appears in the lists. Krelage reproduces only the first page of the 1708 price list. The entire list was sold to British buyers with the breakup of Krelage's library.

Bradley (1728) reproduces the 1722 bulb catalogue of a Haarlem florist. The majority of the hundreds of bulbs in this catalogue were offered at prices of less than one guilder, and only one, Superintendant Roman, sold for 100 guilders. The list, however, does contain prices for 25 bulbs which appeared in the 1637 tulip speculation.

Krelage (1946) also reproduces a 1739 Haarlem price catalogue of hyacinth and tulip bulbs. Of its several hundred different bulbs, only six names match those of bulbs traded in 1637. Interestingly, it offers Semper Augustus bulbs for 0.1 guilders.

TABLE 4
Tulip prices, weights, dates, and sources

Date	Tulip	Price	Weight	Price/ Aas
01-Jun-36	Admirael Liefkens	6.6	1	6.6000
				11.796
05-Feb-37	Admirael Liefkens			11.8000
05-Feb-37	Admirael Liefkens	4400	400	11.0000
05-Feb-37	Admirael Liefkens	1015	59	17.2034
02-Jan-37	Admirael de Man	15	130	0.1154
02-Jan-37	Admirael de Man	90	1000	0.0900
				0.938
05-Feb-37	Admirael de Man	250	175	1.4286
05-Feb-37	Admirael de Man	800	1000	0.8000
05-Feb-37	Admirael de Man	175	130	1.3462
05-Feb-37	Admirael van Enchuysen	5400	215	25.1163
05-Feb-37	Admirael van Enchuysen			28.0000

TABLE 4—continued
Tulip prices, weights, dates, and sources

Date	Tulip	Price	Weight	Price/Aas
05-Feb-37	Admirael van Enchuysen	900	8	112.5000
05-Feb-37	Admirael van Hoorn	230	1000	0.2300
05-Feb-37	Admirael van Hoorn	200	440	0.4545
01-Dec-34	Admirael van der Eyck	80	80	1.0000
01-Dec-34	Admirael van der Eyck	66	20	3.3000
27-Jul-36	Admirael van der Eyck	2.5	1	2.5000
				4.487
05-Feb-37	Admirael van der Eyck			4.5000
05-Feb-37	Admirael van der Eyck	1620	446	3.6323
05-Feb-37	Admirael van der Eyck	1045	214	4.8832
05-Feb-37	Admirael van der Eyck	710	92	7.7174
01-Dec-36	Bleyenburch (Laeten)	350	4 tulips	
28-Dec-36	Bleyenburch (Laeten)	120	104	1.1538
05-Feb-37	Blijenburger (Vroege)			3.5000
05-Feb-37	Blijenburger (Vroege)	1300	443	2.9345
05-Feb-37	Blijenburger (Vroege)	900	171	5.2632
05-Feb-37	Bruyne Purper	2025	320	6.3281
05-Feb-37	Bruyne Purper			10.3000
05-Feb-37	Bruyne Purper	1100	50	22.0000
05-Feb-37	Bruyne Purper	1300	60	21.6667
10-Jul-12	Caers op de Candelaer	24		
02-Jan-37	Centen	40	1000	0.0400
15-Jan-37	Centen	72	530	0.1358
22-Jan-37	Centen	380	3000	0.1267
05-Feb-37	Centen	400	1000	0.4000
05-Feb-37	Centen	4300	10240	0.4199
02-Jan-37	Coorenaerts	60	1000	0.0600
22-Jan-37	Coorenaerts	220	1000	0.2200
				0.4760
05-Feb-37	Coorenaerts	550	1000	0.5500
05-Feb-37	Coorenaerts	4800	10240	0.4688
10-Jun-36	English Admiral	3	1	3.0000
05-Feb-37	English Admiral	700	25	28.0000
05-Feb-37	Fama	605	130	4.6538
05-Feb-37	Fama	700	158	4.4304
05-Feb-37	Fama	440	104	4.2308
02-Jan-37	Generalissimo	95	10	9.5000
05-Feb-37	Generalissimo	900	10	90.0000
02-Jan-37	Gheele Croonen	24	10240	0.0023
05-Feb-37	Gheele Croonen	1200	10240	0.1172
08-Dec-36	Gheele ende Roote van Leyden	260	578	0.4498
02-Jan-37	Gheele ende Roote van Leyden	46	515	0.0893

TABLE 4—continued
Tulip prices, weights, dates, and sources

Date	Tulip	Price	Weight	Price/Aas
02-Jan-37	Gheele ende Roote van Leyden	100	1000	0.1000
				0.7541
05-Feb-37	Gheele ende Roote van Leyden	700	1000	0.7000
05-Feb-37	Gheele ende Roote van Leyden	140	400	0.3500
05-Feb-37	Gheele ende Roote van Leyden	550	515	1.0680
05-Feb-37	Gheele ende Roote van Leyden			0.5800
05-Feb-37	Gheele ende Roote van Leyden	235	240	0.9792
12-Nov-36	Ghemarm. de Goyer	70	357	0.1961
04-Feb-37	Ghemarm. de Goyer	36	1 bulb	
05-Feb-37	Ghemarm. de Goyer	250	1000	0.2500
05-Feb-37	Gouda			7.5000
01-Dec-34	Gouda	45	30	1.5000
01-Dec-35	Gouda	2.1	1	2.1000
29-Aug-36	Gouda	3.75	1	3.7500
25-Nov-36	Gouda	446	66	6.7576
09-Dec-36	Gouda	600	400	1.5000
12-Dec-36	Gouda	520	48	10.8333
02-Jan-37	Gouda	20	4	5.0000
29-Jan-37	Gouda	100	7	14.2857
05-Feb-37	Gouda	3600	1000	3.6000
05-Feb-37	Gouda			5.0600
05-Feb-37	Gouda	1500	244	6.1475
05-Feb-37	Gouda	1330	187	7.1123
05-Feb-37	Gouda	1165	160	7.2813
05-Feb-37	Gouda	1165	156	7.4679
05-Feb-37	Gouda	1015	125	8.1200
05-Feb-37	Gouda	765	82	9.3293
05-Feb-37	Gouda	635	63	10.0794
05-Feb-37	Gouda	225	4	56.2500
29-Sep-36	Groote Geplumiceerde	140	2000	0.0700
12-Jan-37	Groote Geplumiceerde	300	2000	0.1500
				0.3667
05-Feb-37	Groote Geplumiceerde	300	400	0.7500
05-Feb-37	Groote Geplumiceerde	280	1000	0.2800
05-Feb-37	Groote Gepulmiceerde	300	1000	0.3000
15-Jan-37	Jan Gerritsz	230	288	0.7986
05-Feb-37	Jan Gerritsz	734	1000	0.7340
05-Feb-37	Jan Gerritsz	210	263	0.7985
05-Feb-37	Jan Gerritsz (Swijmend)	210	925	0.2270
05-Feb-37	Jan Gerritsz (Swijmend)	51	80	0.6375
05-Feb-37	Julius Caesar	1300	187	6.9519
18-Dec-35	Latour	27	16	1.6875

TABLE 4—continued
Tulip prices, weights, dates, and sources

Date	Tulip	Price	Weight	Price/ Aas
05-Feb-37	Latour	390	450	0.8667
16-Jan-37	Le Grand	90	122	0.7377
22-Jan-37	Le Grand	21	185	0.1135
24-Jan-37	Le Grand	480	1000	0.4800
				0.948
05-Feb-37	Le Grand	500	350	1.4286
05-Feb-37	Le Grand	780	1000	0.7800
24-Jan-37	Macx	12	400	0.0300
03-Feb-37	Macx	400	2000	0.2000
				0.3666
05-Feb-37	Macx	300	1000	0.3000
05-Feb-37	Macx	300	1000	0.3000
05-Feb-37	Macx	390	700	0.5571
06-Jan-37	Nieuwburger	125	425	0.2941
				0.497
05-Feb-37	Nieuwburger	500	1000	0.5000
05-Feb-37	Nieuwburger	390	495	0.7879
05-Feb-37	Nieuwburger	235	500	0.4700
05-Feb-37	Nieuwburger	430	1000	0.4300
05-Feb-37	Nieuwburger	180	495	0.3636
01-Dec-36	Oudenaerden	600	10240	0.0586
02-Jan-37	Oudenaerden	70	1000	0.0700
22-Jan-37	Oudenaerden	1430	5120	0.2793
30-Jan-37	Oudenaerden	2200	4864	0.4523
				0.563
05-Feb-37	Oudenaerden	600	1000	0.6000
05-Feb-37	Oudenaerden	370	450	0.8222
05-Feb-37	Oudenaerden	530	1000	0.5300
05-Feb-37	Oudenaerden	510	1000	0.5100
05-Feb-37	Oudenaerden	5700	10240	0.5566
17-May-33	Parragon Schilder	50	1 Bulb	
05-Feb-37	Parragon Schilder	1615	106	15.2358
16-Dec-36	Petter	172	360	0.4778
05-Feb-37	Petter	900	800	1.1250
05-Feb-37	Petter	730	1000	0.7300
05-Feb-37	Petter	705	1000	0.7050
05-Feb-37	Petter	730	1000	0.7300
05-Feb-37	Rotgans	805	1000	0.8050
05-Feb-37	Rotgans (Violette Gevla)	725	1000	0.7250
05-Feb-37	Rotgans (Violette Gevla)	375	500	0.7500
18-Dec-35	Saeyblom van Coningh	30	7.5	4.0000
05-Feb-37	Saeyblom van Coningh	320	220	1.4545
05-Feb-37	Saeyblom, beste	1000	1000	1.0000

TABLE 4—continued
Tulip prices, weights, dates, and sources

Date	Tulip	Price	Weight	Price/Aas
05-Feb-37	Schapesteyn	235	95	2.4737
05-Feb-37	Schapesteyn	375	246	1.5244
02-Jan-37	Scipio	800	1000	0.8000
12-Jan-37	Scipio	1500	1000	1.5000
				2.5183
05-Feb-37	Scipio	100	10	10.0000
05-Feb-37	Scipio	400	82	4.8780
05-Feb-37	Scipio	2250	1000	2.2500
01-Jul-23	Semper Augustus	1000	1 bulb	
01-Jul-24	Semper Augustus	1200	1 bulb	
01-Jul-25	Semper Augustus	2000	1 bulb	
05-Feb-37	Semper Augustus	5500	200	27.5000
02-Jan-37	Switsers	60	10240	0.0059
15-Jan-37	Switsers	120	9728	0.0123
22-Jan-37	Switsers	280	10240	0.0273
23-Jan-37	Switsers	385	10240	0.0376
01-Feb-37	Switsers	1400	9728	0.1439
03-Feb-37	Switsers	6000	40960	0.1465
05-Feb-37	Switsers	1800	10240	0.1758
06-Feb-37	Switsers	1100	10240	0.1074
06-Feb-37	Switsers	1060	10240	0.1035
09-Feb-37	Switsers	1100	10240	0.1074
02-Jan-37	Viceroy	3000	1000	3.0000
05-Feb-37				6.9470
05-Feb-37	Viceroy	4203	685	6.1358
05-Feb-37	Viceroy	3000	410	7.3171
05-Feb-37	Viceroy	2700	295	9.1525
05-Feb-37	Viceroy	6700	1000	6.7000
10-Jul-12	Vlaems	450	38912	0.0116
02-Jan-37	Witte Croonen	128	10240	0.0125
				0.3455
05-Feb-37	Witte Croonen	300	1000	0.3000
05-Feb-37	Witte Croonen	3600	10240	0.3516
05-Feb-37	Witte Croonen			0.2700
05-Feb-37	Zomerschoon	1010	368	2.7446

NOTES

1. I paraphrase this distinction from Schama (1987), p. 343.
2. Mackay's first edition appeared in 1841. The tulip diffused into Western Europe from Turkey only in the middle of the 16th century. The tulip was immediately accepted by the wealthy as a beautiful and rare flower, appropriate for the most stylish gardens. The market was for durable bulbs. The Dutch dominated the market for tulips, initiating the development of methods to create new flower varieties. The bulbs that commanded high prices produced unique, beautifully patterned flowers; common tulips were sold at much lower prices.
3. Mackay produced no evidence of post-collapse transactions prices of the rare bulbs.
4. After the October 19, 1987, stock market crash, *The Wall Street Journal* (December 11, 1987) evoked the tulipmania; and *The Economist* (October 24, 1987) explained the event as follows:

   > The crash suffered by the world's stock markets has provided a beginning and middle for a new chapter updating Charles Mackay's 1841 book *Extraordinary Popular Delusions and the Madness of Crowds* which chronicled Dutch tulip bulbs, the South Sea bubble.... It was the madness of crowds that sent the bull market ever upward.... It is mob psychology that has now sent investors so rapidly for the exits. (p. 75).

5. Most of this section is reconstructed from the discussions in Posthumus (1929) and Krelage (1942, 1946).
6. The heavier bulbs had more outgrowths and therefore represented a collection of future bulbs.
7. A purchase between September and June was necessarily a contract for future delivery. Also, markets materialized for the outgrowth of the rarer bulbs. The outgrowths could not be delivered immediately, as they had to attain some minimum size before they could be separated from the parent bulb to assure the viability of the new bulb. Hence, the contracts for outgrowths were also for future delivery.
8. Buyers were required to pay one-half stuiver (one stuiver equaled one-twentieth guilder) out of each contracted guilder to sellers up to a maximum of three guilders for each deal for "wine money." To the extent that a trader ran a balanced book over any length of time, these payments would cancel out.
9. All discussions of the tulipmania openly criticize the activity of buying or selling for future delivery without current possession of the commodity sold or an intention to effect delivery. They attack futures markets as a means of creating artificial risk and do not consider their role in marketing existing risks.

10. It is unclear which date was designated as the settlement date in the "college" contracts. No bulbs were delivered under the deals struck in the new futures markets in 1636–37 prior to the collapse because of the necessity of waiting until June to exhume the bulbs. It is also unclear how the settlement price was determined. Beckmann (p. 29) states that the settlement price was "determined by that at which most bargains were made," presumably at the time of expiration of a given contract. Again, this is the standard practice in current futures markets.

11. See Posthumus, p. 442.

12. I have developed much of the following information in greater detail in Garber (1989).

13. Other bulbs are more difficult to classify, encompassing different deals in which either odd weights or standard weights appear.

14. The 3.5 percent suggested settlement does not imply a fall in market prices of 96.5 percent from peak. Since all contracts were legally suspect, buyers had little incentive to settle at any price. Even a slight permanent price decline might have triggered massive defaults. See the penultimate section of this chapter, page 18.

15. This was a return to the pre–1634 situation. Prior to 1634, only a handful of prices are available from recorded sales contracts: a pair of bulbs from 1612 reported by Posthumus (1929) in his contract numbers 3 and 4; a 1625 sale of three bulbs; and a 1633 sale of a pair of bulbs, both reported in Posthumus (1934). Even the series in Figure 1 for the Semper Augustus is based on undocumented stories emanating from the historical authority Wassenaer in the 1620s, as reported by Solms-Laubach (1899, p. 77), among others.

16. This total was not broken down into individual bulb prices. For those few bulbs sold in which the estate held a fractional interest, however, the sales prices were reported (p. 111).

17. For example, Roi de Fleurs would be counted as rare when its price was 251 guilders in 1707. By 1722, its price was 10 guilders, so it would no longer be considered rare. The price declined between 1707 and 1722 by 96 percent and the average annual decline was 21.5 percent. The 21.5 percent annual decline was averaged with similarly computed declines for other rare bulbs to produce an overall average.

18. The plague had marched westward with the armies in Germany, starting in 1630. See Prinzing (1916) on the epidemics of the Thirty Years War. Plague also broke out from 1623–5, 1654–5, and 1663–4, killing in Amsterdam one-ninth, one-eighth, and one-sixth of the population, respectively. See Cooper (1970), p. 76. On life expectancy during the plague years, see Alter (1983).

19. New flower bulb varieties still can carry high prices. Information provided by officials at the Bloembollencentrum in Haarlem indicates that new varieties of "very special" tulip bulbs currently sell for about 5,000 guilders ($2,400 at 1987 exchange rates) per kilo. A small quantity of prototype lily bulbs recently was sold for one million guilders ($480,000 at 1987 exchange rates), an amount which would still buy a modest house in some places. Such bulbs, after rapid reproduction, would ultimately be marketed at relatively low prices.

20. Palgrave's *Dictionary* (1926, p. 182) includes a paragraph on tulips in its section on bubbles, citing Mackay.

21. Burmeister (1980, pp. 264–86) summarizes these models. In his study of manias, Kindelberger (1978) does not include the tulipmania among those episodes examined in detail because "Manias such as...the tulip mania of 1634 are too isolated and lack the characteristic monetary features that come with the spread of banking...." In his article on "bubbles" in *The New Palgrave Dictionary* (1987), however, he includes the tulipmania as one of the two most famous manias.

22. Under the topic "tulipmania" in *The New Palgrave Dictionary* (1987), Calvo does not refer to the 17th century Dutch speculative episode. He defines tulipmania as a situation in which asset prices do not behave in ways explainable by economic fundamentals. He develops examples of rational bubbles, both the explosive and "sunspot" varieties.

23. The discussion in this section is based on Schama (1987), pp. 323–71, and on the translation of de la Vega (1688), pp. xii–xix.

24. For a list of these pamphlets, see the references in Krelage (1942, 1946).

25. Actually, the report is the responsibility of the Market Regulation division and was not explicitly endorsed by the SEC.

REFERENCES

Alter, G. (1983). Plague and the Amsterdam annuitant: A new look at life annuities as a source for historical demography. *Population studies, 37,* 23–41

Azariadis, C. (1981). Self-fulfilling prophecies. *Journal of Economic Theory, 25,* 380–96.

Beckmann, J. (1846). *History of inventions, discoveries, and origins.* 4th ed., vol. 1. London: Harry G. Bohn.

Bradley, R. (1728). *Dictionarium botanicum: Or, a botanical dictionary for the use of the curious in husbandry and gardening.* London.

Braudel, F. (1979). *Civilization & capitalism, 15th–18th century.* Vol. 3, *The perspective of the world.* New York: Harper & Row.

Burmeister, E. (1980). *Capital theory and dynamics.* Cambridge: Cambridge University Press.

Cooper, P. (1970). *New Cambridge modern history.* Vol. IV, *The decline of Spain and the thirty years war.* Cambridge: Cambridge University Press.

de Vries, J. (1976). *The economy of Europe in an age of crises, 1600–1750.* Cambridge: Cambridge University Press.

Dreman, D. (1977). *Psychology and the stock market.* New York: Anacom.

Garber, P. (1989). Tulipmania. *Journal of Political Economy.* Forthcoming.

Kindleberger, C. (1978). *Manias, panics, and crashes.* New York: Basic Books.

Krelage, E. H. (1942). *Bloemenspeculatie in Nederland.* Amsterdam: P. N. van Kampen & Zoon.

Krelage, E. H. (1942). Drie Eeuwen Blembollenexport. *s'Gravenhage.* Vol. 2.

Liste van Eenige Tulpaen.... (1927). In *Economisch-Historisch Jaarboek,* pp. 96–99.

MacKay, C. (1852). *Extraordinary popular delusions and the madness of crowds.* London: Office of the National Illustrated Library, Vol. I (2nd ed.).

Malkiel, B. (1985). The madness of crowds. In *A random walk down Wall Street.* (4th ed.).

Munting, A. (1672). *Waare Oeffening der Planten.* Amsterdam.

Munting, A. (1696). *Naauwkeurige Beschryving der Aardgewassen.* Leyden.

Palgrave, R. H. (1926). *Dictionary of political economy.* London: Macmillan & Co.

Palgrave, R. H. (1987). *The new Palgrave dictionary of economics.* Edited by J. Eatwell, M. Milgate, and P. Newman. London: Macmillan & Co.

Penso de la Vega, J. (1688). *Confusion de Confusiones.* Amsterdam. English translation, Boston: Baker Library, 1957.

Posthumus, N. W. (1926, 1927, and 1934). Die Speculatie in Tulpen in de Jaren 1636–37. *Economisch-Historisch Jaarboek.*

Posthumus, N. W. (1929). The tulip mania in Holland in the years 1636 and 1637. *Journal of Economic and Business History, 1.*

Prinzing, F. (1916). *Epidemics resulting from wars*. Oxford: Clarendon Press.

Register den de Prijsen der Bloemen . . Derde Samenspraeck . . (1926). In *Econo-misch–Historisch Jaarboek,* reprint of Haarlem: Adriaen Roman.

Report of the Presidential task force on market mechanisms. (1988). Washington, D.C.: Government Printing Office.

Rich, E. E., and Wilson, C. H., eds. (1975). *The Cambridge economic history of Europe*. Vol. IV, *The economy of expanding Europe in the sixteenth and seventeenth centuries*. London: Cambridge University Press.

Rich, E. E., and Wilson, C. H., eds. (1977). *The Cambridge economic history of Europe*. Vol. V, *The economic organization of early modern Europe*. London: Cambridge University Press.

Samenspraeck Tusschen Waermondt ende Gaergoedt: Flora. (1637). In *Econo-misch–Historisch Jaarboek, XII,* (1926), reprint of Haarlem: Adriaen Roman.

Samuelson, P. A. (1957). Intertemporal price equilibrium: A prologue to the theory of speculation. *Weltwirtschaftliches Archiv, Band 79, Heft 2,* 181–219; reproduced in *The collected scientific papers of Paul A. Samuelson*. (1966). J. Stiglitz, ed. Cambridge: M.I.T. Press. Vol. 2.

Samuelson, P. A. (1967). Indeterminacy of development in a heterogeneous-capital model with constant saving propensity. In (K. Shell, ed.) *Essays on the theory of optimal economic growth*. Cambridge: M.I.T. Press.

Schama, S. (1987). *The embarrasment of riches*. New York: Alfred Knopf.

Shell, K., and Stiglitz, J. (1967). The allocation of investment in a dynamic economy. *Quarterly Journal of Economics, 81,* No. 4, 592–609.

Shiller, R. (1984). Stock prices and social dynamics. *Brooklings Papers,* No. 2, 457–498.

Shiller, R. (1986). *Fashions, fads and bubbles in financial markets*. Paper prepared for Conference on Takeovers and Contests for Corporate Control, February 1986.

Shiller, R. and Pound, J. (1986). Survey evidence on diffusion of interest among institutional investors. Cowles Foundation Discussion Paper No. 794.

Solms-Laubach, H. Graf (1899). *Weizen und Tulpe und deren Geschichte*. Leipzig.

Tweede Samenspraeck Tusschen Waermondt ende Gaergoedt. (1926). In *Economisch–Historisch Jaarboek,* reprint of Haarlem: Adriaen Roman.

U.S. Securities and Exchange Commission (1988). *The October 1987 market break*. Washington D.C.: Government Printing Office.

van Damme, A. (1976). *Aanteekeningen Betreffende de Geschiedenis der Bloembollen, Haarlem 1899–1903*. Leiden: Boerhaave Press.

van Horne, J. (1985). Of financial innovations and excesses. *Journal of Finance, 60,* No. 3.

CHAPTER 2

HOW THE SOUTH SEA BUBBLE WAS BLOWN UP AND BURST: A NEW LOOK AT OLD DATA

*Larry D. Neal**

We are now to enter upon the year 1720; a year remarkable beyond any other which can be pitched upon by historians for extraordinary and romantic projects, proposals, and undertakings, both private and national; ... and which, ... may serve for a perpetual memento to the legislators and ministers ... never to leave it in the power of any, hereafter, to hoodwink mankind into so shameful and baneful an imposition on the credulity of the people... (Adam Anderson, *Origins of Commerce,* v. 3, pp. 91–2.)

This magisterial pronouncement was made by Adam Anderson in his 1764 work on the age of mercantilism. His detailed description of the events of the South Sea Bubble has remained the authoritative source for all subsequent analysis of this fascinating episode at the dawn of financial capital-

*The author acknowledges with gratitude helpful comments and criticisms of earlier drafts by Jeremy Atack, P.G.M. Dickson, Robert Flood, Virginia France, Charles Kahn, Charles Kindleberger, and Eugene White, as well as by participants in seminars at the Cliometrics Conference at Miami University, Columbia University, University of Chicago, Harvard University, University of Illinois, Northwestern University, Vanderbilt University, and Yale University. Research support was provided by the University of Illinois Research Board, the Bureau of Economic and Business Research, and the National Science Foundation (SES 83-09211 and SES 85-20223).

ism. Anderson's theme is simply that an inner ring of the South Sea directors bribed the government into allowing them to hoodwink the holders of the existing government debt. This was the immediate, politically palatable, verdict made as well by Robert Walpole. By his leadership in the financial reconstruction that followed the collapse of the Bubble, Walpole became the longest ruling Prime Minister in British history. All subsequent historians have echoed his verdict with minor variations of emphasis upon the political intrigues of the time, general corruption in the government and the society, the peculiar nature of the South Sea Company, or the infections from international speculative fevers.[1]

The standard accounts emphasize a swindle of the stock buying public by a subset of the directors of the company, and widespread bribes to high officials, Court favorites, and members of Parliament that were in some cases quite large. It is not clear, however, that swindling and bribery were the primary elements in the bubble. While the Directors of the Company were deprived of all of their property, save the £5 to £10,000 capital necessary for an eighteenth century London gentleman, the Company did retain its charter, the government debt was exchanged for South Sea stock, and foreign investors who had been attracted to the London stock market during the Bubble continued to invest in English securities on a much larger scale after the end of the Bubble.

My interpretation, based upon analysis of the daily stock prices, exchange rates, and transfers and mortgages of Bank of England stock, emphasizes, by contrast, the technical aspects of the Bubble and the structural features of the securities and money markets of the time. In my interpretation, a good deal of the traditional evidence on the South Sea Bubble takes on a different meaning. It appears to be less a tale about the perpetual folly of mankind and more one about financial markets' difficulties in adjusting to an array of innovations.

After the Glorious Revolution of 1688, British government finances were gradually reorganized during the next twenty-five years, and the London capital market responded to these changes. A new financial system based upon large scale use of foreign bills of exchange, easily transferable shares of joint-stock corporations, and securely serviced long-term government debt grew up to accommodate the government's financial needs. But its inadequacies and innovational vigor led directly to the South Sea Bubble. What this financial system required was another financial instrument to complete the existing structure. But this instrument was only created in the aftermath of the bubble in the form of South Sea Annuities. These were the first perpetual, as opposed to term or life, annuities issued to individuals as government debt.

THE PIPE, THE BOWL, AND THE SOAP

The motivation for the South Sea scheme in England was essentially the same as for the Mississippi Bubble in France that began in 1719—to refinance the immense debts accumulated by the governments during the War of the Spanish Succession (1702–13).[2] This war increased the British national debt from £16.4 million to £53.7 million.[3] For the British, the new long-term debts were accumulated largely as the £10 million capital of the South Sea Company formed in 1711 and the £13.33 million of Long Annuities.[4]

The South Sea Company was proposed in 1710 by George Caswall, a London merchant, financier, and stock broker, and John Blunt, a London scrivener turned stock broker. These two individuals remained the leading forces in the Company until the collapse of the Bubble in October 1720. In 1710 they proposed to the new government of Robert Harley that the £9.47 million of outstanding short-term war debts, not funded by a specific tax, be converted into equity in a new joint-stock company. This was the South Sea Company which would enjoy the future profits anticipated from a monopoly on English trade to the Spanish Empire *and* the current cash flow on a perpetual annuity from the government paying £576,534 annually.[5] This was the same technique that underlay the founding of the Bank of England in 1694 and the New East India Company in 1698. The intention was to relieve the government's debt burden by substituting long-term debt at 6 percent for high interest short-term debt. The new Company could raise working capital on the security of its annuity from the government to exploit its monopoly privileges. At the same time, the public was able to exchange their short-term government debentures which were written in odd sums, deeply discounted, and difficult to transfer for fungible and easily transferred shares in the Company. These new shares were worth at least the annuity held by the Company and promised further gains if the Company made profits from its trade monopoly. The South Sea Company proved to be a success as a long-term funding operation of the government debt—97 percent of the short-term debt was subscribed into its stock by the end of

1711. However, the government quickly fell into arrears on its payment of the annuity to the Company so its stock did not reach par until October 1716.[6]

It is clear that from the start the value of the stock was driven by the expected value of the annuity payments. These were simply 6 percent on the nominal capital of the Company, which in turn paid a 6 percent dividend to its stockholders. But while the original short-term debt was selling at one-third discount, the shares of the South Sea Company gradually rose to a premium of one-third. The implied difference in yields to public holders of government debt, 9 percent to 4.5 percent, measures, in large part, the advantages of liquidity the South Sea Company shares provided to the public holders of government debt.

By contrast, the Company's trade with the Spanish Main was not successful and the Company failed to turn a profit on this monopoly. Trade did not begin until 1714 and was severely restricted in the years 1714–16 by Spanish officials in America. By mid-1716, direct negotiations with Spain had resolved most issues in favor of the Company, but hostilities soon arose between the English and Spanish governments. Although these culminated in a decisive English naval victory in the Battle of Cape Passero in late 1718, the South Sea Company's ships and assets were seized by Spain.[7] The Directors then turned their attention to further conversion of government debt, the one thing they could do well.

The second form of government debt incurred during the War of the Spanish Succession was annuities. These financial instruments had been introduced into British finance by William III in 1694. Purchased in any denomination desired, an annuity guaranteed a fixed payment in pounds sterling to the registered owner. These payments were made so long as the nominee was alive in the case of life annuities, or as long as the stated term of the annuity in the case of term annuities. The owner of either was given a Standing Order to be presented at the Exchequer to claim the semi-annual payments. In the case of life annuities, each time the owner, or his/her agent, generally one of the London goldsmiths, collected the payment, evidence had to be presented that the nominee was alive. This was usually a note from the parish priest or local Justice of the Peace. All the life annuities created during the War of the Grand Alliance (1688–97) had a reversionary clause that enabled annuitants to convert to a fixed term annuity upon payment of an additional lump sum. The costly procedure for life annuitants, which required them to produce semi-annual notes proving that the nominees were alive, led to the voluntary conversion to long-term annuities within a few years. Only term annuities were offered the public during the War of the Spanish Succession.

The Standing Orders for any annuity, life or term, at the Exchequer were assignable, but only in whole, not in part. This made them awkward to handle as legacies where there was more than one heir. Since they were in odd sums, they were not easily traded. Moreover, the assignments or transfers of the Standing Orders were not recorded by the Exchequer. The Exchequer maintained only the initial subscription ledgers and recorded the payments made against the Standing Orders presented at each payment period. So while transfers were possible, they were very cumbersome and it was expensive to prove title after a transfer or assignment had been made. As a result, transfers of Exchequer annuities were much fewer than those of shares in the joint stock companies, occurring probably at one-tenth the rate.[8]

After the Treaty of Utrecht in 1713, a substantial boom occurred in the London stock market which affected the shares of all the joint-stock corporations and raised the average price of a share from 100 to 120 percent of par by early 1717.[9] Consequently, the government expected it could reduce its debt service by buying up high-interest, but difficult to trade, debt with new issues of low-interest, readily marketable, debt. It began this operation with the Conversion Acts of 1717. This legislation permitted the conversion of several minor types of government obligations—the Lottery Loans of 1711–12 and the Bankers' Annuities of 1705 for redeemable annuities yielding 5 percent. These were managed by the Bank of England instead of the Exchequer. This meant transfers were recorded and the annuities could be assigned in part as well as in whole. Overall, the floating debt of Exchequer bills was reduced substantially, a Sinking Fund established for reducing the National Debt, and annual debt service reduced 13 percent.[10]

Walpole had also originally proposed to convert the Long Annuities with terms of 99 years issued during the War of the Spanish Succession into the new redeemables, but this part of his proposal was dropped after he was forced to resign from the government in April 1717.[11] The Long Annuities could not be redeemed without the consent of the holders and so they were known as the Irredeemables. Since these annuitants received nearly a 7 percent yield on the original capital lent, they needed a guarantee of substantial capital appreciation to compensate for the lower interest of 5 percent that the government was proposing to pay. But it is still not clear why this part of Walpole's conversion proposal was dropped. Much has been made of the high interest received by the annuitants, but more, it seems, should be made of the annuitants' relative inability to cash in on the capital gains other asset-holders were enjoying in the rising market of the time. The new 5 percent redeemable annuities managed by the Bank had risen four percent above par by the end of 1717 and their owners could readily cash in, as contrasted with the difficulties faced by the holders of Irredeemables. It may be that the London goldsmiths who held so many of the Standing Orders saw conversion as a loss of substantial fees they charged to the owners and were able to muster enough political force to block conversion. Or it may be that the supporters of the former Tory government were especially concentrated among the annuitants and resisted having part of their portfolios administered by Whig institutions. At any rate, the failure to convert the Irredeemables was a major piece of unfinished business which became more irksome as the stock market continued to advance. It even became a source of strategic weakness relative to France when the success of John Law's "System" for converting France's debt became apparent.

From its beginning, the South Sea Company was primarily an organization for the conversion of government debt. It resumed its activities in this arena after Walpole was removed from office. In 1719, it carried out a conversion of the Standing Orders from the 1710 Lottery into new stock issued by the Company. This was a simpler version, indeed a trial run, of the grandiose operations the Company was to attempt the following year. In early 1719, the Treasury proposed to the Company that payments of £135,000 annually on the annuities created by the Lottery Loan of 1710 should be capitalized at 11-1/2 years purchase and an equivalent £1,552,250 South Sea stock offered to the annuitants. The annuitants would gain only a small percentage (3.48 percent) over their original investment of £1.5 million. But this was a higher price than they could get on their annuities since the annuity payments had fallen into arrears. Moreover, they would gain a permanent asset for one due to expire in 23 and 3/4 years and they would be able to sell it more easily whenever it rose in value. In fact, South Sea stock was selling at 114 percent of par when the annuitants who converted received it in December 1719. Nearly 70 percent of the Lottery Loan was converted on these terms. By this voluntary conversion, the government reduced its annual payments of £94,330 on the Orders to

£54,240 and moreover it could now repurchase the debt it owed the South Sea Company whenever it chose. This gave the government the prospect of eventually retiring all its debt, which was seen as a great virtue at the time. But it also gave the government the power to undo the South Sea Company if its trade monopoly or financial influence was abused.

The South Sea Company benefited as well. It had contracted to increase its capital by £2.5 million if all the annuities were converted (by adding to the £1,552,500 of annuities converted, a sum of £168,750 for arrears, and a permanent loan to the government of £778,750). Since only 69 percent of the annuities were turned in, all these amounts were scaled down proportionately. The Company's capital was increased by £1.75 million, £1.08 million were given to the former annuitants along with another £117,912 to them for arrears of interest, and the Treasury was loaned £544,142. The latter sum was obtained by selling £520,000 of new stock at the current price of 114, realizing £592,800. So the Company was left with an immediate profit of £76,180.[12]

Everybody—proprietors, government, and Company—seems to have gained, and substantially, considering the modest amount of debt converted. If we compare the present value of the gains of all the participants using a 9 percent discount rate, the proprietors gained £324,527 (the excess of the market value of their South Sea stock over the old value of their annuities), the government saved £309,683 (the difference in present values of their annual payments), and the Company gained an increase in its minimum fundamental value (that derived solely from the annual payments received from the government) of £985,982, with an immediate gain of £76,180.

Part of the overall gain was due to a general rise in the securities market of the time, but it was principally achieved by the exchange of a more modern financial instrument—the perpetual, funded, and easily transferable share in a government chartered joint-stock company—for an instrument equally recent but encumbered by antiquated procedures for payment and transfer—the term annuity administered by the Exchequer. The improved liquidity of government debt provided a gain that was shared by all parties. Nevertheless, the great bulk of the annuities were left outstanding. So much larger opportunities for financial improvement were still present and the South Sea Company intended to exploit them in the plan it offered the government in late 1719.

BLOWING BUBBLES

The mechanics of the South Sea Company's new scheme were very similar to the 1719 conversion, only on a grander scale with much greater possibilities of profit. All the government's remaining debt except that owed to the Bank of England and to the East India Company, the other two chartered companies entrusted with administering the national debt, was to be subscribed into South Sea stock. Holders of the £16,546,202 of redeemable government stock handled by the Bank of England would have no choice but to subscribe or to be bought out by the government on worse terms. However, the annuitants holding £15,034,688 worth of Irredeemable annuities would have to be tempted to convert their securities. The South Sea Company was authorized to issue new stock up to the nominal par value of the Redeemable government debt they converted and whatever proportion of the Irredeemables they induced to convert.[13]

But, and this was the fatal attraction and duplicity of the scheme, the South Sea Company could set whatever conversion price they wished for the shares given to the debtholders in exchange for the old annuities. The higher the price the Company could charge without discouraging the Irredeemables from converting, the more of the new capital issue would be left to them to be used as they wished. If, for example, they set the conversion price of South Sea Stock at the current market price of 135, £20 million of debt could be converted by issuing only £14,814,815 of new stock, leaving £5,185,185 for other uses. In the initial proposal presented January 22, 1720, they envisaged enough profit to warrant paying the government up to an additional £1,500,000 on the Redeemables and another £1,578,752 if all the Irredeemables were turned in for the privilege of carrying out the scheme. The Bank of England on January 27 countered with an even more generous proposal. The South Sea Company in its response on February 1 raised its ante to over £7,500,000.[14] As events would later reveal, competition from the Bank forced the South Sea Company into promising too much. The House of Commons happily accepted the South Sea's proposal and it was enacted into law April 7, 1720.

The formal conversion operation began with the first subscription of stock on April 14. This issue of new stock was intended to raise some working capital for the Company and so only money payments were accepted. None of the annuities was converted in this operation. The intended amount of new stock was £2 million, but it was quickly oversubscribed—the first quantitative sign of the extent of public enthusiasm for the scheme based on the proven advantages of increased liquidity and the prospect of monopoly profits. It was also the first indication of the inadequacy of the Company's bookkeeping facilities for carrying out the conversion scheme. The amount of new stock issued was small relative to the total that would later be issued, but it was large enough to pay the bribes that had been promised to Members of Parliament and government officials and to buy up enough Redeemables to satisfy the government's requirement. Converting the Redeemables purchased into new equity would increase the value of the company so long as the new shares commanded a premium. This could be maintained if the the old shares still had a premium over par, and this was likely since the working capital obtained from the first subscription could be used to support the price of the existing stock. The new stock was not actually entered into the ledgers and available for transfer until December 1720, so only demand for the existing stock was increased, not the supply in the hands of the public. The price rose correspondingly, from 288 on April 13 to 335 by April 27.[15]

On April 28, the Company held the first registration of the Irredeemables. These were in two categories: the Long Annuities that had been issued for terms of 99 years and the Short Annuities issued for terms of 30 years. The government had agreed it would owe the Company 20 years of annuity payments or "purchase" on all the Longs it converted and 14 years' purchase on the Shorts. In its turn, the Company offered the Long annuitants 32 years' purchase and the Short annuitants 17 years' purchase, meaning it offered both classes better terms than it was getting from the government. It then apparently took away this concession by charging both classes of annuitants £375 for each £100 of new South Sea stock subscribed. On this day, however, shares in the existing South Sea stock were selling between 335 and 343, so the price charged the annuitants for their new South Sea stock would have been seen as reasonable if the current market price could be expected to rise further.[16] So it is not surprising that £9,454,744 of the Irredeemables, or 63 percent, were subscribed, nearly the same proportion as with the Lottery Loan conversion the year before. This was an overwhelming response and the Redeemables were still awaiting their deliverance!

A second "money subscription" was held the day after the first registration of annuities, April 29, and it was quickly over-subscribed even though the price per £100 share was now raised to £400 while the current price of original stock was only £340. The announced issue this time was only £1 million, but the amount actually issued came to £1.5 million. Public enthusiasm for the South Sea conversion was mounting. The amount of new capital at a minimum would be equal to the Redeemable debt outstanding plus the Irredeemables subscribed, or £25 million. The first two Money Subscriptions were together only £3,750,000, well below the eventual total of new stock that would be created. The terms of purchase for the Money Subscriptions were very generous and amounted to buying on margin albeit with fixed margin calls at regular intervals. Only one-tenth to one-fifth of the sale price was paid at the time of subscription and the remaining payments were stretched out to three years. These subscriptions would have been most attractive to speculators anticipating further rises in the price of South Sea stock and wanting to leverage their purchases as much as possible. But, since the total sold on margin at this time amounted to only slightly over 10 percent of the total capital that would be in existence at the end of the debt conversion, it does not seem plausible that the money subscriptions were the primary contrivance used to blow up the bubble. They were mainly a device for attracting speculators, but not the primary cause of the bubble itself.

Yet bubble there was. The price of South Sea stock continued to rise sharply while the price of the underlying annuities was stable. The bubble seems to have reached its peak just after the third money subscription on June 17. The highest price often quoted is 1050 found for June 24 in Freke's *Price of All Stocks*, but the more reliable source, Castaing's *Course of the Exchange*, gives a peak of 950 on July 1. Freke's price included the dividend which had been announced as 10 percent in stock,[17] while Castaing's price did not include it. But the jump is remarkable in both sources and we can have no doubt that a new element was operating in the market. The new factor is that the transfer books for existing South Sea stock were closed on June 23 to prepare and pay the Midsummer (June 29) dividend. So the price from June 24 until August 22 when the transfer books were re-opened is not the spot price as before, but rather the price "for the open[ing]" of the transfer books.

If we imagine that the spot price was unchanged throughout the summer, the difference between the time price (for delivery two months hence) and the spot price reflects either a very high implicit interest rate or a rising expected dividend rate. If the spot price was constant throughout this gives a truly enormous forward premium by any standards, modern or historical, which is difficult to accept. But the spot price may well have been constant, given that the next spot price on August 23 (740) was only slightly less than the last spot price on June 22 (765) and that the total sums to be converted were known with some precision after the registration of Irredeemables on April 28.[18] Moreover, the prices of the underlying annuities began to sag at this time (Figure 1) and the prices of Bank and East India stock also began to fall (Figures 3a and 3b). So it is likely that one of the most dramatic parts of the bubble, the final leap upwards after June 22, is in large part illusory and reflects not so much a buying mania as a desperate credit crunch in the London money market.

The foreign exchange rates of the period give us other evidence that a liquidity squeeze of unprecedented magnitude was pressing upon the bubble in the price of South Sea Company stock. The rates of London on Amsterdam plotted in Figure 2 indicate a credit crunch in London from the time of the Third Money Subscription on. Comparing the London-Amsterdam exchange rate and the graph of South Sea stock prices, it appears that an influx of foreign speculators came to England in March. Both the price of South Sea shares and the English pound appreciated throughout the spring of 1720. By the first half of May, both South Sea stock and the London-Amsterdam exchange rates leveled off. There then followed a marked decline in the pound sterling from 36s. 3d. in April 22 to 32s. 4d.[19] on November 8 and 11, the lowest level of the century. Note that the first major fall of the pound sterling occurs just before the Third Money Subscription and the pound reaches a very low level at that time. This dates the beginning of the credit crunch in the London market.

The prolonged fall of the pound is interrupted by several sudden appreciations of the pound including one at the time of the Third Money Subscription. The long decline was interrupted by at least five sharp recoveries. These appreciations, however, are always followed by an equally sudden depreciation back to the original exchange rate or lower. These shocks in eighteenth century exchange rates usually signaled a scramble for liquidity in the country whose currency appreciated. Since short-term liquid assets were few, a scramble for liquidity in London would focus on those bills of exchange drawn abroad for payment of pounds in London that had been presented to bill brokers but had not yet been paid off. The price of these bills would be driven up and this would appear as a rise in the exchange rate of the pound. But since the fundamental value of the pound had not changed, and in fact was falling at this time, the exchange rate

FIGURE 1
South Sea stock and annuities

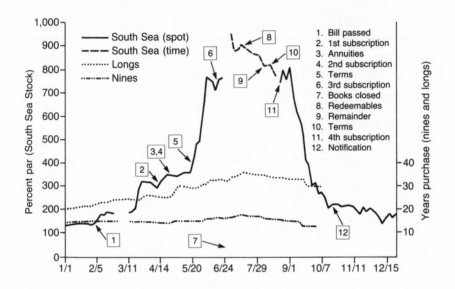

FIGURE 2
London–Amsterdam exchange rate

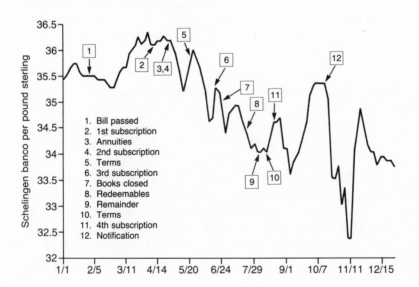

FIGURE 3A
Castaing's share prices for Bank, EIC, and SS

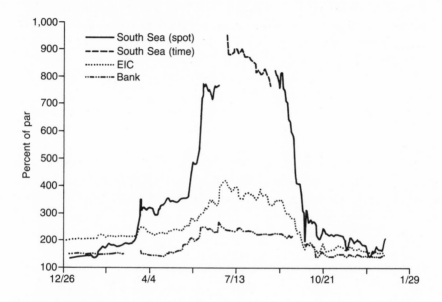

FIGURE 3B
Freke's share prices of Bank, EIC, and SS

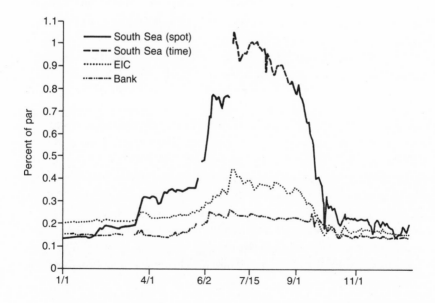

would revert to its equilibrium level as soon as letters from London had reached the merchant correspondents abroad and fresh bills had been drawn on them. The equilibrium level might not be the previous level given the credit manipulations of this period in France and England. Thanks to the sedate pace of business correspondence relative to the posting of exchange rates semi-weekly at the Royal Exchange in London, the time series for each currency in this period show characteristic blips when capital market disturbances occurred.[20]

The foreign exchanges thus provide us strong evidence that credit became increasingly tight at the peak of the South Sea bubble. This supports our thesis that the sharp increase in the forward price of South Sea stock on June 24 was due to a contraction of supply in the credit markets causing the forward premium to rise enormously. The alternative explanation requires continuing increases in the demand for South Sea stock, but this is inconsistent with the exchange rate evidence.

Before June 23, however, there undoubtedly were demand shifts for South Sea stock fueled, according to most accounts, by the increasing amounts the Company loaned on its stock. It was this injection of fresh funds into the stock market that apparently caused the bubble in South Sea stock that occurred in the preceding month of May, before the transfer books were closed and while prices were still based on spot transactions. The first lending on stock began April 21, or as soon as cash became available from the First Money Subscription on April 14. The terms were that for each £100 of stock deposited, £250 would be loaned, repayable in four months at 5 percent interest. A limit of £500,000 was set to be loaned, but nearly a million was actually loaned.[21] This, according to Scott, had a double-barreled effect. It withdrew some £400,000 of stock from the supply available to the market and it pumped another £1,000,000 of purchasing power into the demand for South Sea stock.[22] Dickson emphasizes the demand aspect more than the supply—the stock mortgaged was clearly unlikely to be sold in any event—but lacks specific evidence on stockjobbing by the South Sea directors or their agents. On May 19 the South Sea Company announced the next conversion of debt and the very favorable terms that were being given to the long-term and short-term Irredeemables registered on April 28. They continued to grant more loans to aid buyers of additional stock. These fresh loans were made at £400 for each £100 of shares. It was no doubt the demand for these loans that caused the Third Money Subscription of June 17 to be taken. This was the bubble mania at its peak. Five millions of stock were subscribed (but as in the first two subscriptions, not actually delivered) at 1,000 percent. Since ten percent was required as down payment, the Company took in exactly £5 million of cash. According to Anderson, of this sum, "the managers lent out in one day three millions, for supplying the stock market with cash."[23] By the end of June another £1,750,000 was loaned out, and by August 1st the total that had been loaned by the South Sea Company on its stock *and on its subscription receipts* amounted to over £11,200,000.[24]

It is important to note here that the South Sea Company was forbidden by its charter from engaging in banking activities, so these loans had to be financed somehow by the South Sea Company. Elias Turner, George Caswall, and Jacob Sawbridge took over the Sword Blade Company in 1712. The latter two, directors of the South Sea Company during the bubble, became a bank and the major stockbroking firm of the period, issuing its own notes which were accepted by the South Sea Company as cash payment. The Sword Blade Company allowed the South Sea Company's scheme to work by providing ready credit. When the Sword Blade Company failed on September 24 under the pressure of the Bank of England demanding redemption of its notes in specie or Bank of England notes, the South Sea scheme came to an end.

To recap, the bubble blowing to June 23 was driven primarily by the lending of money on the mortgage of existing stock, and partly by the Third Money Subscription. We can see the effects of these devices in Figure 3 which compares the prices of South Sea shares with those for East India Company and Bank of England shares. Each rose in three spurts—the second half of March, the second half of May, and during June. The first was due primarily to international speculators moving from Paris to London, the second to increased participation by Dutch investors and the beginning of loans by directors of the company on security of South Sea stock, while the third arose from an immense increase in loans on stock, subscription receipts, and verbal subscriptions.[25]

POPPING BUBBLES

There are two features in this account that need to be emphasized: (1) the market's expectation of the proportion of the Irredeemables that would be converted and (2) the market's expectation of the premium over par that

South Sea stock would command. My reinterpretation finds that most of the uncertainty about the market fundamental was removed early in the bubble because of the high proportion of the Irredeemables that were subscribed at the beginning and the favorable terms given to these annuitants. These fundamentals were markedly better than had been expected, and they impelled a rapidly growing number of investors to participate. The actions of the South Sea directors from the Third Money Subscription on can be interpreted as an effort to limit participation. But it appears that in mid-summer the actions of the General Court of the South Sea Company reflected more the urges of the mob than the machinations of Blunt, Caswall, and Sawbridge. The Third Money Subscription was a mistake, unlike the First and Second Subscriptions which were appropriate steps at the time and very conservative. The Third was a mistake primarily because the very high price demanded for the stock, which may have been intended to discourage further participation, backfired by draining £5 million from an already over-extended money market. Although these funds were lent out as soon as possible, all the proceeds failed to halt the liquidity scramble it had initiated. By this time, new investment opportunities had arisen to compete with the South Sea Company, the so-called "bubble companies" that began to be promoted in the London stock market. The most important of these were two marine insurance companies which received their charters in June and began to be traded on July 1. Now payments on the First and Second Subscriptions in South Sea stock, the equivalent of margin calls, fell due, and the liquidity squeeze was on.

The sharp rise and fall in Amsterdam rates in mid-August is a clear signal that the financial panic had begun. This was produced unintentionally by the directors of the South Sea Company, when they invoked a writ of *scire facias* on August 18 against the York Buildings Company and the New River Company. These were old chartered companies like the Sword Blade Company which had changed activities from building waterworks to underwriting insurance. They were attracting speculators away from the South Sea Company, which now charged them with violating the Bubble Act by engaging in insurance activities not specified in their charters. The Bubble Act, enacted in June, prohibited any chartered joint-stock company from engaging in activities outside those authorized in its original charter. This was ironic since the charter of the Sword Blade Company, long acting as banker for the South Sea Company, only authorized it to make sword blades. So it too was technically operating in violation of the Bubble Act.

The price of South Sea stock dropped sharply from the last half of August through the middle of October. On September 24 the Sword Blade Company suspended payments, intensifying the scramble for cash in a tight money market. This marks the final collapse of the South Sea Bubble.

What role was played by the Bank of England in all this? Most accounts simply say that the Bank was fortunate that its counterproposal to Parliament was not accepted on February 1 and that it withdrew in the nick of time from taking over a large part of South Sea stock in mid-September. It was not until 1723 that the Bank engrafted part of South Sea stock into its own capital on much more favorable terms. Yet, the Bank stock participated in the general stock market rise, even if the bubble in its price was very mild compared to that in South Sea stock (Figures 3a and 3b). The Bank also encouraged speculation by allowing its stockholders after May 10 to borrow on security of their shares. The terms were conservative, compared to those offered by the South Sea Company, but were quickly liberalized so that eventually a total of 962 mortgages were made, amounting to 29 percent of the Bank's transferable stock.[26]

Analyzing the pattern of mortgaged Bank stock indicates that the heaviest demanders of credit were stockbrokers. The leader far and away is Samuel Strode, with a total of £75,000 mortgaged. Another major borrower is Matthew Wymondesold, infamous as the broker for John Aislabie, Chancellor of the Exchequer, who bought heavily into South Sea stock at the outset of the bubble and took £20,000 of South Sea stock as late as the Third Subscription.[27] The striking thing about the large sums borrowed by the brokers, however, is that they were all repaid promptly upon the calls to put up 25 percent of the value of stock made by the Bank in late September, despite evidence that a large number of borrowers failed to respond in a timely fashion and had 25 percent of their stock sold off between the end of October and April.[28]

Legend, incorporated into the standard accounts of the South Sea bubble, has it that the knowledgeable and canny investors, meaning wealthy City men represented by the Bank of England's Directors and wealthy Dutch merchants, sold their South Sea stock at high prices and invested their gains in safe, staid Bank of England stock.[29] The transfer records of stock in the Bank of England, however, tell a different story. To analyze how the South Sea bubble was popped, it is most relevant to view the trading activities of the Directors of the Bank and the 163 individuals who gave an address in the Netherlands. For these two groups, I have calculated the number and value of their purchases and their sales on a daily basis. The trading activities of the Directors are summarized in Figure 4. The Directors took longer positions in the stock of the Bank immediately before the closing of the transfer books on March 8 and up to May 20 after the transfer books were re-opened on April 8. After that, it appears they reduced their holdings, perhaps to increase their purchases of South Sea stock or annuities. After the end of August, they reduced their holdings considerably, presumably to cover speculative losses in other assets. In sum, the Directors of the Bank stayed with their investment in Bank stock in the early stages of the South Sea bubble, abandoning it only in the most exciting period of the bubble, and then were forced to liquidate their holdings of Bank stock after August as the final collapse of South Sea prices and the other bubble companies occurred.

Legend also has it that the canny Dutch bought South Sea stock and sold out at the peak. This is consistent with their transactions of Bank stock. They bought when the price rose, sold during the price plateau of early summer, and then bought back heavily during the low prices of the autumn. In fact, the Dutch ended up with cumulated holdings exceeding those of the Directors (Figure 5). Does this mean as a group they were even smarter than

FIGURE 4
Bank directors' holdings of bank stock

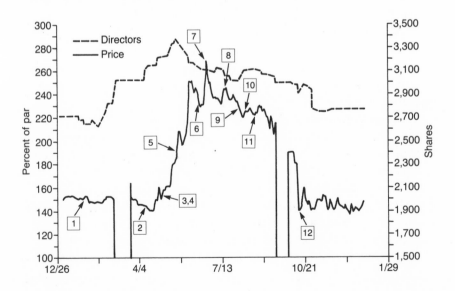

the Bank's Directors, or even the South Sea Directors, since they did not get fined for illegal participation in the South Sea fraud or in any of the dubious bubble companies?   Perhaps, but it seems more likely that they found themselves as a group locked into holding South Sea stock due to the paper losses they had sustained. The sales of Bank stock could have been to cover subscription calls on South Sea stock. Evidence for this comes from the fluctuations in the Amsterdam-London exchange rate that coincide with subscription payment dates on South Sea stock. The build-up of Bank stock may also have been in anticipation of the engrafting of South Sea stock onto the Bank's capital, a scheme suggested in September 1720 but not realized until 1723. The bulk of the Amsterdamers' purchases were in units of £1,000, exactly the amount required to vote in the semi-annual General Courts that would decide the role the Bank should play with respect to the South Sea Company and the remains of the government's debt conversion. By the end of November, the accumulated shares of the Dutch exceeded the total held by the Bank's Directors. This pattern is less consistent with cautious or canny behavior on the stock market than it is with investors feeling they are locked into a dubious investment and are determined to influence the eventual outcome by voting upon decisions now being made

FIGURE 5
Amsterdamers' holdings of bank stock

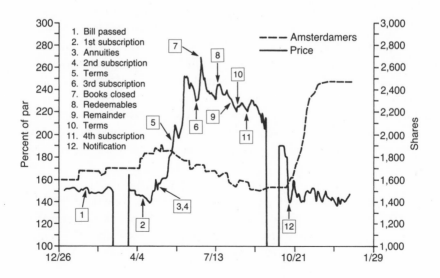

by the strongest institution emerging from the collapse—the Bank of England.

CLEANING UP

The minutes of the Court of Directors show that the Bank's relation with the South Sea Company was generally accommodating before the Bubble and most likely until the suspension of payments by the Sword Blade Company bank on September 24. There is no mention of the South Sea Company as such in the year 1720 until the minutes of the emergency meeting of September 24. The Bank was then taking in payments for subscribing £3,775,000 of new stock that would be used to buy up part of the South Sea Company's stock. The General Court of the Bank became alarmed when notes it had taken in payment, drawn upon Turner and Caswall and Company, were not accepted when presented to the Sword Blade Company. There is a note written in the margin of the General Court's minutes, "Sword Blade Company don't pay"!

During the next week, the Bank's Directors took action on all fronts to confront the liquidity crisis caused by the failure of the South Sea Company's banking affiliate. They did this by accumulating their own resources, and in the process made the crisis worse. By November 10, the Bank had gained strength and the Directors made a bold move. They agreed to advance to the South Sea Company the deposit money remaining from their mid-September subscription, but the Governor, John Hanger, reported that he "did not think fit for the proposal to proceed further in that manner." By November 17 a formal offer to the South Sea Company was approved, which insisted upon much stiffer terms to the South Sea Directors. Part of the Bank's aggressiveness appears to have stemmed from large loans it had obtained in November through Andrew Pels and Sons in Amsterdam, the leading Dutch merchant bankers. Dutch influence was being exerted from the much larger presence of Dutch merchants or their attorneys in the General Court at this time.

The next two years were given over to extended negotiations between the Bank and the South Sea Company. It was not until the end of 1722 that the new set of Directors of the South Sea Company could bring themselves to acknowledge the control now being exercised by the Bank. The Bank's capital was increased by £3,409,000 while that of the South Sea Company was further reduced by £4 million. The final step in reconstruction was to split the £32 million of capital stock in half in Midsummer 1723. One-half remained the trading stock of the Company, but the other half became fixed interest stock, called the "South Sea Annuities." These were, in fact, perpetual annuities and were greatly favored by conservative Dutch investors over the next quarter century. This was the final financial innovation to emerge, and it completed a structure of marketable, liquid financial instruments for the British government that proved its worth in each war for the next two centuries. Henceforth, the Exchequer, Army, and Navy could issue bills in times of emergency. These could then be retired from the proceeds of selling new issues of perpetual annuities, which could be retired at the government's discretion or left in circulation. The Bank of England created its first perpetual annuities in the Three Per Cents of 1726, but these were still irredeemable. The Bank followed up by issues of redeemable, perpetual, three percent annuities in 1727, 1731, 1742, 1743, 1744, 1745, 1750, and 1751. The latter issues were the basis for the most popular government security of the next 150 years when they were combined into the Three Per Cent Consol by the Consolidating Act of 1751.

CONCLUSION

The South Sea Bubble should be viewed not simply as a wild mania or as a massive swindle. These played a role, but the driving force in the bubble was the technical problem of converting government war debts that were predominantly short-term, high-interest, and difficult to trade into easy-to-exchange, low-interest, long-term securities. All parties—the government, the public, and the South Sea Company—could gain from such a conversion by sharing the benefits of increased liquidity. Earlier conversions had been successful, but the bubble was created because the South Sea Company overreached itself and promised more than it could deliver to all the interested parties. Part of the rise in share prices was justified by the benefits of increased liquidity. However, the Company's machinations to meet its commitments could not succeed and provoked a financial crisis. This popped the bubble and delivered the Company into the hands of its archrival, the Bank of England.

NOTES

1. The standard accounts are Adam Anderson, *Origin of Commerce,* Vol. 3, 1st ed. (London, 1764); John Carswell, *The South Sea Bubble* (London: Cresset Press, 1960); P. G. M. Dickson, *The Financial Revolution in England: A Study in the Development of Public Credit, 1688-1756* (London: Macmillan, 1967); Viscount Erleigh, *The South Sea Bubble* (New York: G.P. Putnam's Sons, 1933); William Robert Scott, *The Constitution and Finance of English, Scottish and Irish Joint-Stock Companies to 1720,* 3 vols. (Cambridge: Cambridge University Press, 1910); and John G. Sperling, *The South Sea Company: An Historical Essay and Bibliographical Finding List* (Boston: Harvard Graduate School of Business Administration, 1962).
2. Dickson, pp. 91–2. Cf. Earl F. Hamilton, "Origin and Growth of the National Debt in Western Europe," *American Economics Review, 37* (May 1947) 118–30.
3. Hamilton, p. 127.
4. These required annual payments of £666,566 by the government until the end of the century. Evaluating the payments at 20 years' purchase gives the capital sum of £13.33 million.
5. This annuity from the government yielded 6.09 percent to the Company on its nominal capital of £9,471,324.
6. Sperling, pp. 1–3, 25.
7. Sperling, p. 24.
8. Dickson, pp. 457–67. Based on the sole remaining transfer books from the Exchequer for this period, those of Bankers' annuities created in 1705, only 4 percent of the nominal capital was transferred annually, compared to 44–50 percent of capital transferred for the Bank of England, the East India Company or the government stock of 1717 administered by the Bank in the same manner as its own stock. Dickson, p. 466.
9. Larry Neal, *The Rise of Financial Capitalism* (forthcoming), ch. 3.
10. Dickson, p. 87.
11. Dickson, p. 85.
12. This is derived by subtracting the £544,142 paid to the Treasury from the £592,800 realized from the sale of the £520,000 stock (£48,658) and then adding the value of the remaining £24,142 stock at 114 percent of par (£27,522). Dickson (p. 89) gives a figure of £242,240 for profit on the whole operation, but he includes in this £193,583 of claims the Company had against the government which they wrote off as part of their payment. This would be appropriate only if the Company had already written off their claims previously and now found a way to realize them.
13. There is an historiographic dispute on this point. My interpretation agrees with Scott's (Vol. III, p. 308) and Anderson's. Eli Heckscher, "A Note on South Sea

Finance," *Journal of Economics and Business History,* Vol. 3 (1931), however, asserted that Scott was mistaken and that the South Sea could increase its capital stock without limit. Dickson (p. 129, fn. 4) apparently agrees with Heckscher. Heckscher's argument was based on his reading of the authorizing statute, 6 George I, c. 4, section 48. This section allows the company to raise "any Sums" they may need by calls upon existing stockholders. This follows section 47 which states the penalty to be paid by the Company if they fail to take in long annuities and clearly refers to their recourse available to pay the penalty. This is not an issue of new capital stock but a call, or tax, to be levied on existing stock and was a feature also of the East India Company and the Bank of England. Section 30 of the Act clearly sets the limit on the new capital stock that can be issued. Section 58 goes further and specifies that the government may cancel the augmented capital from section 30 in whole or in part after June 24, 1727. (*The Statutes at Large from the Fifth to the Ninth Year of King George I,* Vol. xiv, Cambridge: Joseph Bentham, 1765.)

14. The clearest description of the proposals is by Sperling, p. 28.
15. These figures are in percent of par value or, in the convention of the time, as the pounds sterling required to purchase £100 par value of stock. Stock could, however, be purchased in smaller units or even fractions since all transfers were made simply by recording ledger entries under the accounts of both buyer and seller.
16. Castaing (1720), no. 36. Freke's competing price list, used by Scott in his classic history of the bubble, shows the range to be £332 to £344 (Freke's *Prices of Stocks,* no. 89).
17. Anderson, Vol. 3, pp. 95, 97.
18. While the first registration of the Redeemables on July 14 brought in only £11,240,145 of them or two-thirds of the total possible, the second registration of both the Redeemables and the Irredeemables on August 4 brought in together £5,371,071 of additional government debt, only slightly more than the £5,306,057 possible if all the remaining Redeemables (mostly held at the Exchequer) had been forced to convert.
19. These are the quantities of Dutch bank money at 2 months' usance that could be purchased for one pound sterling in London. See John McCusker, *Money and Exchange in Europe and America, 1600-1775: A Handbook* (Chapel Hill, NC: University of North Carolina Press, 1978), pp. 42–45, for a full discussion.
20. T. S. Ashton, *Economic Fluctuations in England, 1700–1800* (Oxford University Press, 1959), p. 113, explains this feature of eighteenth century exchange markets, although he notes the same thing happened in August 1914 when the pound appreciated sharply for a very brief period. Ashton gives credit to Jacob Viner for the explanation of this non-intuitive result. A full analysis of them for the 18th century can be found in Eric Schubert, "The Ties That Bind: Foreign Exchange Markets in Eighteenth Century Europe," unpublished Ph. D. thesis, University of Illinois at Urbana-Champaign, 1986.

21. Scott, Vol. 3, p. 318. Anderson puts the amount actually loaned at £900,000 (Vol. 3, p. 95).
22. Scott, Vol. 3, p. 318.
23. Anderson, Vol. 3, p. 97.
24. Sperling, p. 32.
25. Dickson, pp. 140–43.
26. Computer analysis of Bank of England Transfer Books M and S, 2nd series, nos. 35 and 41. For transferable capital, see Fairman, p. 51.
27. Dickson, p. 96.
28. Bank of England, General Court Book H; entries for 29 September, 13 October, 25 October 1720, and 6 April 1721.
29. William Fairman, *The Stocks Examined and Compared...*, 7th ed. (London, 1824), p. 51. "Amidst the general speculation excited by the subscription scheme, some of the more cautious persons sold out of South Sea Stock at very high rices, and bought into Bank Stock; this naturally caused a considerable rise of the latter, which got up to 260 per cent."

DISCUSSION

COMMENT ON WHO PUT THE MANIA IN TULIPMANIA

Frederic S. Mishkin

Peter Garber's work on the Dutch tulipmania of 1634–37 in this book and his paper in *The Journal of Political Economy* is in the best tradition of revisionist economic history. By revisionist, I mean that it reevaluates an important historical episode using a new perspective based on modern analysis.

Why is it important to reevaluate the tulipmania legend? Because the tulipmania story is often raised as an example to convince us of the irrationality of financial market behavior. After all, investors in the Dutch tulip market in the 1630s must have been crazy (i.e., irrational) if they were willing to pay the equivalent of $50,000 in gold for a single tulip bulb.

Because historical examples like the tulipmania are so graphic, they have a powerful impact on the way the public and even professional economists think about financial market behavior. Professional economists often ignore the importance of rhetoric—that is, the way an argument is presented—in how ideas get accepted. Yet as McCloskey (1985) has argued, rhetoric has an important impact on the way economists think. Indeed the tulipmania legend has been an important part of rhetoric today and in the past that leads many to be convinced of market irrationality and the dominance of investor psychology and fads in financial market behavior.

Because the tulipmania legend has been such an important part of the rhetoric to persuade us of the irrationality of market behavior, a reexamination of the episode which suggests that the tulip market was far less irrational than the legend suggests can have an important impact on the way people evaluate financial market behavior today. Garber's work on removing some of the mania from the Dutch tulipmania legend is thus not an irrelevant exercise in economic history. It forces us to reconsider our priors about the irrationality of financial market behavior in both the distant as well as the recent past, and can thus subtly influence our views on how to deal with potential market crashes in the future.

What immediately convinces most hearers of the tulipmania story that the market was irrational is the incredibly high prices that some tulip bulbs fetched at the peak of the market. How could a bulb that sold for over 5,000 guilders in 1637 be worth only one-tenth of a guilder in 1739 and be rationally priced? Such pricing behavior of an asset like a common stock or a piece of art like a Rembrandt (which is closer to what a beautiful tulip is) just seems impossible to explain by saying the market fundamentals are driving the price.

What Garber does not emphasize enough in his chapter, although it is implicit in his discussion, is that a tulip bulb is a fundamentally different kind of asset than a Rembrandt or a common stock. *In contrast to these other assets it can keep on reproducing itself, leading to exponential growth in the quantity of the asset.* Thus, one tulip bulb asset, say, over a hundred-year period, can produce millions of the same bulbs. The net result is that even though one hundred years down the road the price of an individual bulb descended from the original bulb is only a tiny fraction of the initial bulb price, the high price of the original bulb is completely sensible. The reason is that the present value of all the millions of descendent bulbs produced from the original bulb can be an extremely high figure indeed.

The pricing phenomenon that Garber describes for tulip bulbs in the seventeenth century is one that we see all the time today with similar assets that can reproduce themselves. Garber has a delightful footnote that informs us that a small quantity of prototype lily bulbs recently sold for close to $500,000, a price that would enable one to buy a pretty decent house (though not a palatial one) even in the New York suburbs. Similarly, we often see that prize bulls sell for what seems to a native New Yorker to be astronomical prices. Successful thoroughbred race horses, such as Secretariat, also often sell for tens of millions of dollars, even though their possible earnings on the racetrack are only a small fraction of their price.

Are these examples of irrational pricing behavior? Just ask any bulb grower or breeder and he or she will tell you that such high prices of prize bulls, bulbs, or horses are appropriate, given the market fundamentals. Since the present value of the offspring of these particular assets is so high, the market price of these assets should also be high.

Although Garber demonstrates that much of the pricing of Dutch tulip bulbs in the 1630s was not irrational, particularly of the rare varieties which were traded by the reputable dealers, some crazy pricing behavior for cheaper bulbs does not seem to be evident. Garber does point out, however, that bulb contracts were not continuously marked to market, required no margins to enforce compliance, and were in effect legally unenforceable. Thus, trades conducted by parties not normally engaged in the tulip trade, and thus who had little cost to reneging on bulb contracts if they went sour, were possibly more akin to a gambling game rather than to serious market transactions.

Garber's reevaluation of the tulipmania legend does not completely destroy the position that there was irrationality in the Dutch tulip market in the 1634–37 period, but he does show that it is no longer an obvious case for wild market irrationality. Why is it then that the tulipmania legend has persisted for so long? Garber gives quite a neat explanation for this also. Just as we see today that special interest groups are trying to use the stock market crash of 1987 to justify government action that will benefit them financially, this was also the case in the capitalist Dutch society of three hundred years ago. The Dutch oligarchy, whose views of the speculation in the tulip market of the 1630s are the source of the tulipmania legend, wanted to discourage new emerging markets that they did not control in order to channel funds into activities in which they could make profits. A similar phenomenon has occurred in the aftermath of the stock market crash. Organized stock exchanges would like to see new regulations which would hamper the growth of emerging markets in financial futures and options, thus limiting some of their competition. Maybe Garber should add to his title the old adage, "the more things change, the more they stay the same."

Garber's work on the tulipmania legend is an important service both to the economics profession and to the general public. Setting the record straight on the Dutch tulip market of the seventeenth century may help promote more sober discussion of what happened on October 19, 1987.

REFERENCES

McCloskey, D. (1985). *The Rhetoric of Economics*. Madison, Wisconsin: University of Wisconsin Press.

Garber, P. (1989). Tulipmania. *Journal of Political Economy, 97,* No. 2.

DISCUSSION

EARLY ASSET BUBBLES

Forrest Capie

The emphasis in both these chapters is on rational explanation of two episodes that in the conventional accounts of financial history have a wild reputation. I found the emphasis of these chapters well placed and the arguments convincing, but would like nevertheless to suggest the danger of overstating the rational aspect. My comments are primarily on the South Sea Bubble with some thoughts on the tulipmania.

Professor Neal is rapidly making this field of early eighteenth-century European finance his own. He has produced many papers and dealt with many parts of Europe. His chapter, then, is part of a much larger research project. Although it may not always show, there is an enormous amount of detailed work and data lying behind his chapter. A first comment is that the reader is not fully informed in the chapter, and that may be a result of the author's assuming greater knowledge in the reader than is justified; he has certainly assumed more knowledge in the discussant than is warranted. The argument of the chapter is that what we observe in 1720 has more to do with technical difficulties in the new and rapidly developing financial sector than it has to do with wild speculation. The conventional story of skulduggery is played down.

The conventional picture begins in the late seventeenth and early eighteenth centuries when the British government had run up debts in wars and was running into difficulties in servicing these debts. A common way out of this problem at the time was to confer trading privileges on a company in exchange for that company's taking over the debt. The specific proposal on this occasion was that the South Sea Company be given a monopoly of trade in the South Seas and that they should be allowed the task of converting the outstanding government debt. Whereas more recent conversions had involved exchange of low-interest stock of longer duration for existing high-interest stock, the bait in the South Sea case was not of a longer dated stock but of an equity that carried the prospect of substantial capital appreciation. This prospect of capital appreciation had an excellent chance of being realized since the South Sea Company was a huge, prestigious, government-backed joint-stock company. The scale of the proposed conversion was also huge—all government debt not held by the big joint-stock companies. It totaled £31 million out of a total debt of around £50 million at a time when national income was of the order of £200 million.

The populace swallowed the story of vast fortunes to be reaped, so enthusiastically indeed that South Sea Company shares soared in price and the capital gains were enormous. But two points have usually been given prominence in previous studies. The first is that there were huge bribes paid to public officials, presumably to stop them revealing the true nature of the activities. The second is perhaps best expressed in an earlier historian's words:

> By an astonishing parliamentary oversight, or criminal omission the amount of South Sea Stock to be given in exchange for the various loans to be converted was not fixed; so the higher the stock stood above par the less the company might hope to offer.[*]

The central question in this episode arises out of the nature of the conversion operation. What was it that encouraged people to exchange the asset they had for another, at the prices recorded? Were they duped—that is, given false or inadequate information? Was there remarkable innovation? Or were they just plain silly, that is to say, irrational? Perhaps a bit of all three. It would be gratifying, of course, if we could indicate the relative importance of each.

---

[*]J. H. Clapham (1945), *The Bank of England: A History,* Vol. 1 (Cambridge: Cambridge University Press), p. 84.

In the South Sea episode it was a promise of capital gain that was the inducement. The question then becomes: were the new financial instruments on offer so desirable that the price they rose to was sensible in terms of fundamentals? That is, did the clamor for them as reflected in their price (that took even the issuers by surprise) suggest a reasonable valuation of their marketability, security, and underlying value in terms of an expected stream of dividends from profitable South Sea ventures? If the answer is yes, then we support the view of sophisticated investors behaving rationally, buying new instruments at correct prices. The innovations allowed welfare gains all round. This may be a large part of the explanation but two questions arise: why were bribes and lies and incomplete information part of the stock in trade of South Sea Company directors? (One figure used for bribes is £1.5 million, which is a staggering amount for the time.) Second, what grounds did investors have for believing in a future stream of dividends that would yield a present value compatible with the prices they were paying?

Professor Neal does concede that some swindle was involved. Can we come any closer to attaching a measure to how much goes down to swindle, how much to technical change, and how much to gullibility?

There are several questions on points of detail. How did the government succeed in converting high interest debt to low interest? And how did this in any case reduce the debt service burden? Wouldn't the price it issued the new stock at have left debt service charges unchanged? (The most recent British conversion operation was that of 1932 when 28 percent of the massive national debt was converted from a 5 percent coupon to a 3-1/2 percent coupon. One important and quite widely accepted account of that episode is that it was patriotism that did the trick. While the calculation is difficult it seems more likely that the authorities took advantage of expectations of falling prices. In other words, such conversions are possible but only in certain conditions. We cannot assume that such conversions are always possible.

Is this conversion a case of genuine financial innovation rather than what has been going on recently under that name? Financial innovation is a phrase widely used to describe almost any new instrument or arrangement in the financial markets. But much of what has been going on recently has been attempts to find ways around regulation. The regulation involves welfare losses and the innovation may take us back to the original starting welfare position but has nevertheless involved some misallocation of resources. Genuine innovation would result in a higher welfare point.

There was a bubble we are told, since South Sea stock rose above the underlying annuity, but surely a difference in price between stocks can arise when the annuities are less marketable than the other stock. One of the most dramatic parts of the bubble is explained by reference to a credit crunch. But how could a credit crunch be connected with a price rise? And continuing, foreign exchange rates are cited as supporting evidence—they reflect "a liquidity squeeze of unprecedented magnitude" that pressed on the Bubble. How could a liquidity squeeze affect one stock only? Does theory predict that profits are distributed randomly? Is it not the case that an efficient market can still allow for a rent on ability, and that some participants can reap above-normal profits at least for a short time?

On turning to tulips, I could not help thinking about paintings. I noticed the other day that in Christie's International magazine for October/ November 1988 that there are estimates for some paintings due to come up at the New York sale on November 9th. One is by Barnett Newman—two yellow stripes on a white background, acrylic on canvas—for which the conservative firm of Christie's estimates that someone will pay $1.5 million. Highlight of the New York sale will be a "Frieze" by Jackson Pollock for which $6 million is expected (that is, around 300 times an average annual income). At the risk of being labeled philistine, I wonder if these prices will always hold, that at some future date, possibly not far off, some paintings like these will be difficult to get rid of. What will historians make of this "Abstract Bubble"? What are the fundamentals here? Are they the words of the current arbiters of taste? Might it not appear quite similar to much of the tulip experience of the seventeenth century—that is, that for a considerable part of the experience of rising prices there really is not much in the way of fundamentals to get hold of, just prices rising so long as the belief was that they would continue to rise.

There are one or two general points about the tulip chapter. I do not think that Professor Garber is entirely fair on the historian. Skepticism is surely the hallmark of the historian. Distrust of an inside story is the historian's starting point. Second, sixteenth and seventeenth century markets had been troubled by merchants endeavoring to manipulate prices by cornering supply (of goods such as spices) and by spreading rumors. Perhaps there is some case to be made for those seeking a regulatory framework—they could have been seeking rules rather than discretion.

Lastly, the view that bubonic plague helps explain the wild activity is surely not very convincing.

History can be thought of as society's memory. If it is fuzzy or inaccurate we may be condemned to relive it. There does seem to be a danger that the application of some recent developments in economics, such as extreme versions of the rational expectations approach, are in danger of depriving us of manias, panics, crashes, and even modest booms and slumps. This may not be helpful in terms of society's memory. But perhaps a certain amount of this is a matter of semantics or of emphasis. Those who argue that it is rational to buy when prices are rising if the expectation is that prices will keep rising sound entirely reasonable. Those who say it is folly are surely simply shifting the emphasis to the fact that we do not know when the terminal condition, that is the change in fashion or whatever, will come. To describe all of these episodes as rational surely stretches the definition of rationality to an unhelpful extent.

PART 2

THE STOCK MARKET IN THE NINETEENTH CENTURY

CHAPTER 3

THE PANIC OF 1873

Charles P. Kindleberger

The panic of 1873 fits somewhat uneasily into a conference on crashes in the American stock market. In the first place the panic was international as many others have been including 1890, 1929, and 1987. The title of this chapter might properly be called "The panics of 1873," since there were panics in Vienna and Berlin, as well as in New York. Secondly, the United States' end of the troubles was felt in the bond market, more than that for equities, and even in the market for urban building sites, especially in Chicago. These differences from the focus of the conference, or extensions, do not seem to me sufficient reason to abandon the study. The panics of 1873, 1890, and 1929 are of particular interest for their international character and because each was followed by fairly deep depression on a global scale. Thus, 1873 is worth reexamination.

The international connections of the crash are of particular interest. National observers repeatedly insist that financial crises within their borders are of purely local origins and consequences. This has been claimed especially for 1866 with the Overend, Gurney failure in London, the *corso forzoso* (forced circulation or abandonment of the silver standard) in Italy on the one hand, and for the 1890 Baring crisis and its 1893 aftermath in London, Argentina, Turin, Melbourne, New York, and probably also Johannesburg. The connections among Vienna, Berlin, Frankfurt, and New York in 1873 were more readily recognized.[1] Friedman and Schwartz (1963) insist that the 1920–21 and 1929 stock market crashes originated solely in the United States, pointing to the gold inflows of the periods as proof. But connections between financial markets and macro-economies extend beyond those running solely through money flows. Booms and busts can both be spread by money movements, to be sure, but also by arbitrage in internationally traded commodities and securities, by the foreign-trade multiplier connecting incomes in two countries through trade between them, and especially by psychological responses in one or more markets to trouble in another. The market (or markets) that follows marks down its prices along with prices in the originating one, shifting both demand and supply curves, if one needs to think in those terms, without transactions between the markets necessarily taking place. Especially of relevance to 1873, one market may precipitate a recession, a depression, and even a crash in another by halting lending to it at a time when the earlier recipient had come to depend on a regular flow. The panic of 1873 provides a striking example of R.C.O. Matthews' dictum, applied by him to 1936–39, to the question whether the trouble started in Britain or in the United States:

> It is futile to draw any hard-and-fast rule assigning to either country causal primacy in the cycle as a whole or its individual phases. (1954, p. 69)

I start with a model which is perhaps familiar to those who know my book *Manias, Panics and Crashes: A Study of Financial Crises* (1978). There is a "displacement" or autonomous event or shock that changes investment opportunities. Some old lines of investment may be closed down, but especially some new are opened up. Prices in the new lines rise. Gains are made. More investment follows. The process can cumulate, accelerate, pick up speed, become euphoric, and verge on irrationality. To quote from the *Chicago Tribune* of April 13, 1890, on the contemporary land boom:

> In the ruin of all collapsed booms is to be found the work of men who bought property at prices they knew perfectly well were fictitious, but who were willing to pay such prices simply because they knew that some still greater fool could be depended on to take the property off their hands and leave them with a profit. (Hoyt, 1933, p. 165)

A stage of "overtrading" or "overshooting" equilibrium levels may be reached. After a time, expectations of continued price rises in the asset weakens and may even be reversed. The period in which expectations are weakening is known as "distress." The expectations that had led to a crescendo of movement out of liquid assets such as money into long-term or equity assets reverse themselves, gradually or precipitously. If the reversal is precipitous, there is a crash and perhaps a panic.

In the history of manic episodes followed by market collapse, it is often clear what the displacement was. The period leading up to 1873, on the other hand, had a great many, making it difficult to rank them in importance. In chronological order there were:

1. the end of the Civil War in the United States;
2. the Prussian–Austrian war of 1866;
3. the Overend, Gurney crash in Britain in 1866;
4. the *Wunderharvest* of wheat in Austria in 1867, a year when the rest of Europe experienced short crops, which gave a lift to Austrian railroad traffic and exports;
5. the opening of the Suez canal in 1869;
6. the Franco–Prussian War in 1870–71;
7. the astounding success of the Thiers *rentes*, issued in 1871 and 1872 to recycle the five billion franc indemnity paid by France to Prussia;
8. the Chicago fire of October 1871;
9. the mistake of German monetary authorities in paying out gold coins minted from a portion of the indemnity payment before the silver coins to be withdrawn had been retired;
10. relaxation of German banking laws;
11. the Credit Mobilier scandal in the finance of the Erie and Union Pacific railroads;
12. the United States claims against Britain for having outfitted and supported the Confederate naval vessel *Alabama* that preyed on Northern shipping;
13. the Grange movement in the west with farm groups fighting the expanding railroads regarded as avaricious monopolies by legislating limits on the rates charged for handling, storing, and shipping farm products.

Of particular importance in the relations between Europe and the United States was that different countries in Europe participated in the boom at its height in 1872–73 in varying degrees. France was relatively depressed as it sought to raise a portion of the indemnity through taxation. Britain had already been through a railway mania in 1847, with a moderated reprise in 1857, so that it was not caught up in a domestic-investment euphoria in the same way as Germany, Austria, and Hungary. Moreover, it had just experienced the Overend, Gurney panic of 1866, largely associated with foreign investment in the Mediterranean, especially Egypt and Greece, and in shipping, and was in consequence wary of investment excitement. Britain functioned in fact to a degree as a balance wheel between Central Europe and the United States, absorbing U.S. government and railroad bonds sold by German investors to acquire funds for investment at home (Simon, 1959 [1979], pp. 101, 127, 145) and fine-tuned the short-term capital market as the French indemnity transfer took place to a large extent through sterling bills. It did so by frequent changes of the Bank of England discount rate—24 in 1873 alone.

Foremost among the displacements in 1871–72 in Europe was the payment of the five billion franc indemnity of France to Prussia that the latter shared with other German states as the Reich was founded. Significant monetary changes followed from the payment of 512 million francs in gold and silver, plus the drawing of gold from London with sterling exchange. This part of the payment was connected with German monetary reform, the adoption of the gold standard, and the expansion of the money supply through the issuance of gold coin before calling in the silver, widely noted as a mistake (Akerman, 1957, p. 341; Wirth, 1890, pp. 456–8; Zucker, 1975, pp. 68–9). In three years the circulation of thalers, later renamed marks, rose from 254 million to 762 million (Wirth, 1890, p. 438).

The bulk of the rest of the indemnity was paid off by September 1873 recycling. The French raised two massive bond issues at home (the Thiers *rentes*) in June 1871 and July 1872 that were subscribed to by French investors, some of whom sold their European securities to acquire the money to do so, and by investors, banks, and speculators all over Europe. The real transfer occurred later as French investors reconstituted their portfolios of foreign securities, and foreign purchasers of the *rentes* sold them to take their profit and repatriated the funds.

The proceeds of the indemnity in Germany were used to pay off the domestic and foreign debts of the German states. One billion marks of German state securities were estimated to have been held in Austria and the redemption of this amount led to a new boom in Austrian railroads. The Austrian railroad system had already been expanded by sixteen percent in mileage and thirty-eight percent in traffic between 1864 and 1867, the latter largely the result of the *Wunderharvest*. The liquidation of German securities led Austrian investors to a new wave of railroad investment that spread to the related industries of iron and steel and rolling stock, and especially to a major expansion in financial institutions, both general banks

and a specialized type, the *Maklerbank*, or broker's bank, that loaned to purchasers of securities.

In Germany itself there was a boom in banking, in railroads, and especially in construction. The formation of the Reich with Berlin as its capital attracted large numbers of people to that city and in due course banks from other cities. Along with mixed banks like the Deutsche Bank, formed in 1872 to compete with London in the financing of German foreign trade but inevitably drawn into domestic lending by the boom, there was created a class of so-called *Baubanken*, or construction banks, that ostensibly financed building but more than anything else financed speculation in building sites. A class of millionaire peasants developed that sold their farm land in the periphery of cities, especially Berlin, and so-called "tent-cities" were built, along with barracks to accommodate the workers that poured in. Rents in Berlin doubled and trebled in a short time, and calculable reality gave way to fantasy (Pinner, 1937, pp. 202–4). Among the foremost of the *Baubanken* was one Quistorpische Vereins-Bank of Berlin with twenty-nine subsidiaries in the field of real estate, construction, and transport. Its shares went from 191 on April 1, 1873, to 25 1/2 the following October 10 (Pinner, 1937, p. 205; Oelssner, 1953, p. 257). After paying out dividends of twenty, thirty, or forty percent per annum in 1872 the prices of *Baubanken* shares fell after September 1873 to fifty, twenty, ten, or five percent of nominal capital (Pinner, 1937, p. 203). In the early years, Berlin was called "Chicago on the Spee" (the river) (Stern, 1977, p. 161).[2]

The period from 1871 to 1873 is called the *Grunderzeit*. This term derived not from the founding of the German Reich, as in *Reichgrundungszeit* (Bohme, 1966). It refers instead to the founding of companies but especially of banks (Good, 1984, p. 164). In Austria, 1,005 companies with a nominal capital of 5,560 million gulden were chartered beween 1867 and 1873, including 175 banks with a nominal capital of 1.3 billion gulden, and 604 industrial firms with nominal capital of 1.5 billion gulden survived to 1874. In North Germany 265 companies with a nominal capital of 1.2 billion marks were founded in 1871; in Prussia 481 firms with a capital of 1.5 billion marks were chartered in 1872, followed in 1873 by 196 companies valued at 166 million thalers (Wirth, 1890, pp. 466–71). The data are partial and not comparable. Detailed data for Prussia in 1872 include forty-nine "banks and credit institutions" with 345 million marks in capital, and sixty-one *Baubanken* with a capital of 227 million.

The boom in the new Reich and in Austria had the usual characteristics: widespread participation in speculative investments, service of distinguished names—largely of nobility—as members of company boards as shills to engender inventor confidence, swindles of all kinds. Wirth observes that there was an epidemic desire to become rich, and that the easy credibility of the public was never greater in any epoch. To get high returns many people "would throw their money out the window" (pp. 502–9). Edmund Lasker, a member of the Prussian House of Delegates from Magdeburg, called attention in February 1873 to a series of scandals in railroad and financing involving German nobility. The most notable was the Arnim affair, "the most celebrated scandel of the 1870s," involving a diplomat in France who was accused of arranging the indemnity negotiations so as to affect the stock market in which he had a position. Lasker also denounced collusion in the manipulation of securities between railroad promoters and officials of the Ministry of Commerce (Stern, 1977, pp. 234–42).

Distress appeared in the late summer and early fall of 1872. Wirth observed that the bow was stretched so taut in the fall of 1872 that it threatened to snap (p. 508). In Austria trade and speculation had been triumphant in 1871 and most of 1872, but at the first sign of trouble railroad securities receded into the background and more speculative bank, construction, and industrial companies moved to the foreground. Already in the second half of 1872 textile firms found themselves in difficulty.

In the fall of 1872 the magic word, according to Marz, was *Weltausstellung* (World Exhibition) to open May 1, 1873, in Vienna to celebrate the twenty-fifth year of the accession to the imperial throne of Francis Joseph (Marz, 1968, p. 172). Hotels, cafes, and places of amusement were built in abundance for the Exhibition, which was expected to attract hundreds of thousands of visitors from all over Europe and to promote widespread prosperity. These hopes were widely exaggerated.

The Creditanstalt pulled back from participation in the market to ready itself to provide help if it were needed (Marz, 1968, pp. 177–78). Other money-center banks prepared to serve as lenders of next-to-last resort, including the largest New York banks (Sprague, 1910, pp. 15, 95, 147, 153, 230, 236–37, 239, 253, 273–74; summarized in Kindleberger, 1978, pp. 169–70). A stock market panic nearly broke out in the fall of 1872, and again on April 10, 1873, but the market held on, waiting for the *deus ex machina* sought in the opening of the Exhibition (Wirth, 1890, p. 519). This period of distress has been called "a silent moratorium" (Wirth, 1890, p.

508). On May 1, 1873, the Exhibition duly opened. No brilliant success was evident for the first week and on May 9 the stock market collapsed, one of a series of Black Fridays.

Berlin hung on until September 1873, when it collapsed simultaneously with the failure of Jay Cooke & Co. in Philadelphia and the closing of the New York Stock Exchange. *Baubanken* continued to lend; prices to rise. The wholesale price level rose from 107 in 1870 to 133 in 1872 and 141 in 1873.[3] For industrial materials alone the price level went from 121 in 1870 to 159 in 1872 and 167 in 1873.[4] Wirth observed that the handwriting on the wall should have been clear to all after the revelation of the scandals of Strousberg in 1872, the failure of the Deschauer Bank in Munich, and the Lasker speech of February 1873, but capital continued to be withdrawn from the solid paper of the Reich to be invested in new ventures. Interest rates tightened. In September the bourse collapsed (Wirth, 1890, p. 513).

The financial crises in Austria and German were primarily asset-market phenomena with little or nothing to do with constriction of the money supply (Wirth, 1890, p. 515). Money in circulation in Austria rose slightly in the second quarter of 1873 (Wirth, 1890, p. 537). The course of the money supply in Germany in 1873 is too difficult to pin down. Reichsbank figures for gold reserves and circulation do not begin until 1876 (Deutsches Bundesbank, 1976, section A and B.1). In 1870, before the founding of the Reichsbank in 1875, there were thirty-eight banks of issue, with notes in circulation rising from 300 million thaler in that year to 450 million in 1872 (Zucker, 1975, p. 78). As already noted, coins in circulation rose from 250 million to three times that amount between 1870 and September 1873. When the last payment on the French indemnity had been paid on September 5, 1873, it is true that the foreign exchanges turned against Germany and it lost several hundred million marks in a few months.[5] How much of this occurred before the stock market crash of September 15 is not evident, but the accounts place no stress on the gold outflow as a precipitant of the collapse. As in Austria, there was no remarkable internal drain.

The relevance of this negative information is to Anna Schwartz's attempted distinction between "real" and "pseudo" financial crises, echoed by Michael Bordo, who calls the former "true" financial crises. Real or true financial crises have bank panics that produce runs out of ordinary money into high-powered money such as bank notes, or in the circumstances of the development of banking at the time, gold coin. Pseudo crises do not have such drains (Schwartz, 1986; Bordo, 1987, p. 3). Both economists are convinced monetarists, and seem to need to fit financial crises into a monetarist framework. It is not clear that they get much support from the Central European crisis of 1873. Bordo's agreement with Schwartz seems a little forced since a reduction in the money supply is sixth in his list of ten elements of a financial crisis, following behind (presumably in order of importance, although possibly chronologically) a change in expectations, fear of insolvency of financial institutions, attempts to convert real and/or illiquid assets into money, threats to the solvency of commercial banks and other financial institutions, and bank runs (pp. 2–3).[6] The crises in Germany and Austria (and the United States) seemed real to contemporaries, conformed to Bordo's elements and Goldsmith's definition, and produced a depression lasting to 1879, even though on Schwartz's monetarist definition it would have to be scored as a pseudo crisis.

The themes of my work on the 1930s and on financial crises generally are that when there is no lender of last resort to halt the collapse of banking institutions they lead to extended depression (1986, chapter 14; 1978, chapter 10). In 1931 the actions of the lenders of last resort, the United States and France, were too little and too late. In the 1890 Baring crisis, the position was belatedly saved by the rapidly rising production of gold in South Africa, but only after financial crises in Australia and the United States in 1893 and a depression that extended to 1896. In 1873, a feeble effort was made to staunch the wound to the financial system in Austria: a support fund (*Aushilfsfond*) of 20 million gulden was established with the national bank contributing five million, the state three million, and the Credit-Anstalt two million to be lent on solid securities. Suspension of the Bank Act, on the analogy of Bank of England action in 1847, 1857, and 1866, was discussed on Sunday, May 11, 1873, and put into effect the next day, but the limit to the issuance of uncovered gulden notes was set at 100 million, a limit that violated the Bagehot prescription that the lender of last resort should lend freely. Marz comments that the suspension of the Bank Act was awkward in meeting the needs of the moment because the crisis was due to overproduction, not to a scarcity of money (1968, p. 179).

Money shrank after Black Friday. In October following the German crash, it became apparent that the Bodenkreditanstalt and its associated banks were in trouble. This time the government helped on a more generous scale because much of the lending by the group had been on domain lands (owned by the emperor) which were regarded abroad as equivalent to government debt. Marz hints that the greater governmental energy in saving this banking group may have been the consequence of the felt need to protect highly placed persons who had gambled with the Bankverein's money (p. 181). The lender-of-last-resort function tends as a rule to raise the insider-outsider problem of who should be saved, an inescapable political aspect.[7]

Lender-of-last-resort steps were virtually excluded in Germany which was in the process of consolidating the thirty-odd principalities and free cities into the Reich. Thirty-eight banks of issue—although only one, the Prussian National Bank, was of any size—were joined to form the Reichsbank which opened its doors in 1876. There was also the clumsily handled transition from bimetalism to the gold standard. Transitions, it is generally recognized, make decisive action in crises difficult.[8] In addition to the major transitions in Germany, there were financial innovations that confused matters—continuous legislation with regard to coinage, the retirement of small notes and of foreign coins (Borchardt, 1976, pp. 6ff), and financial deregulation which stimulated the formation of the *Baubanken*. Innovation in banking tends to be underpriced and to lead to what Adam Smith and the classical economists call "overtrading" (Bank for International Settlements, 1986, chapter 10). The German economy was suffused with vigor partly as a consequence of the founding of the German empire and eventually pulled itself out of the slump. It is hard to find in the literature, however, a recognition of the role of the lender of last resort.

One tragic aspect of the German depression from 1873 to 1879 is that it turned German public opinion against liberalism (Lambi, 1963, chapter vi). Some observers attribute the shift of Bismarck's trade policy from one of low tariffs to the notorious tariff on rye and iron to this shift. Agriculture in particular had not been helped by the boom, except for peasants around cities, and was prepared to desert free trade when its exports gave way to import competition from new lands. In addition, the depression gave rise to a wave of anti-Semitism on the ground that Jewish speculators had been prominent among the beneficiaries and swindlers during the boom (Lambi, 1963, p. 84; Good, 1984, p. 163).

Connections between economic conditions in Germany and Austria and those in the United States went back to the end of the Civil War in 1865. Central Europe was depressed from 1866 to 1869, partly as a result of the Prussian War against Austria, and this, combined with recovery in the

United States, produced a large-scale movement of capital westward to New York from Cologne, Berlin, and especially Frankfurt. Matthew Simon estimates the total capital inflow into the United States from June 1865 to June 1873 as roughly $1 billion, starting relatively slowly at about $100 million a year, picking up to $175 million in 1869, and reaching a peak of $259 million in 1872 before declining to $114 million in 1873 and $100 million in each of 1874 and 1875.[9]

Most of this investment up to 1870 was in U.S. government bonds issued during and after the war, notably the 5–20s (five percent, twenty-year bonds) issued in 1862, 1865, and 1867. Immediately after the war these bonds fell in price to very low levels and were bought speculatively. Later the U.S. govenment ran sizeable budget surpluses from 1866 to 1871 and reduced its gross debt from $2.7 billion at the end of 1865 to $2.3 billion six years later. The gold agio declined from a high of 185 percent in 1865 to 25 percent in 1869–70 and 11 percent in 1874–75, and there were assured opportunities for gain (Simon, 1955 [1979], pp. 34, 113). The flow from Central Europe had slowed down in 1866 with the Prussian attack on Austria and did so again in July 1870 at the outbreak of the Franco-Prussian War. Panics such as Overend, Gurney and war scares produce two effects on capital movements, according to Simon (p. 92): (1) capital flight which stimulated the purchase of American securities, and (2) the "liquidity motive," building up cash on hand. Which motive dominates in a given situation may depend on a variety of factors. From 1866 to 1869 depression in Europe produced more capital flight than hoarding of cash (p. 97). In 1870, however, the liquidity motive prevailed (p. 101). The rise in the prices of U.S. government bonds and the possibilities of a boom in railroads also played a part in the earlier period, a pull as opposed to a push. In 1870 the disturbed market in Europe meant that the U.S. Treasury's attempt to refinance outstanding debt by issuing $200 million of 10–5s, $300 million of 15–4-1/2 s, and $1 billion of 30–4s resulted in failure (p. 105).

The proceeds of bonds sold by United States investors to Europe or redeemed by the U.S. government were largely invested in U.S. railroads, pushing their way west. The railroad network expanded rapidly after the Civil War, from 35,000 miles at the end of 1865 to 53,000 miles five years later and 70,000 miles at the end of 1873 (Bureau of Census, 1949, p. 200).

Jay Cooke & Co. got its financial start by a major innovation in the marketing of U.S. war bonds in aggressive domestic sales campaigns designed to appeal to the general public rather than merely established financial circles. His success did not make him a favorite of established bankers like Drexel in Philadelphia and Morgan in New York. Like the Pereire brothers in France who failed in 1868, he was an "active" banker, rather than a passive one like the Drexels, Morgans, and Rothschilds in Paris (Gras in Larson, 1936, p. xi; Larson 1936, pp. 86–87, 433). The financial history of the nineteenth century is sometimes written in terms of bankers' quarrels, and the distinction between active and passive bankers is echoed in the current controversy whether bankers lending to the Third World in the 1970s were "loan pushers" or "wallflowers, waiting to be asked to dance" (Darity and Horn, 1988).

Cooke's success in marketing U.S. government bonds at home meant that he was late in moving in two other directions, in selling bonds abroad and in entering the market for railroad bonds. When he did move in the latter direction, the eastern railroads such as the Baltimore & Ohio backed by the Brown Brothers, the Chesapeake & Ohio by Alexander Brown, and the Pennsylvania by Drexel already had established connections, as did some newer lines—the Rock Island (Henry Clews), the Union Pacific (the Ciscos), and the Central Pacific (Fisk and Hatch) (Larson, 1936, pp. 245, 257). In addition the Central Pacific and the Union Pacific had governmental subsidies (Larson, 1936, p. 259). Like latecomers in many businesses, Jay Cooke was forced to take what was left over and palpably more risky in his case, the Northern Pacific. This led westward from Duluth, Minnesota, through sparsely settled country. Its hope was to sell land from the abundant grant as the lines reached further west. Land offices were opened in Germany, Holland, and Scandinavia to attract settlers. These efforts did not help to sell Northern Pacific bonds. Its competitors, the Missouri Pacific and the Union Pacific, lay in more settled territory, and their bonds proved more attractive. Furthermore, European investors held U.S. railroad bonds in considerable disrepute, especially after the Erie, Union Pacific, and Credit Mobilier scandals of 1868 and 1872. Cooke failed to enlist the support in Europe of the Rothschilds or Bleichroeder and was forced to form a connection with a new house, Budge, Schill & Co. of Frankfurt. When the Franco-Prussian War broke out the prospect of selling Northern Pacific bonds in Germany evaporated.

Cooke had many other troubles. An absentee president of the line incautiously bought supplies with cash well in advance of need rather than inducing suppliers to grant long credits or accept bonds. His brother Henry, who ran the Washington lobbying office, lived high and was a drain.

Substantial investments in advertising and gaining the support of newspapers in Europe failed to pay off after the U.S. railroad scandals. Bit by bit, Jay Cooke & Co. found itself advancing capital to the Northern Pacific for construction. In the fall of 1872 the London partner Fahnestock observed that it was cruel to the depositors to use their money to support Northern Pacific bonds, and that the railroad should go to the market to borrow at any price. The near panic in the market of September 1872 made this impossible. Both Northern Pacific and Southern Pacific pushed for congressional subsidy of $40,000 a mile, but the scandals in Erie and the Union Pacific made Congress leery.

The scramble to keep Northern Pacific and Jay Cooke & Co. afloat lasted until September 1873 when the storm broke in the second week. The Grange movement in the west attacked railroad rates. Money was tight as funds were withdrawn from the east to finance an early, heavy harvest. The New York Warehouse and Security Company, formed to lend on grain and other farm produce, suspended on September 8 because of bad loans to the Missouri, Kansas & Texas Railroad. On September 13 the banking house Kenyon, Cox & Co. failed as a result of endorsing a note of the Canada Southern railroad for $1.5 million which the latter could not pay. Jay Cooke & Co. closed its doors on September 18, and Fisk and Hatch on the next day, Black Friday. They were followed by the Union Trust Company and the National Bank of the Commonwealth on Saturday, September 20. The stock market was closed that day and remained so for ten days.[10] *The Commercial and Financial Chronicle* for September 20, 1873, blamed the crash on the excessive tightness of the money market that prevailed without interruption from September 1872 to May 1873, making it impossible for railroad companies to borrow on bonds. Several banking houses negotiating large railroad loans or intimately connected with the building of the roads became involved because of their endorsement of loans and their borrowing on call loans collateralized by railroad securities. "In this delicate situation, the equilibrium was liable to be violently disturbed" (Sprague, 1910, p. 36). The newspaper account makes no reference to the decline in foreign lending from Europe, but it is clear that the tightness of money rates in the market from September 1872 to the following May is associated with the decline in foreign funds.

The collapse of the bond and stock markets in New York in September 1873 also put an end to the land boom in Chicago. Public participation in land buying, according to Hoyt (1933, p. 100) began about 1868 when many cases of large profits made in land since 1861 became common knowledge. In 1871 one writer claimed that every other man and every fourth woman had an investment in lots. The Chicago fire of October 8, 1871, destroyed 17,450 of the 60,000 homes in the city, but the fire accentuated rather than slowed down the growth of the city, with a year of "hectic borrowing" from the East, and the spending of $40 million for new construction (Hoyt, 1933, p. 102). Population in a belt within three to five miles of the center grew from 8,000 in 1860 to 55,000 in 1870 and nearly 100,000 in 1873. Land prices went from $500 to $10,000 an acre between 1865 and 1873 in the fashionable residential area of the South Side. Some land near the village of Hyde Park rose from $100 to $15,000 an acre (Hoyt, 1933, pp. 107–9). The euphoric aspect of the boom and the dangerous position of land speculators in the summer of 1873 is described by Hoyt in terms of

> municipal extravagance, excessive outlays on magnificent business blocks built at high cost on borrowed money, lavish expenditure on street improvements in sections where they were not required, overextended subdivision activity, and a disproportionately large amount of real estate purchases on small down payments—all these had been the result of the extreme optimism of the times (p. 117).

In the summer of 1873, the upward movement of land values stopped as falling wages limited the cash resources of prospective buyers. Moreover, as Hoyt commented, when land values ceased to rise the desire to purchase land fell off sharply as expectations of a fall replaced those of a rise. There was a lull in activity from May to September 1873 when the Jay Cooke failure was made known and then precipitated a collapse in land values and building prices.

At first on such occasions as 1837, 1857, 1873, 1893, and 1929, the stock market crash shatters the hopes of gain but has no other result. Debts contracted to purchase land or buildings are for a term not on demand. There is no forced selling and no forced liquidation. Owners of real estate, indeed, tend to congratulate themselves that they escaped more lightly than the owners of stocks or of defaulted bonds. There follows, however, a process of attrition (Hoyt, 1933, p. 400). The decline of industry lowers prices. Unemployment induces recent immigrants to return. Gross income from rentals declines sharply, but expenses of interest and taxes remain the same. Landholders retain their ownership until the constant attrition of interest charges, taxes, and penalites or the inability to renew mortgages brings foreclosures that squeeze out the equities above the mortgage. Hoyt notes that it takes about four or five years to complete this process and thoroughly deflate land values (pp. 119, 124). This process often cripples banks. In Chicago in 1933, 163 out of 200 banks suspended.[11]

It would be useful to have a comparable study of land values in Britain and Vienna in the years after the crash of 1873. I call attention to the spread of deflation from the bond and stock market in New York to the market for real estate in Chicago, as it may furnish food for thought about the delayed effects of the October 19, 1987, decline in the stock market on the markets for office buildings, condominia, shopping malls, hotels, and the like, especially luxury housing. There is, of course, the major difference that real estate today has built-in lenders of last resort in the Federal Deposit Insurance Corporation and the Federal Savings and Loan Insurance Corporation, troubled as those institutions are.

NOTES

1. The exception is Emden who calls the Jay Cooke failure independent of the Viennese *krach* (1938, p. 183).
2. I come later to the 1873 real estate boom in Chicago, the third of five in a century, that evokes Chicago as the standard of real estate mania (Hoyt, 1933).
3. 1800 = 100.
4. By 1879 the two indexes had fallen to 93 and 95, respectively (Jacobs and Richter, 1935, p. 81).
5. Wirth claims that this was because Berlin was the dearest city in the world (p. 459).
6. Compare Goldsmith's definition that includes no mention of money: "a sharp, brief, ultracyclical deterioration of all or most financial indicators—short-term interest rates, asset (stock, real estate, land) prices, commercial involvements and failures of financial institutions." Goldsmith regards financial troubles of the 1960s and 1970s in the United States as at most potential or near crises and does not regard foreign exchange difficulties as a necessary concomitant of financial crises (1982, p. 42).
7. In a passage that evokes the plight of the thrift institutions in California and the Southwest today, Marz observes that the Credit-Anstalt tried (in vain) to rescue the *Baubanken*, including among its tools the device of merging them (p. 179).
8. In the Great Depression in the United States there were three such, from the monetary leadership of the Federal Reserve Bank of New York to that of the Federal Reserve Board in Washington, from retiring President Herbert Hoover

to Roosevelt who was elected in November 1932 but only took office six months later, and from the international economic leadership of Britain, which yielded it in the summer of 1932 to that of the United States which picked up the burden piecemeal between 1936 and perhaps the Lend-Lease Act of 1941 or the Marshall Plan of 1947.

9. All fiscal years, ended June 30.

10. This move was later agreed to have been mistaken insofar as it induced a panic withdrawal of brokers' loans in October 1929 for fear of a closing of the exchange.

11. It is interesting to note that real estate had been the largest single factor in the failure of 4,800 banks in the three years from 1929–32 (Hoyt, 1933, p. 401).

REFERENCES

Akerman, J. (1957). *Structure et cycles economiques*, Vol. II. Paris: Prosses universitaires de France.

Bank for International Settlements (1956). *Recent innovations in international banking*. (Cross report. Prepared by a study group established by the Central Banks of the Group of Ten Countries.) Basel: Bank for International Settlements.

Bohme, H. (1966). *Deutschlands Weg zur Grosmacht, Studien zom Verhaltnis von Wirschaft und Staat wahrend der Grundungszeit, 1848–1861*. Cologne: Kiepenheuer & Witsch.

Borchardt, K. (1976). Wahrungs–und Finanzpolitik von der Reichsgrundung bis zum I Weltkrieg. In Deutsche Bundesbank, *Wahrung und Wirtschaft in Deutschland, 1876–1975*. Frankfurt am Main: Fritz Knapp.

Bordo, M. D. (1987). Financial crises: Lessons from history. Unpublished paper presented to the 5th Garderen Conference on International Finance, Erasmus Universiteit, Rotterdam.

Bureau of the Census, Department of Commerce (1949). *Historical statistics of the United States, 1789–1945*. Washington, DC: U.S. Government Printing Office.

Darity, W., Jr., and Horn, B. L. (1988). *The loan pushers: The roie of commercial banks in the international debt crisis*. Cambridge, Massachusetts: Ballinger.

Deutsche Bundesbank (1976). *Deutsches Geld–und Bankwesen in Zahlen, 1876–1975*. Frankfurt am Main: Fritz Knapp.

Emden, P. H. (1938). *Money power of Europe of the nineteenth and twentieth centuries*. London: Sampson, Low, Marston & Co.

Friedman, M. and Schwartz, A. J. (1963). *A monetary history of the United States, 1867–1960*. Princeton: Princeton University Press.

Good, D. (1984). Comment. On H. P. Minsky, The financial instability hypothesis: Capitalist processes and the behavior of the economy, in C. P. Kindelberger and J. P. Laffargue (eds.), *Financial crises: Theory, history and policy.* Cambridge: Cambridge University Press.

Gras, N.S. B. (1936). Editor's introduction. To H. M. Larson, *Jay Cooke, private banker.* Cambridge, Massachusetts: Harvard University Press.

Hoyt, H. (1933). *One hundred years of land values in Chicago: The relationship of the growth of Chicago to the rise in its land values, 1830–1933.* Chicago: University of Chicago Press.

Jacobs, A.,and Richter, H. (1935). Die Grosshandelspreise in Deutschland von 1792 bis 1934. *Sonderhefte des Instituts fur Konjunkturforschung, 37.*

Kindelberger, C. P. (1978). *Manias, panics and crashes: A history of financial crises.* New York: Basic Books.

Kindelberger, C. P. (1986). *The world in depression, 1929–39.* Berkeley: University of California Press (revised ed.).

Lambi, I. N. (1963). *Free trade and protection in Germany, 1868–1879.* Wiesbaden: Franz Steiner.

Larson, H. M. (1936). *Jay Cooke, private banker.* Cambridge, Massachusetts: Harvard University Press.

Marz, E. (1968). *Oesterreichesche Industrie–und Bankpolitik in der Zeit Franz Joseph I. Am Beispiel der k. k. priv. Osterreischischen Credit-Anstalt fur Handel und Gewerbe.* Vienna: Europa.

Matthews, R.C.O. (1954). *A study in trade-cycle history: Economic fluctuations in Great Britain, 1832–1842.* Cambridge: Cambridge University Press.

Oelssner, F. (1953). *Die grossen Weltkrisen im Lichte des Structurwandels der Kapitalistwischen Wirtschaft.* Zurich and Leipsig: Max Niehans.

Schwartz, A. J. (1986). Real and pseudo financial crises. In F. Capie and G.E.G.E Woods (eds.), *Financial crises and the world banking system.* London: Macmillan.

Simon, M. (1955 [1979]). *Cyclical fluctuations and the international capital movements of the United States, 1865–1897.* New York: Arno Press.

Sprague, O.M.W. (1910). *History of crises under the national banking system.* For the National Monetary Commission, reprinted 1968, New York: August M. Kelley.

Stern, F. (1977). *Gold and iron: Bismarck, Bleichroder and the building of the German empire.* London: Allen & Unwin.

Wirth, M. (1890). *Geschichte der Handelskrisen.* (3rd ed.) Frankfurt am Main: J. D. Sauerlander. (Reprinted 1968, New York: Burt Franklin).

Zucker, S. (1975). *Ludwig Bamberger, German liberal politician and social critic, 1823–1899.* Pittsburgh: University of Pittsburgh Press.

CHAPTER 4

FINANCIAL MARKET PANICS AND VOLATILITY IN THE LONG RUN, 1830–1988

Jack W. Wilson
Richard E. Sylla
*Charles P. Jones**

Interest in the volatility of asset market returns has increased greatly since the stock market crash of 1987. A crash almost by definition represents increased volatility. But what exactly is the relationship of increased volatility to panics and crashes? Does increased volatility precede, coincide with, or follow these crises? How has volatility changed over the long sweep of asset market history? These are among the questions we address in this chapter.

Our specific concern is with the so-called era of the National Banking System between the Civil War and World War I. In this era financial panics and stock market crashes were linked to one another, and crashes occurred with greater frequency than they have since 1914. While primary emphasis is on the relationship of pre-1914 panics and crashes from the perspective

*We wish to thank our colleagues Marie Davidian and David Dickey for their advice on the measure of volatility with these time series data. Dickey was especially helpful in the comparisons of the volatility measure when using monthly average data as opposed to end-of-month data. We also thank Michael Bordo, Gary Gorton, and Kenneth Snowden for useful comments.

of volatility, our data extend backward to the 1830s and forward to the present. We therefore also present a long-term historical perspective on volatility in the National Banking System regime in relation to what preceded and what came after it.

PANICS, CRASHES, AND VOLATILITY

The stock market crash of October 1987, like that of 1929, was surprising, as well as unsettling, because it was both unexpected and unprecedented in post-Depression market behavior. Before 1914, financial panics and the stock market crashes that accompanied them occurred every ten to twenty years. They were unsettling but not especially surprising. They were expected to happen every so often; the only real question was when? Nonetheless, they grew tiresome. Therefore, in the aftermath of the great panic and crash of 1907, the problem of panics was studied intensively by a blue-ribbon National Monetary Commission, and by 1914 a solution was legislated and put in place—the Federal Reserve System. Pre-1914 banking panics occurred when panicky depositors descended upon their banks demanding cash. Banking panics, in turn, were intimately related to crashes in other financial markets. The Fed, the bankers' bank, was created to ensure that soundly managed but illiquid banks would always be able to obtain enough cash to meet depositor demands.

The great stock market crash of 1929, coming after the 1914 reform, embodied two surprises. Stocks fell more in October and November of that year than they had in any previous two-month period in our monthly data set, which extends back to January 1834. And the 1929 crash, unlike most pre-1914 crashes, was unrelated to a banking panic. While a series of banking panics were associated with the 1929–33 slide into depression, they commenced well after the stock market crash. Before 1914 panics and crashes typically occurred around the same time.

The Great Depression diverted attention away from the causes of the Crash and toward the causes of the Depression. As a consequence the unique (until 1987) features of the Autumn 1929 crash have been insufficiently studied. The Depression also led to financial reforms, as had the panic of 1907. Deposit insurance, provided by the FDIC created by the Glass-Steagall Banking Act of 1933, allayed the fears of bank depositors after they learned that the Fed was not completely reliable. Glass-Steagall also separated commercial and investment banking. The Securities Act of

1933 established disclosure rules for new issues. The Securities Exchange Act of 1934 created the SEC and required that publicly held companies report to it and to stockholders on operating results and balance sheets. The Banking Act of 1935 strengthened the powers of the Fed and centralized them in Washington, D.C. These reforms were meant to put an end to panics and crashes, and many believed that they had—until October 1987.

Given all the defense mechanisms in place—the Fed, the FDIC, and the SEC among others—the 1987 crash is especially perplexing. One contributing factor cited at the time, that the Fed inadvertently promoted the crash by raising its discount rate some weeks before, is far too simple. It is also a feature of the story of the 1929 crash. The problem in each case is that the Fed raised the discount rate on previous occasions without causing a stock market crash. After the crash of 1987, the lack of a ready and tested explanation, coupled with a perception that market volatility had increased around the time of the crash, led to a fingering of volatility itself as a prime suspect. Evidence on volatility in 1987 is mixed but could be construed as favoring the charge; for example,

> [V]olatility, measured as one-month price swings, during the 12 months prior to October 1987 was quite average compared with the period since 1926. On the other hand, if recent volatility is compared with the last 25 years, the year ending October 1 stands out somewhat more. Additionally, ... with respect to fluctuations within months, the preceding year was indeed extraordinary when viewed against the last quarter century (Feinstein, 1987, p. 42).

As to why volatility increased, the official Report of the Presidential Task Force on Market Mechanisms (Brady Commission) pointed to the new techniques of programmed trading such as portfolio insurance and market index arbitrage, and—in a repeat of post-1907 and post-1929 events—called for reining them in through regulatory reform. Other analysts question both the diagnosis and the prescription (Santoni, 1988; Shiller, 1988).

The difficulty of resolving the role of volatility in the 1987 crash suggests to us that examination of volatility in the context of earlier crashes and panics is worthwhile. Studying earlier crashes as case studies yielded up by market history can establish whether there are general patterns in the relationship of volatility to crashes and whether a particular case such as October 1987 was typical or atypical. We begin with panics and crashes during the National Banking era, and then widen the study to survey the last one and one-half centuries of market history.

PANICS AND CRASHES IN THE NATIONAL BANKING ERA

Four major financial panics accompanied by stock market crashes occurred in the National Banking era. Although signs of impending crisis may have been evident in earlier months and the effects of a panic may have lasted into later months, generally accepted dates of the crises are September 1873, May 1884, July 1893, and October 1907. Thus, there were four major crises in 34 years, or roughly one every decade. One, the 1884 crisis, was confined mostly to New York City banks and markets; in the other three the panics spread throughout the country as banks suspended the conversion of depositors' balances into cash. Although numerous other periods of financial stringency occurred in the era, none is customarily described as a major crisis. The National Banking regime had certain characteristics pertinent to understanding its panics and crashes (Sylla, 1975). There was no central bank, a difference between the United States and other leading economies such as Great Britain, France, and Germany. Instead of one central reserve bank functioning as a lender of last resort in panics, the United States had a pyramided reserve system with a number of large New York City banks at the apex of the pyramid. All banks held some cash reserves, but a large part of reserves was held as deposits (interbank balances) at other banks. The National Banking System formalized this arrangement by allowing country banks to hold reserves in the form of reserve city bank balances, and reserve city banks to hold reserves as balances in central reserve cities (primarily in New York City).

The reserve pyramid came about because the same dollar of cash in the till or vault of a large New York City bank could be counted not only in the reserve of that bank but also in the reserve of a reserve city bank maintaining a New York balance as well as in that of a country bank maintaining a balance in the reserve city bank. Thus, the large banks, mostly national banks in New York City, became the ultimate reserve holders under the National Banking System.

What induced banks all over the United States to hold reserves in other banks rather than as vault cash? It was the payment of interest on interbank balances. And what enabled the banks at the center to pay interest on interbank reserve balances that could be recalled at any time, and often were, by interior banks? It was the existence of the call loan market at the stock exchange in New York City where such loans, payable on demand, were made to those who bought securities on margin. In theory, if such a loan was called by a bank, another such loan could be had or, barring that, the securities being carried could be sold and the loan repaid with the proceeds. Since a large proportion of the liabilities of New York banks were interbank deposits from interior correspondents, it was natural that a large proportion of New York bank assets took the form of call loans. For example, on September 12, 1873, just before that year's crisis broke out, O.M.W. Sprague (1910, p. 83) reports that 31 percent of New York bank loans were demand (call) loans.

The call loan market establishes a connection between bank panics and stock market crashes during the National Banking regime but it does not establish the nature of that connection. To contemporary observers interested in the problem of banking panics and its solution, the nature of the connection seemed obvious and fundamental. Agriculture loomed larger in the economy of the National Banking era than it does today, and the annual agricultural cycles—Spring planting and Autumn harvesting and crop moving—created seasonal credit demands. When interior banks called home New York reserve balances at these times, the New York money market experienced tightness. When the tightness became extreme, and particularly when the difficulties or insolvencies of some banks or other firms become known, a panicky scramble for cash would break out. Call money rates would soar, and securities would be dumped at rapidly falling prices—that is, they would crash. The line of causation ran from banking panic to stock market crash. That is why many believed that the creation of the central bank would eliminate both panics and crashes.

We now know that did not happen. Both 1929 and 1987 witnessed crashes without banking panics. This suggested to us that an alternative interpretation of panics in the National Banking regime might be worth exploring. The stock market is widely believed to forecast future events such as recessions, depressions, and liquidity problems. Expectations of sharply reduced earnings, for example, would cause stocks to decline or possibly even crash. Such stock market behavior would signal, if not actually cause, an increased probability of defaults on bank loans. When the public—more specifically, holders of bank deposits—realized that the stock market was making such a forecast, the result could well have been runs on banks and, in the extreme, a full-fledged banking panic. Speculative advances of stocks fueled by extensions of bank credit at rising interest costs could have a similar result if the deposit-holding public perceived that speculative loans threatened the margin of safety in bank reserves. Extreme tightness in the money market and difficulties or insolvencies of firms could then trigger a market crash and an ensuing banking panic. The line of causation in these alternative scenarios runs from stock market problems (excessive speculation, declines, possibly crashes) to banking panics.

Evidence from earlier writers makes far from clear which of these two scenarios relating panics and crashes is more plausible. This may be illustrated by referring to the work of Sprague, the historian of crises under the National Banking System for the National Monetary Commission. Sprague subscribed to the first scenario, that banking panics led to stock market crashes. For each major crisis, however, he presents evidence consistent with a reversal of the relationship. For example, he cites the following passage from the *Banker's Magazine* of May 1873, four months before the September crisis:

> [T]he stock exchange and its members have absorbed a large portion of the capital which is demanded for the legitimate wants of trade and commerce. The country bankers, far and near, have been importuned to place their cash balances in Wall Street, instead of keeping them at home, the promise of high rates of interest creating inducements for the transfer of capital to New York.... The principle is a vicious one, because the same money serves a double purpose, but at great risk. The exchange transactions with New York are so heavy and so constant, that balances in Wall Street are by the country banker considered as cash in hand. The result has been that these immense accumulations of capital owned in the South and West, instead of being "cash on hand," are loaned out "on call" by the city banker, thereby contributing to a fatal inflation of prices. The country banks thereby contribute indirectly to the stock gambling in New York in order to realize interest on their daily balances here.... The merchant can afford to pay 6 percent, rarely more, per annum. The stock operator who bids for a rise in market values, offers 6 percent per month in many instances.....
>
> Is it surprising, with such prospects for money, that capital concentrates here from the wilds of Maine, the recesses of Connecticut, the prairies of the West, or the tobacco fields of the South to be used at 1 or 2 percent per month, instead of 6 percent at home (Sprague, 1910, p. 30)?

Some of the phrasing of this passage as well as the events being generally described could support an interpretation that excessive stock speculation was underway well before the banking panic of September 1873.

The panic of May 1884 definitely appears to have spread from the stock market to New York's banks. The New York banks were in a strong reserve position, according to Sprague, right up to the May panic. The stock market, on the other hand, was weak, in part because coinage of silver dollars under the Bland-Allison Act led foreign holders of American securities, fearful of U.S. commitment to the gold standard, to return the securities.

> At length, the strain of successive breaks in prices on the stock exchange brought about the downfall of a number of speculators whose plans might have proved successful if general conditions had been such as to lead to a rise in security values (Sprague, 1910, pp. 109–10).

One of these was the brokerage firm of Grant and Ward, "a firm better known for its personnel than for the scope of its business," according to Sprague (1910, p. 110), referring presumably to former president Ulysses S. Grant. Revelations of illegal check certifications, defalcations, and bank and broker suspensions soon followed. The Clearing House Association quickly agreed to issue clearing house loan certificates, a method of economizing on bank resources, and the panic subsided, having been contained in New York (Sprague, 1910, pp. 111–15).

Foreign fears about a U.S. commitment to maintaining the gold standard were also a factor in the 1893 panic. By the end of 1892, European investors were dumping their American securities, depressing the New York market. In February 1893, the Philadelphia and Reading Railroad failed, giving rise "to doubts of other companies, particularly of the industrials, and the course of the stock market was depressed and downward through March and April" (Sprague, 1910, p. 167). In early May, National Cordage Company failed; the May 6, 1893, *Commercial and Financial Chronicle* reported:

> Again our market has passed through a severe stock panic, and again the prodigious vitality of bankers and brokers has been abundantly demonstrated. On such an enormous and precipitate shrinkage in values it is very remarkable that so few houses have failed, and those that were compelled to suspend were more or less loaded up with the stocks of those companies which proved to be the bane of the market..... The open-market rates for call loans during the week on stock and bond collateral have ranged from 4 to 40 percent, the average being 6 percent (Sprague, 1910, pp. 160–61).

Not until late July, however, did bank runs and failures along with failure of the Erie Railroad produce a collapse of stock prices, and not until the first week of August did the nation's banks, following the New York banks' lead, suspend conversion of deposits into cash (Sprague, 1910, pp. 175–78).

In 1907, not one but two stock market crashes occurred before the main panic and crash in October. Late in 1906 the Bank of England raised its discount rate from 4 to 6 percent and discouraged the London market from accepting American finance bills (loans collateralized by American securities). Borrowing shifted to New York until February and March, when New York banks contracted such loans. The result was, in Sprague's words,

> ... the so-called "rich men's panic" of March, 1907. Never before or since have such severe declines taken place on the New York stock exchange. The most notable decline was in the case of Union Pacific shares, which fell over 50 points within less than two weeks. Probably no one security had been used so extensively as collateral in finance-bill operations....

> While the course of prices on the stock exchange after the March panic was upward, the market manifested great sensitiveness at all times. Early in August came another decline, which wiped out more than the gain of the preceding months (Sprague, 1910, p. 241).

The banking panic and suspension of cash payments throughout the country did not come until late October, the suspension itself lasting until January 1908.

We do not mean to suggest that such evidence as the foregoing should persuade one that preceding stock market events led to both banking panics and stock market crashes under the National Banking regime. We merely suggest that such a scenario, based upon literary evidence from that era and the experience of 1929 and 1987, is as plausible as the traditional position that bank panics caused stock market crashes.

We propose to examine the validity of these two scenarios by studying the volatility of asset returns—stocks, bonds, commercial paper, and call money—before, during, and after the panics of 1873, 1884, 1893, and 1907. In particular, we argue that the traditional position is consistent with a finding of no unusual volatility of stock returns before a panic/crash, but sharply increased volatility during and possibly after it. In contrast, a finding that stock returns were unusually volatile in the months preceding a panic/crash would be consistent with a theory that the behavior of the stock market itself promoted the subsequent bank panic and stock market crash.

ANALYSIS OF VOLATILITY, 1866–1913

In this section we present and discuss asset returns and their volatility in the panic/crash periods of 1873, 1884, 1893, and 1907. We have assembled data on the monthly returns of stocks, Aaa bonds, and commercial paper, and a monthly average call money interest rate. Sources and descriptions of the data are given in the Data Appendix.

Extremes of monthly asset returns for the years 1866 through 1913, a period of 48 years or 576 months, are presented in Tables 1 to 4. Tables 1 to 3 present the 25 lowest and the 25 highest monthly returns for stocks, bonds, and commercial paper. Table 4 gives the 50 highest monthly call money interest rates during the period. In studying the tables, recall that the panic months are September 1873, May 1884, July 1893, and October 1907.

Table 1 clearly establishes that banking panics and stock market crashes occurred together. Four of the eight lowest monthly stock returns during the years 1866–1913 were in the months banking panics occurred. One of the eight, October 1873, is the month after the panic, and two of the remaining three, May 1893 and March 1907 (the "rich men's panic"), fall in the same year as, but before, the panic, as does the ninth lowest monthly

TABLE 1
The 25 lowest and 25 highest stock price changes, 1866 through 1913

Year	Month	Lowest Return	Rank	Year	Month	Highest Return
1907	10	−10.8514%	1	1879	10	10.8824%
1907	3	−9.7987	2	1901	6	9.9678
1893	7	−9.4340	3	1873	12	9.5385
1893	5	−8.8993	4	1901	4	8.4437
1873	10	−8.6721	5	1891	9	8.0605
1884	5	−8.5575	6	1900	11	7.8512
1880	5	−7.9137	7	1899	1	7.6923
1873	9	−7.7500	8	1906	8	7.4074
1907	8	−7.4809	9	1877	8	6.9869
1890	11	−7.3350	10	1898	5	6.8120
1877	6	−7.1730	11	1893	9	6.6869
1877	4	−7.0588	12	1897	8	6.6852
1899	12	−6.7308	13	1896	11	6.6667
1901	7	−6.7251	14	1908	11	6.6066
1896	7	−6.6092	15	1884	8	6.4067
1869	9	−6.4913	16	1885	11	6.3131
1884	6	−6.4171	17	1898	12	6.3084
1876	9	−6.0127	18	1877	9	6.1224
1877	2	−5.9441	19	1881	1	5.9574
1907	11	−5.8052	20	1904	10	5.9423
1895	12	−5.6911	21	1900	12	5.9387
1903	6	−5.5556	22	1885	10	5.8824
1896	8	−5.5385	23	1895	5	5.6980
1911	9	−5.4201	24	1882	7	5.6893
1877	3	−5.2045	25	1885	8	5.5710

return, August 1907. Of the nine lowest returns, only May 1880 is unconnected with a financial panic. Two more of the 25 lowest returns came in the month after the panic, June 1884 and November 1907.

The list of highest monthly stock returns in Table 1 shows a tendency, but not a marked tendency, for stocks to rally two or three months after a panic: December 1873, rank 3; September 1893, rank 11; and August 1884, rank 15. Only 1907 fails to show a good post-panic rally; it appears to have been the worst of the 48 years for the stock market. The non-panic year 1877, like 1907, had 4 of the 25 lowest monthly stock returns, but unlike 1907 it also had two of the 25 highest. It was a year of general deflation, strikes, and other unrest.

The data on monthly bond returns in Table 2 tell a story similar to that of stock returns. All four of the panic months are in the 18 lowest bond returns. A small difference from stocks is the tendency of bonds to

TABLE 2
The 25 lowest and 25 highest Aaa bond returns, 1866 through 1913

Year	Month	Lowest Return	Rank	Year	Month	Highest Return
1873	10	−4.1236%	1	1874	1	3.9196%
1896	8	−2.4319	2	1870	2	3.7627
1907	11	−1.9494	3	1872	1	3.4114
1893	7	−1.6777	4	1873	12	3.3920
1884	6	−1.1941	5	1879	2	2.7477
1893	8	−1.1460	6	1866	5	2.6326
1873	9	−1.0652	7	1908	1	2.6009
1871	10	−1.0308	8	1893	9	2.5007
1898	4	−0.9811	9	1867	7	2.4054
1896	7	−0.9588	10	1879	5	2.3917
1898	3	−0.9526	11	1881	5	2.3355
1879	9	−0.8358	12	1879	1	2.2744
1884	5	−0.8246	13	1868	1	2.1886
1887	9	−0.8080	14	1880	11	2.1735
1881	9	−0.7996	15	1866	7	2.0805
1866	12	−0.7828	16	1874	2	2.0511
1879	3	−0.7616	17	1869	5	2.0233
1907	10	−0.7142	18	1907	12	2.0085
1876	9	−0.6445	19	1870	3	1.9370
1893	6	−0.6404	20	1874	11	1.9362
1907	3	−0.6363	21	1891	1	1.9275
1869	10	−0.6158	22	1896	11	1.8925
1913	3	−0.5968	23	1893	11	1.8437
1886	9	−0.5305	24	1872	7	1.7917
1877	3	−0.5227	25	1868	2	1.7408

experience their worst declines in the month after the panic/crash rather than contemporaneously. Four of the six lowest monthly bond returns during 1866–1913 came in the months immediately following the panic months in 1873, 1884, 1893, and 1907. The likely explanation is the scramble for liquidity that led banks and other investors to dump bonds in response to panics. But like stocks, bonds tended to have good rallies in the months after panics, as can be seen in the list of the 25 highest monthly bond returns. Seven of the 25 highest monthly bond returns occurred two to five months after the panics of 1873, 1893, and 1907.

The commercial paper returns of Table 3 show that the worst three months were panic related, and one more month of the worst 25 (May 1893) was close to a panic. On the other side, the highest nine months of commercial paper returns, meaning the months when commercial paper interest rates dropped the most, came in the months following panics. These

TABLE 3
The 25 lowest and 25 highest commercial paper returns, 1866 through 1913

Year	Month	Lowest Return	Rank	Year	Month	Highest Return
1893	7	−2.6675%	1	1893	9	5.3438%
1907	11	−2.1037	2	1873	12	2.9993
1873	9	−1.9016	3	1908	1	2.9570
1871	10	−0.5933	4	1907	12	2.5253
1868	11	−0.2444	5	1873	11	2.2268
1893	5	−0.2387	6	1873	5	2.1781
1879	8	−0.2355	7	1893	8	1.8404
1872	9	−0.1921	8	1893	10	1.7614
1877	8	−0.1601	9	1874	1	1.6970
1896	1	−0.1393	10	1869	12	1.6936
1898	3	−0.1379	11	1869	5	1.6023
1896	8	−0.1147	12	1896	11	1.5825
1879	3	−0.1023	13	1873	1	1.5089
1886	8	−0.0911	14	1868	12	1.5008
1876	9	−0.0859	15	1872	1	1.4562
1909	10	−0.0147	16	1870	2	1.3606
1898	4	0.0156	17	1896	2	1.3407
1881	8	0.0172	18	1893	11	1.3327
1895	12	0.0260	19	1872	12	1.3142
1869	6	0.0393	20	1870	1	1.3120
1866	11	0.0424	21	1871	1	1.3055
1882	8	0.0431	22	1872	5	1.2725
1878	9	0.0490	23	1891	1	1.2311
1888	9	0.0586	24	1868	5	1.1831
1890	11	0.0637	25	1898	5	1.1792

drops in short-term interest rates, like the post-panic bond rallies, are indicative of the depressed general economic conditions that typically followed the major financial panics. The brief panic of 1884, which was confined to New York, had no noticeable impact on commercial paper.

There is a tendency for soaring call money rates to be associated with panic months, but it is not as strong as one would expect from the traditional theory that crises typically spread from the banking system to the stock market through the call loan mechanism (see Table 4). Although two of the three highest monthly call loan rates came in the panic months of 1884 and 1873, none of the 50 highest comes in any months of 1893, and the only two "shows" for 1907 (ranks 18 and 33) came in the two months after the panic, not during or before it.

Our measure of volatility identified as belonging to a particular month (e.g., volatility in September 1873) is the annualized standard deviation of

TABLE 4
The 50 highest call money interest rates, 1866 through 1913

Rank	Year	Month	Rate	Rank	Year	Month	Rate
1	1884	5	163.40%	26	1868	3	16.70%
2	1873	4	87.50	27	1872	3	16.40
3	1873	9	72.05	28	1880	4	16.15
4	1872	12	58.68	29	1881	8	15.60
5	1881	2	50.12	30	1871	1	15.40
6	1879	11	45.80	31	1880	3	15.25
7	1879	10	40.10	32	1872	2	14.90
8	1872	4	36.25	33	1907	12	14.60
9	1872	9	35.20	34	1905	12	14.20
10	1868	11	35.00	35	1872	1	14.10
11	1887	6	33.26	36	1881	10	13.55
12	1873	10	31.20	37	1873	11	13.50
13	1869	6	30.10	38	1879	9	12.55
14	1886	12	28.69	39	1872	11	12.30
15	1880	11	22.00	40	1867	10	11.45
16	1873	3	21.35	41	1880	12	11.10
17	1868	12	20.55	42	1883	3	10.87
18	1907	11	19.80	43	1882	11	10.75
19	1869	1	18.40	44	1873	12	10.75
20	1870	12	18.40	45	1873	1	10.55
21	1881	12	18.28	46	1879	12	10.30
22	1871	12	18.15	47	1890	8	10.10
23	1873	2	18.00	48	1899	12	10.10
24	1868	4	17.40	49	1902	9	10.00
25	1881	3	17.15	50	1889	12	9.87

monthly returns for that month and 9 of the previous 11 months. The high and low returns for the previous 11 months are discarded, as is done in the judging of sports competitions such as diving and gymnastics. The measure is a variant of the standard deviation measure used in a number of volatility studies (e.g., Feinstein, 1987; Shiller, 1988). We call it the "trimmed annualized standard deviation" (TASD). A detailed description of TASD and its relation to the literature on volatility is presented in the Technical Appendix.

In developing the TASD we had in mind two purposes of our project. To study the behavior of asset returns and their volatility in and around panic months, we require a measure of volatility that changes from month to month. Our measure, which is in the nature of a moving average, does. Without trimming, however, the extreme volatility characteristic of a panic month would carry over into a pure moving average measure of volatility in subsequent months, leading to a bias in favor of a conclusion that volatility was high after panics. Our trimming procedure, which not necessarily but in fact leads us to drop the panic month from our post-panic monthly volatility measures, eliminates this bias.

The 50 months of highest volatility for stocks, bonds, and paper during 1866–1913 are presented in Table 5. This table shows that for stocks and bonds the months of greatest volatility tended to be in the year following the panic year, while for commercial paper and call money the months of greatest volatility tended to be coincident with, or closely following, the panic month itself.

Figure 1 portrays asset volatility (stocks, bonds, and paper) for four 10-year periods centered on each of the panic months. In the panels of Figure 1, the hatch marks for years on the horizontal axes are located at June of each year, and the vertical lines mark each of the four panic months. The vertical volatility axes are comparable, so direct comparisons of volatility levels across the four panic periods can be made visually.

In general, the asset volatility relationships are what one would expect: the four panels of Figure 1 all indicate that monthly stock returns were considerably more volatile than monthly bond and paper returns, and that long-term bond returns were somewhat more volatile than short-term paper returns. Call money returns, on the other hand, exhibited such extreme measures of volatility that it was not convenient to graph them in Figure 1.

The four panels of Figure 1 support two general points about panics and crashes in the National Banking era. First, while volatility increased

TABLE 5
The top 50 months of volatility for stocks, bonds, and paper,
1866 through 1913

	Stocks			Bonds			Paper		
Rank	Year	Mo.	Stocks	Year	Mo.	Bonds	Year	Mo.	Paper
1	1908	5	16.2433	1873	10	5.1473	1893	9	5.2125
2	1908	6	15.6801	1874	1	4.1399	1893	7	3.2602
3	1908	7	15.6239	1874	6	4.0149	1873	9	3.0964
4	1908	4	15.4590	1870	2	4.0121	1873	12	2.8656
5	1908	2	15.0509	1874	7	4.0041	1907	11	2.7715
6	1908	1	15.0179	1874	8	3.9859	1908	1	2.5623
7	1901	7	15.0078	1874	5	3.9853	1874	3	2.3766
8	1878	1	14.2182	1874	2	3.9037	1874	1	2.3706
9	1877	10	14.1960	1874	3	3.8780	1874	4	2.3598
10	1877	12	14.1921	1874	4	3.7958	1874	2	2.3493
11	1877	11	14.1841	1866	1	3.7295	1908	10	2.2734
12	1873	12	14.1461	1873	12	3.6842	1893	11	2.2527
13	1908	3	13.9722	1866	2	3.5088	1894	2	2.2375
14	1901	8	13.7695	1866	5	3.3517	1894	1	2.2339
15	1901	10	13.7645	1874	9	3.2913	1908	11	2.2322
16	1877	8	13.7459	1894	4	3.2334	1893	12	2.2206
17	1877	9	13.7238	1894	2	3.2135	1894	4	2.2003
18	1907	12	13.5497	1893	9	3.2087	1908	9	2.1874
19	1893	9	13.5273	1894	3	3.1960	1894	3	2.1753
20	1908	9	13.0782	1893	12	3.1684	1908	8	2.1637
21	1908	8	13.0658	1908	1	3.1577	1908	7	2.1601
22	1901	9	13.0519	1894	1	3.1481	1893	10	2.1537
23	1878	2	13.0206	1866	6	3.1173	1908	6	2.1468
24	1896	11	12.8153	1866	9	3.1104	1908	2	2.1274
25	1894	4	12.5641	1881	9	3.0704	1908	4	2.1268
26	1901	5	12.4214	1866	8	3.0685	1908	5	2.1260
27	1894	3	12.3836	1894	5	3.0654	1907	12	2.1259
28	1901	11	12.3543	1893	11	2.9869	1874	9	2.1214
29	1891	9	12.2079	1879	9	2.9852	1908	3	2.1011
30	1884	8	12.1837	1896	8	2.9804	1874	7	2.0859
31	1898	5	12.0430	1874	10	2.9739	1874	6	2.0430
32	1901	12	12.0014	1866	12	2.9629	1874	8	2.0361
33	1901	6	11.9526	1879	11	2.9519	1874	5	2.0144
34	1902	1	11.8947	1879	12	2.9512	1874	10	1.9985
35	1878	3	11.8415	1879	10	2.9497	1873	11	1.9552
36	1893	12	11.8154	1881	10	2.9477	1894	5	1.9278
37	1874	8	11.8127	1870	4	2.8830	1873	5	1.9115
38	1902	2	11.8042	1866	7	2.8746	1894	6	1.8928
39	1880	5	11.7880	1870	3	2.8724	1894	7	1.8689
40	1898	6	11.7863	1866	10	2.8688	1893	8	1.7911
41	1874	7	11.7802	1874	11	2.8547	1870	2	1.6931
42	1874	6	11.7571	1872	1	2.8469	1896	11	1.6278
43	1874	5	11.7442	1896	11	2.7880	1870	1	1.6009
44	1874	4	11.7132	1870	8	2.7807	1869	10	1.5759
45	1893	11	11.7040	1870	6	2.7704	1872	9	1.5749
46	1874	3	11.5068	1908	5	2.7412	1869	12	1.5644
47	1894	2	11.5040	1894	6	2.7194	1869	9	1.5279
48	1874	2	11.4914	1866	11	2.7094	1894	8	1.5118
49	1901	4	11.4480	1908	7	2.6665	1871	10	1.5107
50	1902	3	11.4422	1870	5	2.6663	1869	8	1.4993

FIGURE 1
**Asset volatility for stocks, bonds, and paper for 10-year periods
centered on the panic month**

A. Asset volatility encompassing the panic of 1873

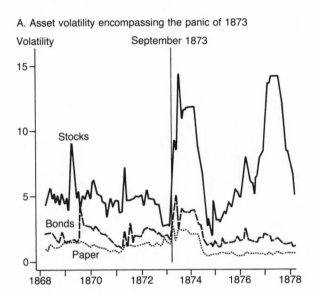

B. Asset volatility encompassing the panic of 1884

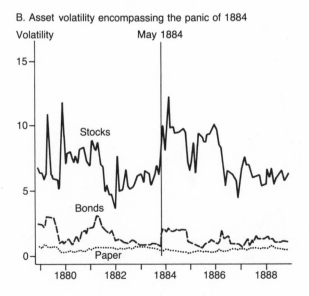

FIGURE 1—continued
Asset volatility for stocks, bonds, and paper for 10-year periods
centered on the panic month

C. Asset volatility encompassing the panic of 1893

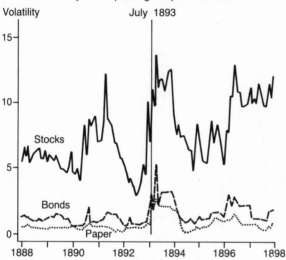

D. Asset volatility encompassing the panic of 1907

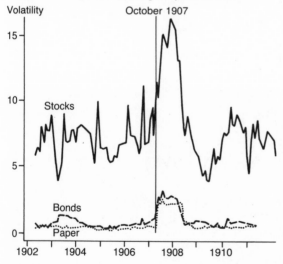

sharply in the months of panic, volatility was not unusual prior to the panic months themselves. In other words, it would have been difficult if not impossible to forecast any of the panics or associated stock market crashes on the basis of unusual prior volatility because there was none. The panic of 1893 might be viewed as an exception to this generalization because volatility jumped up in May, two months before our panic month. Sprague, however, identified May as the first phase of the 1893 panic, and we also would note that the May 1893 level of volatility, while high, was less than that in September 1891 (a high return month) and that of the months after the July 1893 panic. The 1907 panel shows two volatility spikes (March and August) before the October panic, but they were not unusual spikes for that period.

The second general point is that while volatility leaps up from prior typical levels in the month of the panic, the peak of volatility comes after the panic months, from two to seven months later. In the panics and crashes in the National Banking era, increased volatility of stock, bond, and paper returns was essentially a post-panic phenomenon.

We conclude that neither of the two hypotheses relating banking panics to stock market crashes is fully supported by the volatility evidence from the National Banking era. The traditional hypothesis that banking problems led to stock market crashes receives its strongest support from the experience of 1873, in which asset volatility was atypically low in the months before the panic. In 1884 volatility was normal before the outbreak of the panic, but the historical record does not indicate any systemic problems in banking that year, so neither of the two hypotheses is supported. The hypothesis that asset market volatility led to banking problems receives some support from the experiences of 1893 and 1907. In each of these two cases stock and bond return volatilities increased before the outbreak of the banking panic; however, the pre-panic volatility increases were not unusual in either case.

LONGER-TERM PERSPECTIVES ON VOLATILITY

In the early stages of our work for this paper, an amusing thing happened to us. We had intended primarily to study the panics and crashes of the National Banking era. Some of our monthly asset return data, however, extended from the 1830s to the present. We anticipated no problems in working with the complete data set because, we reasoned, surely the famous panics/crashes of 1873, 1884, 1893, and 1907 in the Age of the Robber Barons would stand out markedly in data covering a century and a half of U.S. financial history. And so we asked our computer to calculate the volatility of monthly stock returns for each of the 1,844 months from January 1835 through August 1988, and to print out the top 100 months of stock volatility. To our considerable surprise, we found in our top 100 not a single month from the years 1866–1913 (see Table 6). In order to rescue our research mission, we then decided to study 1866–1913 using only the data from those years, the results of which work have been presented in the previous section.

One learns in science, of course, never to discard unanticipated experimental results, no matter how irregular they might appear to be. If monthly stock returns were not notably volatile in 1866–1913, when were they? Table 6 gives the answer. No less than 67 of the top 100 months of stock volatility were in the years from 1929 through 1940, and fully 44 of the top 50 months fall in that period of Crash, Depression, and New Deal. Most of the top volatility months not contained in the 1929–40 period came before the Civil War, clustering around the panic of 1837, the depression of the early 1840s, and the panic of 1857. Nine of the top 100 months of volatility come after World War II. Eight of them are in 1974–75, and the ninth, the most volatile month since the 1930s, is October 1987. But October 1987 ranks only 43rd of the 1,844 months for which we can measure stock volatility.

For the entire one and one-half centuries, the volatility measures we calculated from monthly stock returns are portrayed in Figure 2. The period 1929–40 stands out as exceptional.

Our finding that volatility of stock returns was relatively low in the National Banking era and relatively high since the 1920s needs to be qualified in two respects. Both are discussed in the Data Appendix. First, we are not dealing with an unvarying set of stocks but with varying stock indexes extending far back into financial history. Before 1890, the underlying stock data are mostly from the railroad sector because rails were the main stocks customarily traded in the early decades we cover. The number of stocks in the indexes we use also declines as we go back in time. What effects the changing number and sectorial composition of stocks over time have on our return and volatility results cannot be determined.

The second qualification is that the end-of-month data we use for the period from 1926 to the present are inherently more volatile than the

TABLE 6
The 100 months with the highest measure of stock price
volatility—January 1834 through August 1988

Rank	Year	Mo.	Volatility	Rank	Year	Mo.	Volatility
1	1933	4	57.3899	51	1837	12	24.7801
2	1933	5	54.7984	52	1837	11	24.7335
3	1932	8	54.2944	53	1932	2	24.6284
4	1933	6	53.9899	54	1842	5	24.4471
5	1932	7	50.2864	55	1934	7	24.3944
6	1933	7	49.0640	56	1939	3	24.3192
7	1932	10	47.6105	57	1931	7	24.0453
8	1932	9	47.5364	58	1931	8	23.9813
9	1932	11	47.2036	59	1934	6	23.7036
10	1933	2	47.0073	60	1939	9	23.6188
11	1933	3	46.1105	61	1938	10	23.5226
12	1933	1	45.9814	62	1857	11	23.2559
13	1932	12	45.9206	63	1931	2	23.1156
14	1933	9	37.2824	64	1975	6	22.9140
15	1934	1	36.4229	65	1930	8	22.8265
16	1938	6	35.6280	66	1975	5	22.6930
17	1933	10	35.4034	67	1975	7	22.5206
18	1933	8	35.1612	68	1975	4	22.4803
19	1933	12	35.1357	69	1938	5	22.4385
20	1933	11	35.1033	70	1842	1	22.4093
21	1931	9	34.8590	71	1837	1	22.2993
22	1934	3	33.3079	72	1931	5	22.1818
23	1934	2	33.2039	73	1843	5	22.0735
24	1837	7	31.7253	74	1975	3	22.0449
25	1932	5	31.5477	75	1858	5	21.9583
26	1931	12	29.5022	76	1858	4	21.7183
27	1938	7	28.6056	77	1930	4	21.6624
28	1932	4	28.4941	78	1858	7	21.5958
29	1938	8	28.4406	79	1975	2	21.5714
30	1934	4	28.4151	80	1858	6	21.5467
31	1931	11	27.6078	81	1930	3	21.4967
32	1940	5	27.5627	82	1930	10	21.4754
33	1932	1	27.5445	83	1858	3	21.3434
34	1932	6	27.4781	84	1858	2	21.1335
35	1934	5	27.3768	85	1858	8	21.1053
36	1929	10	27.2853	86	1939	1	21.0316
37	1931	6	27.0349	87	1934	8	21.0037
38	1938	4	26.7078	88	1843	12	20.9945
39	1931	10	26.5897	89	1939	2	20.7565
40	1938	3	25.6271	90	1930	5	20.6741
41	1932	3	25.5343	91	1938	11	20.5578
42	1837	8	25.5220	92	1842	2	20.4526
43	1987	10	25.5215	93	1839	2	20.3832
44	1837	9	25.4416	94	1931	4	20.1455
45	1930	9	25.1261	95	1930	2	20.1291
46	1974	10	25.1125	96	1975	1	20.0738
47	1930	6	25.0672	97	1839	1	20.0247
48	1930	7	24.9305	98	1844	1	19.9789
49	1837	10	24.9052	99	1930	1	19.9353
50	1938	9	24.8092	100	1929	12	19.8790

FIGURE 2
Monthly stock price volatility, 1835–1988

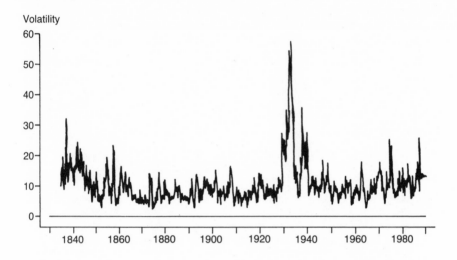

monthly average data that are available to us for pre-1926 years. We know this because we can compare end-of-month and monthly average data for 1926 and later years; when we do, we find that the latter are 20 to 25 percent less volatile than the former. This probably means that the pre-1926 data lead us to underestimate volatility in these years compared both to post-1926 years and to what we would estimate volatility to be if we had end-of-month data before 1926.

Nonetheless, we do think that the National Banking era was less volatile than the post-1926 era. Why? We are able to compare monthly average data (Standard and Poors) for 1926–88 with our roughly comparable monthly average data for the National Banking years, 1866–1913. A statistical F-test for the volatilities of monthly average stock returns in 1866–1913 and 1926–88 indicates that volatility was less in the earlier period at the .01 level of statistical significance. Consequently, we are confident that stock returns in the National Banking era were less volatile than they have been in the past six decades, a conclusion—we shall now see—that is supported by the behavior of the bond market.

What can be said of the volatility of bond returns? Our data on Aaa bonds cover the period from 1857 to the present, or 1,592 months. As with stocks, we again discovered two unexpected results. None of the months in the National Banking years, 1866–1913, are in the top 100 months of bond volatility (see Table 7). And, like stocks, much of the peak volatility in bonds arises in one brief period of about a decade. It is not the 1930s, however, but the most recent decade, 1979–88. Forty-two of the top 50 months of bond volatility in the whole period 1857–1988 covered by Table 7 fall in the years 1979–88. The other 8 of the top 50 come in 1858, following the panic of 1857. If we consider the top 100 months, 66 of them fall in 1979–88. The Civil War years 1861–65 (17 of the top 100) and 1932 (2 months), 1970 (2 months), and 1971 (5 months) are the only other years represented.

The volatility of monthly bond return is portrayed in Figure 3. The historically unprecedented nature of bond volatility in the past ten years is readily apparent. As scholars rather than bond investors, we had no inkling that we were living through a unique period of bond market history.

Compared to stocks and bonds, commercial paper has an unexciting history of returns and volatility since the Civil War. Fully 82 of the top 100 months of volatility in commercial paper returns presented in Table 8 fall into the years 1831–60. Nine of the remaining 18 top months were related to panics under National Banking: 1873–74 (5 months), 1893 (2 months), and 1907–08 (2 months). The remaining 9 are relatively recent, coming in 1980–81. Figure 4 presents a century and a half of the volatility of commercial paper returns.

The volatility histories of stocks, bonds, and commercial paper are thus both similar and different. They are similar in the sense that most of the peak volatilities of the three assets are compressed into relatively brief periods of the one and one-half centuries covered by our data. They differ in the historical timing of the peak volatilities: commercial paper before the Civil War, stocks in the years 1929–40, and bonds in the last decade, 1979–88. Our task in this paper is to describe rather than explain the historical volatility patterns. In the cases of stocks and bonds, however, we note that the former were most volatile during and after a period of unexpectedly severe deflation in the 1930s, whereas bond returns experienced their peak volatility during and after a period of unexpectedly severe inflation in the late 1970s and early 1980s.

The economic history of stock and bond market volatility raises some

TABLE 7
The 100 months with the highest measure of Aaa bond return
volatility—January 1857 through August 1988

Rank	Year	Mo.	Volatility	Rank	Year	Mo.	Volatility
1	1980	4	20.4097	51	1988	3	9.0524
2	1981	11	17.6340	52	1865	2	9.0494
3	1982	10	17.1649	53	1865	3	9.0134
4	1982	8	16.5816	54	1932	8	9.0092
5	1982	9	16.4112	55	1988	1	8.9879
6	1980	8	15.7035	56	1985	2	8.9866
7	1980	9	15.7022	57	1985	1	8.9859
8	1980	7	14.7742	58	1988	2	8.9208
9	1980	6	14.1497	59	1865	1	8.8396
10	1982	11	14.1112	60	1981	6	8.8376
11	1980	12	13.9753	61	1982	1	8.7833
12	1985	5	13.9486	62	1970	12	8.6783
13	1981	1	13.9215	63	1864	10	8.6485
14	1980	5	13.7311	64	1932	9	8.6130
15	1980	10	13.5133	65	1984	8	8.5211
16	1980	11	13.5078	66	1981	7	8.3450
17	1982	12	13.3237	67	1985	3	8.3376
18	1982	7	13.1128	68	1863	4	8.2959
19	1981	3	12.9915	69	1971	5	8.2681
20	1858	3	12.8402	70	1864	12	8.2668
21	1981	2	12.8253	71	1986	9	8.2652
22	1858	4	12.8034	72	1864	11	8.0310
23	1980	2	12.6980	73	1986	1	8.0263
24	1858	5	12.6638	74	1864	9	8.0203
25	1858	2	12.2982	75	1981	9	7.9564
26	1858	6	12.1712	76	1988	6	7.9488
27	1858	7	12.0650	77	1985	4	7.9148
28	1858	8	11.8520	78	1981	8	7.8309
29	1982	6	11.6132	79	1987	9	7.8181
30	1987	4	11.2571	80	1985	12	7.8039
31	1981	4	11.0809	81	1971	4	7.8012
32	1983	7	11.0783	82	1971	3	7.7933
33	1983	5	10.9519	83	1987	11	7.7686
34	1858	1	10.5360	84	1988	5	7.6682
35	1984	11	10.4407	85	1970	8	7.6414
36	1982	3	10.3701	86	1988	7	7.6231
37	1983	6	10.1920	87	1861	10	7.5965
38	1984	12	10.1715	88	1861	9	7.5930
39	1983	4	9.8526	89	1863	1	7.5929
40	1979	10	9.8145	90	1861	7	7.5851
41	1983	3	9.8084	91	1861	8	7.5408
42	1983	2	9.6697	92	1971	2	7.5248
43	1982	5	9.6218	93	1865	5	7.5235
44	1983	1	9.5426	94	1971	1	7.5212
45	1982	4	9.5197	95	1865	4	7.4326
46	1981	5	9.4332	96	1986	5	7.4185
47	1982	2	9.3708	97	1861	5	7.4141
48	1980	3	9.3150	98	1988	4	7.4018
49	1984	9	9.1814	99	1865	7	7.3848
50	1984	10	9.1481	100	1981	12	7.3773

FIGURE 3
Monthly Aaa bond volatility, 1858–1988

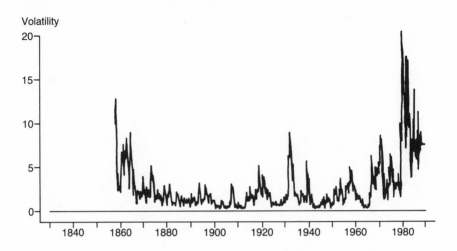

FIGURE 4
Monthly commercial paper volatility, 1832–1988

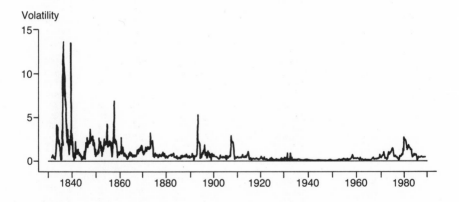

TABLE 8
The 100 months with the highest measure of commercial paper volatility—January 1831 through August 1988

	Lowest				Highest		
Rank	Year	Mo.	Volatility	Rank	Year	Mo.	Volatility
1	1839	12	13.5154	51	1847	3	2.6939
2	1837	6	13.4684	52	1848	12	2.6837
3	1837	7	10.2510	53	1980	5	2.6382
4	1837	9	10.0614	54	1848	10	2.6318
5	1837	8	9.9911	55	1836	9	2.6133
6	1837	1	9.4250	56	1847	1	2.6060
7	1837	10	9.4167	57	1861	1	2.6051
8	1837	11	8.8662	58	1840	10	2.6048
9	1837	12	8.8463	59	1840	11	2.6006
10	1837	3	7.5251	60	1847	2	2.5992
11	1837	4	7.4297	61	1835	2	2.5853
12	1837	5	7.3863	62	1851	11	2.5776
13	1837	2	7.0231	63	1980	8	2.5680
14	1857	11	6.8427	64	1838	6	2.5628
15	1836	11	6.2334	65	1908	1	2.5623
16	1893	9	5.2125	66	1849	3	2.5508
17	1836	12	4.7587	67	1838	3	2.5465
18	1855	1	4.1890	68	1838	8	2.5253
19	1834	2	4.1124	69	1981	2	2.5222
20	1834	9	3.9927	70	1838	9	2.5105
21	1834	8	3.9812	71	1838	10	2.5085
22	1838	5	3.9440	72	1981	3	2.5041
23	1834	6	3.9406	73	1858	6	2.4807
24	1834	7	3.8199	74	1858	8	2.4775
25	1834	10	3.7759	75	1849	7	2.4745
26	1838	4	3.6462	76	1858	7	2.4734
27	1836	10	3.6443	77	1981	1	2.4703
28	1834	11	3.5617	78	1835	3	2.4671
29	1848	2	3.5194	79	1839	1	2.4664
30	1836	6	3.3477	80	1839	2	2.4622
31	1834	4	3.3288	81	1838	7	2.4566
32	1834	5	3.3241	82	1838	1	2.4523
33	1840	8	3.2919	83	1980	9	2.4480
34	1893	7	3.2602	84	1849	9	2.4474
35	1834	12	3.1948	85	1849	6	2.4290
36	1840	7	3.1710	86	1857	12	2.4218
37	1873	9	3.0964	87	1849	4	2.4158
38	1840	4	3.0766	88	1849	2	2.4158
39	1840	5	3.0671	89	1854	12	2.4063
40	1840	6	3.0639	90	1858	4	2.3967
41	1835	1	3.0061	91	1980	10	2.3945
42	1840	9	2.9037	92	1858	3	2.3910
43	1873	12	2.8656	93	1858	2	2.3877
44	1857	9	2.8411	94	1858	5	2.3842
45	1849	5	2.7842	95	1849	10	2.3797
46	1848	11	2.7806	96	1874	3	2.3766
47	1907	11	2.7715	97	1980	12	2.3765
48	1848	9	2.7293	98	1874	1	2.3706
49	1849	1	2.7262	99	1980	11	2.3641
50	1848	8	2.7213	100	1874	4	2.3598

provocative issues. That monthly stock and bond returns had low volatility during the National Banking era compared to earlier and later periods is somewhat of a surprise. Financial panics were more frequent in the National Banking era than before or after, and the traditional historiography of the period emphasizes the antics of the so-called robber barons who, among other things, manipulated financial markets for personal gain without due regard for the public good. Unusually high stock and bond volatilities would be consistent with the frequency of panics and market manipulations. We find the opposite to be the case.

There is a related issue as well. The financial instabilities of the National Banking era led to the reform that established the Federal Reserve System. Further instabilities during 1929–33 led to more reforms: the SEC, the FDIC, and so on. One would have thought that these reforms would have made the stock and bond markets from the New Deal forward in time to the present less volatile than they were in the pre-1914 National Banking era. Again, we find the opposite. Have the financial reforms of the twentieth century in this sense failed? Or have other changes in the way the stock and bond markets function increased volatility more than the reforms reduced it? We do not know the answers to these questions, but we do think that they should be asked.

We conclude our paper with a brief discussion of asset volatility around the time of the 1929 and 1987 crashes, which may be compared with volatility behavior during the panics and crashes of 1866–1913. Figure 5 presents our volatility measures for 10-year periods surrounding the 1929 crash, and for 1968–78, and 1978–88, the last including, of course, the crash of 1987. With regard to 1929, several observations are warranted. First, volatility of stock, bond, and commercial paper returns was not unusual before October 1929. Second, stock volatility was higher after the crash than before. Both of these observations are consistent with our findings for panics and crashes before 1914. Third, stock volatility did not decline one to three years after the 1929 crash, as was typical in the earlier period, but instead rose to new heights in 1932–33, so much so that we had to quadruple the height of the vertical volatility axis compared to our 1866–1913 charts in order to portray it. The persistence of increased stock volatility and its rise to new heights two to three years after the stock collapse are what distinguish the crash of 1929 from earlier crashes.

Asset volatility during the past two decades is presented in the other two panels of Figure 5. The volatility axes in these two panels need to be only twice the height we used for 1866–1913, not four times as in 1929. In

FIGURE 5a
Asset volatility encompassing the Panic of 1929

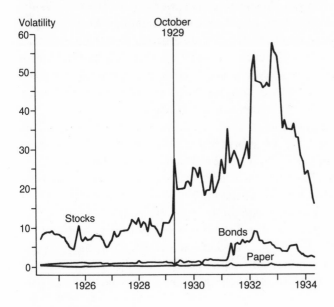

FIGURE 5b
Asset volatility, 1968-1978

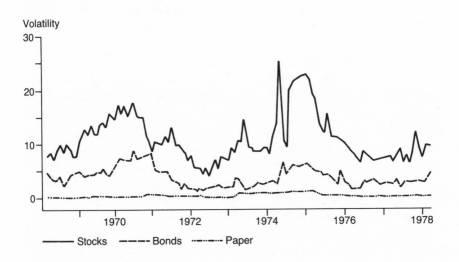

FIGURE 5c
Asset volatility, 1978-1988

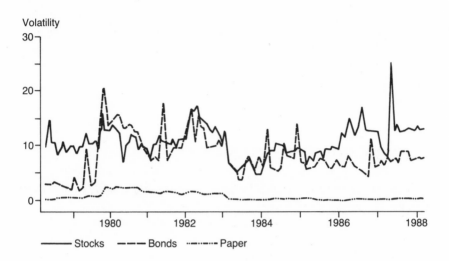

Stocks   – – – Bonds   ·········· Paper

the 1968–78 decade, bond and stock volatility was high during 1969–71 and 1974–75, the years of Vietnam and OPEC among other influences. The most unusual feature of the past decade, apart from the clearly marked spike of the October 1987 crash, is the behavior of bond return volatility. Historically, bond returns have been much less volatile than stock returns; all of our previous figures comparing stock and bond volatilities show this. But from late 1979 to 1986, bond volatility equalled and often exceeded stock volatility, an unprecedented experience.

What of the October 1987 crash? It is like earlier crashes in that market volatility was not at all unusual before October; volatility, in fact, had been declining for some months before the crash. In another respect, however, October 1987 is different from all previous crashes surveyed here. Stock volatility after October 1987 quickly declined to what are normal levels for the recent period. In earlier crashes volatility increased during and after the crash itself. October 1987 appears to move us into uncharted territory in the long history of stock market crashes.

In this chapter we have focused on the volatility of asset returns in panic/crash periods. To close, we present without comment some more conventional charts of the behavior of the stock market—the levels of stock prices in index form—before and after the crashes of 1873, 1884, 1893, 1907, 1929, and 1987 (see Figure 6). The crash month itself is set at 1 in the charts, and marked by a vertical. There is a lot of variety in the behavior of stock prices before and after crashes, more than we find in the volatility patterns. For 1987, of course, we have less than a year of post-crash market behavior. The history of crashes is fascinating, but nothing in it appears to us to offer much guidance concerning which way stock prices will move from current levels.

SUMMARY AND CONCLUSIONS

Our analysis of some 150 years of monthly returns and volatility data leads us to the following conclusions:

1. Pre-1914 banking panics were contemporaneously associated with stock market crashes. The crashes of 1929 and 1987 demonstrate, however, that it is not necessary to have a panic in order to have a crash.

2. Two hypotheses are advanced to relate bank panics and stock crashes. The first, which is traditional, is that panics caused crashes. The second is that increased stock market volatility led to both panics and crashes. Volatility evidence from the National Banking era, 1866–1913, which witnessed panics and crashes in 1873, 1884, 1893, and 1907, does not strongly support either hypothesis. The behavior of volatility before panics was irregular. During and after panics, volatility patterns were more uniform: volatility rose during the panic/crash month and continued to rise during succeeding months before declining to more normal levels.

3. In contrast with impressions one receives from financial and other historians, the National Banking era before 1914 exhibits less, not more, stock and bond market volatility than the period from 1914 to the present. This raises questions about the effectiveness of financial and regulatory reforms that were put in place in 1914 and later years.

4. The past century and a half of financial market history indicates that the highest volatilities of stock, bond, and commercial paper returns were concentrated in relatively brief periods, but also that these brief periods differed for the three assets. Most of the peak volatilities of commercial paper returns occurred before the Civil War. Most of the peak volatilities of common stock returns were concentrated in the years 1929–40.

FIGURE 6
Stock price indexes (Price = 1.0 in crash month)

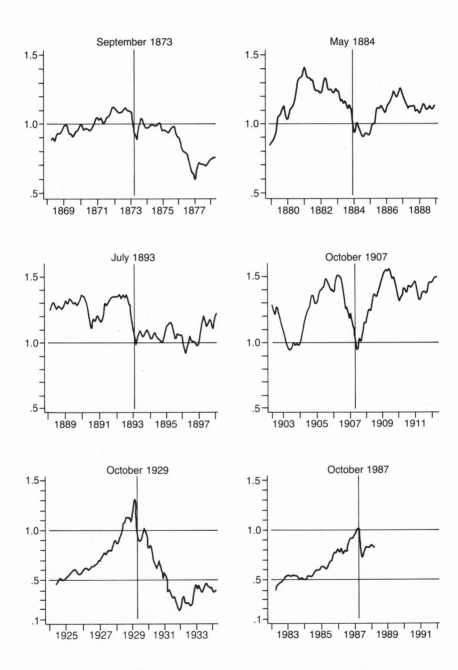

Most of the peak volatilities in bond market returns occurred in the latest decade, 1979-88. These findings raise new questions for financial research.

5. The crash of 1929 differed from pre-1914 crashes. Volatility of stock returns failed to decline one to three years after the crash, as it did in the National Banking era, but instead rose to new heights.

6. The crash of 1987 also differed from earlier crashes. Stock market volatility returned quickly to normal levels after the crash rather than rising to higher levels as happened after the crashes of 1873, 1884, 1893, 1907, and 1929.

DATA APPENDIX

Introduction

All returns and changes in this paper are expressed in monthly percentage form and are based on arithmetic as opposed to logarithmic changes. For bonds and commercial paper, the returns are on a holding period yield basis while for a common stock we use only the appreciation return. For call money, the monthly holding period assumption is not relevant, and the values are expressed in interest rate terms instead of returns.

We have attempted to assemble the highest quality data that are available on a monthly basis, over as long a period as possible. As a general caution, we feel that the quality of the data deteriorates backward in time. Ideally, the data should be end-of-month data; however, most of the early data (at least to the 1920s) are monthly averages or the average of the "high" and "low" for a particular month, and even some of the later data on interest rates are averages for the last full week in the month.

The use of average as opposed to end-of-month data biases the measures of volatility downward. We have experimented with a file of Standard and Poor's composite monthly stock prices both on an average and end-of-month basis from January 1926 through 1987. Using the regular standard deviation of 12 monthly returns as the measure of volatility, the end-of-month measure was greater than the average measure. Based on mean volatility over the period, the end-of-month measure exceeded the average measure by 25 percent, and based on medians, 23 percent.[1] Thus, it is important to consider the definition of the returns measures because they are not comparable between periods if the definition changes from average to end-of-month data. The measures of volatility are comparable over the time periods where the definitions are the same. The description of the data sources below will carefully draw the distinction between average and end-of-month data sources.

Call Money Interest Rates

Frederick Macaulay (1938) and Albert Greef (1938) are used as the two basic sources for the call money interest rates for the period prior to picking up the Federal Reserve sources (1943) in 1919. Macaulay (1938, Appendix Table 10, pp. A141–61) provides a monthly call money interest rate from January 1857 through January 1937. His rates are "renewal" rates on existing call loans, and are monthly averages of daily rates. From 1890 Macaulay's data are identical to the average rates

---

[1] Other experiments with common stocks led to similar conclusions.

on "renewal" loans from Federal Reserve sources. Greef (1938, Table 6, pp. 130–32) presents monthly call money rates, on a "new" loan basis, from January 1866 through December 1935. Greef cites the source of his data as Federal Reserve System publications, and cautions that the "new" rates change to a "renewal" definition in the latter part of the series.[2]

The Fed data (1943) are provided as monthly averages for "renewal" loans from 1890. Beginning in 1919, the Fed data are also available on an average weekly basis for both "new" and "renewal" loans. This series continues until March 1957, when the "going rate" on call loans is substituted (1980, pp. 682–683).

The "new" rates are more volatile than the "renewal" rates and seem more appropriate in expressing the true market conditions; furthermore, the end-of-month data are preferable to the monthly averages. Therefore, we have constructed a monthly series by using Macaulay's average monthly data on "renewal" loans from January 1857 through December 1865, Greef's "new" average monthly rates from January 1866 through December 1918, and the weekly average rates for the last week of the month for "new" loans from the Federal Reserve sources.[3]

Commercial Paper Returns
A monthly series of percentage holding period returns was constructed for commercial paper from January 1830 through June 1988. Although the terms to maturity of the commercial paper were either unknown or changed over time, we have calculated the returns on the assumption of a purchase with five months to maturity (152.1875 days) and sold with four months to maturity (121.75 days). The formula for the acquisition and sales price used was:

$$P = 100 - [100r / (360/d)]$$

where "r" is the market interest rate in decimal form and "d" is days to maturity. The percentage return is calculated on the basis of the sales price in a particular month relative to the purchase price in the previous month.

The source of the early data is Macaulay. In his Appendix Table 10 (1938, pp. A141–61), he provides average monthly values for prime commercial paper from January 1857 through January 1937. He also provides (1938, Appendix Tables 24 and 25, pp. A246–50) the available monthly rates in Boston presented by Erastus Bigelow and Joseph G. Martin. These data (1831 through 1856) are relatively crude, but seemingly all that are available. We have relied in this early

---

[2] By comparing Greef's data with Macaulay's, it can be determined that 1922 was when the change was made (from that date, Greef's data are identical with Macaulay's.)

[3] At the splice dates the rates were very similar, and no adjustment was made to any of the series in the splicing process.

period primarily on Bigelow's end-of-month values, and have had to interpolate in some missing values in 1834 and 1835. These values were spliced to Macaulay's average monthly rates from New York for prime commercial paper in January 1857, with the earlier rates adjusted on the basis of the overlap. Macaulay's definitions of his series is for "choice two name paper" from January 1857 to about 1910 for 60–90-day paper, and from then for "4 to 6 month prime name paper" (1938, Appendix E, pp. A349–51).[4]

As with call money interest rates, the weekly average rates become available from the Federal Reserve sources (1943–86) in January 1919. Also, from January 1890, monthly average interest rates for 4–6 month commercial paper are available from the same source (1943, Table 120). These early monthly average rates differ from the rates reported by Greef and Macaulay, and on average are higher than Greef's rates.[5]

The Fed source lists missing values for the months of November and December 1907, March, October, and November 1908, and October 1909. Given the marked differences between Macaulay, Greef, and the Fed, we checked *Historical Statistics* (1949), which was no help since it provided only Macaulay's data. Therefore, we spliced in commercial paper rates for those dates based upon the Fed's source of Stock Exchange 90-day time loans, using the monthly percentage changes of the overlapping series for the interpolation.

The final series that was constructed included the Bigelow-Martin data from 1831 through 1856, Macaulay's average monthly series through 1889, the average monthly data from the Fed from 1890 through 1918, and the average rate for the last week of the month from January 1919 through June 1988. The resulting series differs from January 1890 through 1918 from that presented by Wilson and Jones (1987).

Corporate Bonds

The bond series is also presented in terms of a one-month holding period percentage return for a bond with a 4 percent coupon, making semiannual payments, with 20 years to maturity. Although this is the standard assumption for calculation in our literature, as exemplified by Ibbotson Associates (1985) and others, it is an approximation to reality. The assumed term and the assumed coupon are not

---

[4] Greef (Federal Reserve Board of Governors, *Annual Statistical Digest, 1983*, Table 1, pp. 81–82) provides a similar monthly series from 1866 through 1935, but it differs from Macaulay's data, showing, on average, higher interest rates. Although both series are monthly averages, it would appear that the Greef series may be based on an "average" lower quality paper than that defined by Macaulay.
[5] Although the three sources allude to similar basic source materials, the data differ. The three series move similarly (but with different magnitudes) over the 1866–1919 period, and we can only conjecture that the differences are due to the different qualities of paper included in their definitions.

adhered to by the available historical evidence. The formula that we use to calculate the acquisition and sale price of the bond, under the assumptions above of a one-month holding period in terms of $100 par, with a $2.00 semiannual coupon payment, and the market interest rate "r" in decimal form, is:

$$P = (2/.5r)\,[1 - (1 + .5r)^{-m}] + 100\,(1 + .5r)^{-m},$$

with "m" being 40 periods at acquisition and 39-5/6 at sale, with an interest return of 33 1/3 cents for the period. The total return is equal to the interest return plus the appreciation return for each month. Although this formulation provides a very close approximation to the price of the 4 percent coupon, 20-year maturity, it is not exact, as shown by Whitmore (1985).

There seems to be no extant monthly series for earlier periods prior to Macaulay's interest rates on railroad bonds beginning in 1857. Therefore, the bond series begins with Macaulay's quotations (1938, Table A10, pp. A141–61) in January 1857, which are continued through January 1937. The bonds included in Macaulay's index enter and exit, and their maturities are varied, but in the main they are high quality debt instruments with maturities of 20 years or more.

The Federal Reserve sources (1943–86) are based on Moody's Aaa series, even to the present day, and begin in 1919. We used the first six-month overlap of the series from January through June to derive a splice factor, and adjusted Macaulay's rates upward by a factor of 3.0845 percent by division. For the period 1919–33 the interest rates are monthly averages, and from 1934 the rates are averages for the last full week of each month.

Stock Prices

We have relied on only four series, Cole and Frickey (1928), Macaulay (1938), Cowles (1939), and the CRSP index returns for the New York Stock Exchange (1987). The Cole and Frickey data are for railroad stocks, which dominated stock market transactions prior to about 1890. We consider their index to be of relatively low quality, but better than any alternative series for the period prior to 1871. The construction of their index, with 1853 = 100, was based on the monthly calculation of an unweighted geometric mean of either the beginning-of-month or middle-of-month bid prices, whichever were available.[6] The earlier data were spliced to the later data on the basis of the overlap of the monthly values in 1853.

Macaulay (1988, Table A10, pp. A141–61) presents a weighted average of railroad stock prices, with the weights being the number of shares outstanding, from

---

[6] We have used their index for 8 stocks for the period January 1834 through December 1853 (Cole & Frickey, 1928, Table 2, Index I, p. 129) and the index for 18 selected stocks from January 1853 through December 1866 (Cole & Frickey, 1928, Table 2, Index IIc, p. 129).

January 1857 through January 1937. It is difficult to ascertain exactly from Macaulay's description, but the data appear to be "average" monthly values.

Cowles' index was formed as the value-weighted index of all stocks that were actively traded on the New York Stock Exchange, and extends from January 1871 through December 1938. Our prices are based on the "All Stocks" series (1939, Table P–1, pp. 66–69), although the composition of the securities in the early portion was dominated by railroad stocks. A complete description of the construction of this index is available in Wilson and Jones (1987).[7]

Beginning in January 1926, we had the choice of two indexes, either the index based upon the Standard & Poor's "500" as regularly updated by Ibbotson Associates, or that available from the index of the New York Stock Exchange securities compiled by CRSP, the Center for Research in Security Prices (1987). Since the coverage of the S&P index has varied from only 90 securities up to 500, and there have been major changes in the industrial composition of the securities included, we chose the broader measure by CRSP, which seems more compatible with the Cowles' data. For 1988, we have used the percentage change in the prices of the NYSE composite index. The CRSP data are end-of-month observations.

We spliced the Cole and the Frickey data to Macaulay's series in January 1857, further spliced to the Cowles' data in January 1871, and finally spliced to the CRSP data in January 1926. Due to the unavailability of dividend returns for the period 1834–70, and the relative low quality of dividend data from 1871, especially until 1926, we measure stock price changes only.

TECHNICAL APPENDIX

Volatility Measurement

Several empirical measures of the volatility in asset returns have been used in past research, all with their origin in the well known definition used by Markowitz (1987), $E(r-u)^2$, the expected variance. Markowitz's variance is an *ex ante* concept, but we are interested in describing volatility in the *ex post* sense, and for market indexes as opposed to individual securities.

Officer's work (1973) on the description of common stock volatility from 1897 to 1969 is a landmark initial point. Officer spliced together several stock index measures over the period, and experimented with the 12-month standard deviation,

---

[7] It is clear that the individual security prices used by Cowles were the average of the high and low prices for each month.

the mean absolute deviation, and fractiles as his measures of volatility, settling on the centered moving 12-month standard deviation of stock price changes in arithmetic form.

Ibbotson Associates' well-known *Yearbooks* (1985, 1986) have included (until quite recently) the standard deviation of the 12 monthly returns for each calendar year for a large number of assets. This descriptive measure is an "annualized" standard deviation derived by calculating the regular standard deviation and multiplying by the square root of 12. Merton (1980) uses a similar measure of volatility, calculated as the average squared deviation of 12 months of logarithmic returns around the logarithmic mean. Merton finds this estimator only trivially biased, and an accurate measure of volatility. Pindyck (1984), in his study of stock volatility relative to inflation, uses exactly the same measure as Merton.

French, Schwert, and Stambaugh (1987) use daily percentage changes in the S&P Composite Index from 1926, measuring the monthly standard deviation from these data as the square root of the sum of the squared daily returns plus twice the product of one day's return with the next day's return. Poterba and Summers (1986) use the same daily data in their study, and measure the monthly stock price volatility as the sum of the squared daily returns divided by the number of trading days in the month. Feinstein (1987), using both monthly and daily data, measures volatility by two alternative means, the standard deviation as well as the absolute value of the percentage return. Shapiro (1988), using annual data from 1871 through 1987, measures volatility as the standard deviation of eleven annual returns.

Schwert (1988) has recently developed a new measure of volatility that is the absolute value of the error of a regression of monthly returns on 12 monthly dummy variables and 12 lagged monthly returns.[8] For our purposes in describing the volatility of different assets at and around periods of panic, Schwert's measure is preferable to the standard deviation. The disadvantage of the standard deviation is the slow rate of decay of an extreme return which remains in the simple measure of the standard deviation for 12 months, creating plateaus of volatility and complicating the problem of placing the measure of volatility in time.[9] The basic shortcoming of the standard deviation in identifying "panic months" is its lack of flexibility temporally, and its resulting insensitivity to specific months.

Although Schwert's measure is highly sensitive to specific months, we have two basic reservations. First, given the R^2 values discussed above, are the absolute values of the errors in a particular month comparable between assets—and for a

---

[8] Using our data the R^2 for the regression for common stocks is only .05, and the absolute value of the errors is, on average, the absolute value of the monthly returns. However, for bond returns the R^2 is .22, and for commercial paper returns the coefficient is .44.

[9] Officer uses the "centered" standard deviation, but would be just as appropriate to place the volatility of the 12 months at the ending month.

single asset is the volatility measure comparable at two points distant in time? Secondly, Schwert's measure is not "time invariant"; therefore, the estimated coefficients in the regression equation, and the resulting absolute values of the errors, depend upon the beginning and ending points of the data set. The fact that we have different beginning and ending points for the assets used in our study is especially troublesome when using Schwert's measure.

Schwert's measure for monthly volatility is solidly based in statistical theory. His model is among the class of parametric models discussed by Davidian and Carroll (1987) in their discussion of variance function estimators. Davidian and Carroll compare many of the models, finding a wide range of robustness among models, and find for many models that "trimming" and/or weighting can lead to large increases in efficiency. The early application of this type of estimator by Schwert likely will lead to better estimates of *ex post* asset risk.

Given the above, we have developed our own measure of volatility tailored to our specific needs for this research project. Since we are only describing volatility, the measure need not possess the statistical properties that would be required if inference were involved.[10]

The basic properties that we seek are:
1. simplicity and understandability,
2. time invariance,
3. flexibility and sensitivity, and
4. comparability between assets.

The measure that we have developed is similar to the standard deviation of monthly returns, but is altered in the spirit of "robust" or "order" statistics as discussed, for example, in Rosenberg and Gasko (1983), Iglewicz (1983), and Hampel, Ronchetti, Rousseeuw, and Stahel (1986). In short, our measure is a nonparametric statistic that avoids many of the inadequacies of the regular standard deviation. For 12 contiguous monthly values, our measure of volatility "belongs" to the ending month. The returns for the ending month and for 9 of the 11 preceding months (after dropping the largest and smallest of those 11 values) are averaged, and the standard deviation of the 10 returns is calculated around the mean of the 10 returns. In order to make the magnitude of the returns comparable to Schwert's measure, and to the annualized standard deviation, the resulting standard deviation is multiplied by the square root of 12. Our trimming of the estimate of the mean and the resulting standard deviation amounts to an 18 percent trim, which is not uncommon in "robust" estimation. However, the requirement that the current month be maintained and the trimming take place with the previous 11 values is

---

[10] We are not testing hypotheses and are more interested with the derivation of a "descriptive" measure of volatility of asset returns as opposed to a "robust" measure.

arbitrary, stylized for our purposes, and intended as a descriptive measure only.

A clearer explanation can be accomplished with an example, and we can also illustrate the similarities of our measure with two alternative measures. For the example, the first column of the table below shows the monthly percentage change in our stock price index (APPR) for the twelve months of calendar year 1987. The returns for the 11 months preceding in 1986 were: 6.94, 5.20, −1.42, 4.63, 1.26, −5.63, 6.85, −8.19, 5.07, 1.36, and −3.01. The second column shows the regular annualized standard deviation (ASD), the third column provides the absolute value of the residual for Schwert's regression (SCHWERT) that we estimated using monthly data from January 1834 through June 1988, and the final column shows our new measure, the "trimmed annualized standard deviation" (TASD).

Using the 11 values listed above plus the January return in column 1 of 12.60 percent, the ASD is 19.65. The ASD is calculated using 12 degrees of freedom and multiplied by the square root of 12 for annualization. In calculating the TASD for January, the 12.60 percent would be combined with the 9 values shown above, after the elimination of the −8.19 and the 6.94, and the annualized standard deviation for the "trimmed" standard deviation is 17.74. In order to calculate Schwert's value, we would have to refer to the 24 estimated regression coefficients and calculate the absolute value of the residual from that regression.

TABLE A–1

Month	APPR	ASD	SCHWERT	TASD
January	12.60	19.65	11.78	17.74
February	3.78	19.11	1.75	13.36
March	2.40	18.81	1.37	12.82
April	−1.80	18.87	1.45	12.92
May	3.00	18.67	3.07	12.56
June	1.36	18.67	.34	12.56
July	4.00	17.23	2.93	9.84
August	3.25	16.61	1.97	8.46
September	−2.30	13.71	2.15	7.98
October	−21.90	26.73	21.98	25.52
November	−7.89	27.79	5.04	12.80
December	6.58	28.45	6.29	13.69

For the calculation of the ASD and TASD for February, the earliest value would be dropped and the February 1987 value added. With the 12 new values, the largest and smallest would be dropped in the calculation of the TASD, which means that January's return would be excluded as the largest return for the 11 months preceding February. Actually, these standard deviations are in percentage terms, the same as the units of measurement of the returns. The volatility measures are seen to be similar in magnitude. The lack of flexibility in the ASD measure is obvious, with the large return in January affecting the measure for the 12-month period, whereas the October change of –21.90 percent will persist for the 11 months following October. The high degree of flexibility in Schwert's measure can also be seen, as can the fact that Schwert's measure is approximately equal to the absolute value of the monthly return. The TASD measure is sort of an "average" between the ASD and SCHWERT, in the sense that it is more flexible than the ASD and less flexible than SCHWERT. The TASD measure is affected in October, but the extreme return will not continue to affect the volatility in future months (unless of course a larger negative return is recorded in the next 11 months). For instance, the November 1987 change was –7.89 percent, which causes the ASD to be 27.79, which is higher than the October value of the ASD, whereas the value for the TASD is 12.80, with the absolute change measure of 7.89, which would be close to Schwert's measure.

The TASD measure seems to work well in serving as a measure for asset volatility for the purposes of this particular research effort. However, its robust qualities for general use in empirical research are yet to be evaluated relative to alternative measures.

This Technical Appendix discussion should suggest that although we understand what Markowitz and others have meant by "risk" in the theoretical and intuitive sense, it is not easily translated into empirical and numerical values with *ex post* data. Markowitz's idea of "risk" is based on an *ex ante* concept, and our ability to measure it with our extant data has been, so far, relatively crudely performed. The measurement of volatility should retain an important place on the agenda of financial research.

BIBLIOGRAPHY

Center for Research in Security Prices (1987). *New York Stock Exchange Monthly File*. Chicago: University of Chicago Press.

Cole, A. H., and Frickey, E. (August 1928). The course of stock prices, 1825–66. *The Review of Economic Statistics, 10, 182–195.*

Cowles, A. A., III & Associates (1939). *Common Stock Indexes.* (2nd ed.) Bloomington, Indiana: Principia Press.

Davidian, M., and Carroll, R. J. (1987). Variance function estimation. *Journal of the American Statistical Association, 82: 400,* 1079–91.

Federal Reserve Board of Governors (1943). *Banking and monetary statistics, 1914–1941.* Washington, DC.

Federal Reserve Board of Governors (1980). *Annual statistical digest, 1970–1979.* Washington, DC.

Federal Reserve Board of Governors (1976). *Annual statistical digest, 1971–1975*. Washington, DC.

Federal Reserve Board of Governors (1979). *Annual statistical digest, 1974–1978*. Washington, DC.

Federal Reserve Board of Governors (1982). *Annual statistical digest, 1981*. Washington, DC.

Federal Reserve Board of Governors (1983). *Annual statistical digest, 1982*. Washington, DC.

Federal Reserve Board of Governors (1984). *Annual statistical digest, 1983*. Washington, DC.

Federal Reserve Board of Governors (1985). *Annual statistical digest, 1984*. Washington, DC.

Federal Reserve Board of Governors (1986). *Annual statistical digest, 1985*. Washington, DC.

Federal Reserve Board of Governors (1976). *Banking and monetary statistics, 1941–1970*. Washington, DC.

Feinstein, S. P. (December 1987). Stock market volatility. *Economic Review* of the Atlanta Federal Reserve Bank, pp. 42–47.

French, K. R., Schwert, G. W., and Stambaugh, R. F. (1987). Expected stock returns and volatility. *Journal of Financial Economics, 19*, 3–29.

Greef, A. O. (1938). *The commercial paper house in the United States*. Cambridge, Massachusetts: Harvard University Press.

Hampel, F. R., Ronchetti, E. M., Rousseeuw, P. J., and Stahel, W. A. (1986). *Robust statistics: The approach based on influence functions*. New York: John Wiley & Sons.

Ibbotson, R. G., & Associates (1985). *Stocks, bonds, bills, and inflation: 1985 yearbook*. Chicago: Capital Market Research Center.

Ibbotson, R. G., & Associates (1986). *Stocks, bonds, bills, and inflation: 1986 yearbook*. Chicago: Capital Market Research Center.

Inglewicz, B. (1983). Robust scale estimators and confidence intervals for location. In D. C. Hoaglin, F. Mosteller, and J. W. Tukey (eds.), *Understanding robust and exploratory data analysis*. New York: John Wiley & Sons.

Macaulay, F. R. (1938). *Some theoretical problems suggested by the movements of interest rates, bond yields, and stock prices in the United States since 1856*. National Bureau of Economic Research.

Markowitz, H. M. (1987). *Mean-variance analysis in portfolio choice and capital markets*. New York: Basil Blackwell Inc.

Merton, R. C. (1980). On estimating the expected return on the market: An exploratory investigation. *Journal of Financial Economics, 8: 4*, 323–61.

Officer, R. R. (1973). The variability of the market factor of the New York Stock Exchange. *The Journal of Business, 46: 3*, 434–53.

Pindyck, R. S. (1984). Risk, inflation, and the stock market. *The American Economic Review, 74: 3*, 335–51.

Poterba, J. M., and Summers, L. H. (1986). The persistence of volatility and stock market fluctuations. *The American Economic Review, 76: 5*, 1142–51.

Rosenberg, J. L., and Gasko, M. (1983). Comparing location estimators: Trimmed means, medians, and trimean. In D. C. Hoaglin, F. Mosteller and J. W. Tukey (eds.), *Understanding robust and exploratory data analysis*. New York: John Wiley & Sons.

Santoni, G. J. (1988). The October crash: Some evidence on the cascade theory. *Review* (Federal Reserve Bank of St. Louis), *70: 3*, 18–23.

Schwert, G. W. (1988). Why does stock market volatility change over time. The Bradley Policy Research Center working paper No. GPB 87–11 (revised).

Shapiro, M. D. (1988). The stabilization of the U.S. economy: Evidence from the stock market. National Bureau of Economic Research working paper No. 2645.

Shiller, R. J. (1988). Causes of changing financial market volatility. Symposium paper for the Federal Reserve Bank of Kansas City meeting at Jackson Hole, Wyoming.

Sprague, O.M.W. (1910). *History of crises under the national banking system.* Washington, DC: National Monetary Commission, U.S. Government Printing Office (Kelley reprint, 1977).

Sylla, R. E. (1975). *The American capital market, 1846–1914.* New York: Arno Press.

U.S. Department of Commerce, Bureau of the Census (1949). *Historical statistics of the United States, 1789–1945.* Washington, DC: U.S. Government Printing Office.

Whitmore, G. A. (March/April 1985). A note on the exact calculation of accrued interest and bond pricing, *Financial Analysts Journal*, pp. 76–77.

Wilson, J. W., and Jones, C. P. (1987). A comparison of annual common stock returns: 1871–1925 with 1926–85. *The Journal of Business, 60: 2*, 329–58.

DISCUSSION

THE PANIC OF 1873 AND FINANCIAL MARKET VOLATILITY AND PANICS BEFORE 1914

Michael D. Bordo

In his interesting chapter Charles Kindleberger documents the events surrounding the international financial crisis of 1873. In a tale similar to an earlier paper (1985) on the international financial crisis of 1893, Kindleberger argues that a series of displacements or shocks touched off an investment boom in Central Europe from 1870 to 1872. The boom ultimately spawned speculative manias in stocks and real estate in Germany and Austria, in turn producing inevitable distress beginning in mid 1872 and a crash in 1873. Events in Germany and Austria, according to Kindleberger, also contributed to a crisis in the United States via international capital flows. In my comment, I initially focus on a number of differences I have with Kindleberger's approach to financial crises and then turn to the events of 1870–73.

Kindleberger's Approach
According to Kindleberger, a whole series of shocks ranging from the end of the U.S. Civil War in 1865 and the Prussian-Austrian War in 1866 to the

Franco-Prussian War of 1870–71 to the Chicago fire of 1871 are responsible for triggering the boom and resulting mania. The problem with this approach is that in every period in history shocks take place, ranging from technical breakthroughs, to wars, natural disasters, and political upsets. How can we identify any one event or series of events as the one that triggered the boom? How can we distinguish between shocks that led to a boom and those that fizzled out? The notion that unanticipated shocks are important in the propagation mechanism of the business cycle is not unattractive, and it is a key element of current research. The problem lies in making the case that a particular shock is the culprit.

Kindleberger views the essence of a financial crisis as a sharp decline in asset values leading to massive wealth losses. These are surely the earmarks but are they the triggers? He treats the role of money and the banking system as secondary. As I have argued elsewhere, reiterating the argument of Anna Schwartz (1986), the essence of a real financial crisis is a scramble for high powered money triggered by the public's fears that they will be unable to easily convert their monetary claims on the banking system into cash. These fears are aroused in the absence of a dependable lender of last resort. As a consequence, the payments system that is crucial to economic activity is impaired.

In 1873, such an event did occur in the United States, but it did not occur in Germany and Austria. What did occur in these countries was a massive disinflation which produced significant wealth losses—concentrated in the highly visible stock and real estate markets. A massive disinflation, like a massive inflation, is inconceivable in a stable money and banking system.

Of course a loss of wealth is serious for the losers. Kindleberger takes for granted that it has systemic consequences. It is not evident that stock markets will have such consequences. In any event, the solution for a loss of wealth is additional work effort and additional saving. The solution for a scramble for high powered money is timely action by a lender of last resort.

Incidentally, Kindleberger misinterprets my list of fundamental elements of a financial crisis as supporting his view, since a decline in the money supply appears sixth out of ten. The list, originally completed for a 1983 conference on financial crises in London, is merely a chronological representation of the stylized facts of financial crises drawn from the literature of which Charles Kindleberger is a leading contributor. The fact that money appears sixth has no relation to its primary role in a financial crisis.

Kindleberger also misinterprets the monetarist view by suggesting that monetary contraction per se is at the heart of a "real" crisis. It is not monetary contraction but the public's apprehension that the availability of the means of payment is in doubt. That is the essence of the monetarist position.

Finally, Kindleberger's emphasis on the international scope of financial crises is sound. The commercial world of 1873 was linked together via the fixed exchange rate gold standard (with the principal exception of the United States), and via arbitrage in goods and assets markets. Thus major shocks in one country were bound to have reverberations abroad.

The Events of 1870–73
The fact that much of the world was on the gold standard during this period suggests some major amendments to Kindleberger's story. As I see it, the main event in Kindleberger's story is the French Indemnity of 1871–72. The transfer of gold to Germany triggered a massive inflation and speculation in 1871–72. This spread to Austria and to the United States via international capital flows.[1] The inevitable overtrading and financial distress occurred in 1872, leading to a collapse in asset prices in 1873 in all three countries.

Kindleberger states that monetary stringency had nothing to do with the events in Central Europe. I disagree. A comparison of R. Tilly's (1973) German money supply series with Hoffman's (1965) GNP implicit price deflator yields almost a perfect correspondence between the annual rates of change of the two series. Thus between 1870 to 1871 and 1871 to 1872, money growth increased from 2.9 percent to 21.7 percent. This of course is Kindleberger's boom. The rate of change of the price level increased from 4.4 percent to 7.8 percent (the WPI from Mitchell (1975) increases even more). Then comparing 1871–72 with 1872–73 money growth drops to 12.69 percent and inflation to 4.4 percent; from 1872–73 to 1873–74 money

---

[1]How important this channel was is debatable since the United States was insulated to a great extent from external shocks by its flexible exchange rate. A more likely story for the U.S. crisis is that it had a life of its own.

growth drops further from 12.6 percent to 2.9 percent and inflation drops to less than one percent. This I would argue is a pretty massive disinflation by any standards that would lead to significant wealth losses and financial distress. However, as Kindleberger correctly notes there was no internal drain. The decline in money was not due to a fall in the public's deposit currency ratio as occurred in 1873 during the "real" financial crisis in the United States, but to a fall in high powered money and the banking system's deposit reserve ratio.

Kindleberger views the French indemnity as the fundamental cause of the boom and bust in Central Europe. An alternative view would give it an important exacerbating feature, making events in Germany (Austria) different only in degree from those in England and other gold standard countries linked together via the standard into a common international business cycle. Indeed, England's money growth and price performances were very similar to Germany's over this period, with rapid money growth 1870–72, monetary deceleration in 1872–74, and the rate of change in the price level conforming. However, the orders of magnitude are much smaller. Also, the NBER reference cycle chronology has the business cycle in both countries peaking at the end of 1872. Thus, evidence of similar money and price level performance in two important gold standard countries in 1871–74 suggests that, absent the Franco-Prussian War, disinflation and possibly financial stress would have occurred anyway in the early to mid 1870s across the gold standard world. The United States during the period 1870–71 to 1873–74 exhibited decelerating money growth and declining prices reflecting its independence from the gold standard world.

One possible explanation why 1872–73 was a period of stress across the world is the operation of the gold standard itself—to which England and Germany (starting in 1871) adhered and to which the United States was attempting to return. World gold production began a secular decline in 1871 which was to continue until 1896. Also, expansion in the world monetary gold stock began to taper off in this period. These movements, in turn, reflect the operation of the commodity theory of money. Gold discoveries in the 1840s and 50s led to a massive increase in the world monetary gold stock in the 1850s and 1860s, raising money supplies and prices across the gold standard world. At the same time, rising prices reduced the purchasing power or exchange value of gold, leading—with a sizeable time lag [up to two decades according to Bordo (1981) and Rockoff (1984)]—to a decline in gold production and the substitution of gold from monetary to nonmonetary uses. The process was aggravated by Germany and other countries joining the gold standard after 1870.

Pressure on the world monetary gold stock was the fundamental cause of world monetary stringency beginning in the early 1870s. The turning point, from secular inflation that began in 1848 to secular deflation, occurred in 1872–73. The disinflation process reduced the balance sheets of many financial institutions as *ex ante* sound investments predicated on rising prices turned sour when the rate of inflation and ultimately the price level declined. Thus the stage was set for financial distress and a strain on the banking system and in the absence of an effective lender of last resort, a financial crisis.

Wilson, Sylla, and Jones, "Financial Market Volatility and Panics before 1914"

This chapter makes two contributions: (a) as a descriptive exercise it documents the pattern of volatility in the United States over a century and a half of stock prices, bond prices and the returns on commercial paper and call loans; (b) it provides evidence on two hypotheses on the relationship between stock market crashes and banking panics. I will comment briefly on both aspects of the chapter.

As a descriptive exercise, the chapter presents a highly useful compilation of historical data on stock prices, bond prices, and returns on other assets. The compilation of data is supplemented by a description of the evolution of the institutions of financial markets. Finally it provides useful measures of the volatility of the different assets from the 1830s to the present.

The volatility measures in turn raise a number of questions that the authors do not provide answers for. One question raised is why the commercial paper market was much more volatile before the Civil War than after. Another question is why stock prices were highly volatile in the deflation years of the early 1930s whereas bond prices were not. A third question is why bond prices were more volatile than stock prices in the inflationary 1970s.

One possible answer to the first question is that commercial paper was the primary method of short-term finance in the pre-Civil War period. After the war more business enterprises were financed by the stock market and its attendant call loan market. Hence, the decline in volatility reflects the decline in the relative importance of the market. With respect to the second and third questions, stock prices may have been highly volatile in the deflation years of the 1930s because stocks turned out to be an important hedge against deflation. Unexpected deflation reduced the value of equities relative to nominal assets such as bonds whose real values increased with falling prices. In the same vein, bond prices were volatile in the 1970s because unanticipated rises in the price level reduced their value and to the extent that returns contained on inflation premium, they did not allow for inflation uncertainty. In fact, real yields were negative.

The author posits two alternative hypotheses on the relationship between stock market crashes and banking panics. The first, attributed to Sprague, suggests that banking panics led to stock market crashes, because faced with a loss of liquidity depositors dumped their securities. As an alternative, the authors argue that stock market crashes led to banking panics because of the close link between the call loan market and bank reserves pyramided in the New York money market and because the decline in securities prices reduced the value of banks' balance sheets leading depositors to become concerned for the safety of their funds. A comparison of the timing of stock price volatility with the incidence of banking panics in the national banking era provides inconclusive results. The Sprague hypothesis holds in 1873 and 1884, while the alternative prevails in 1893 and 1907.

A third view is that both stock market crashes and banking panics are reflections of another more basic phenomenon—an expectation of a decline in economic activity. Schwert (1988) provides evidence linking increasing stock market volatility to subsequent recessions and Gorton (1987) provides evidence that banking panics represent a rational response by depositors wishing to maintain their consumption in the face of an expected recession.

Even more fundamental as a likely cause of declining economic activity and as a determinant of both stock market crashes and banking panics is the behavior of the money stock. Sprinkel (1971) viewed evidence of specific cycle peaks in money growth preceding turning points in stock price indices as early warning for the influence of monetary contraction on the real economy. Friedman and Schwartz (1963) identified severe economic downturns—many of which also contained banking panics—with prior declines in the money supply.

Whether a banking panic accompanies a stock market crash has a lot to do with the presence or absence of an effective lender of last resort.

Historical evidence for a large number of countries that experienced frequent stock market crashes yet no banking panics suggests that the presence of effective procedures to allay incipient depositors' fears is the key (Schwartz, 1986). In addition, there is evidence suggesting that countries with nationwide branch banking systems experienced very few banking panics (Bordo, 1986).

REFERENCES

Bordo, M. D. (1986). Financial crises, banking crises, stock market crashes and the money supply: Some international evidence, 1870–1933. In F. Capie and G. Wood (eds.), *Financial crises and the world banking system*. London: Macmillan.

Friedman, D., and Schwartz, A. J. (1963). Money and business cycles. *Review of Economics and Statistics, 45,* No. 1, part 2 (supplemental).

Gorton, G. (1987). Banking panics and business cycles. University of Pennsylvania unpublished mimeo.

Hoffman, W. (1965). *Das Wachstum des deutschen Wirtschaft seit der Mitte des 19 Jahrhundart.* Berlin: Springer Verlag.

Kindleberger, C. P. (1984). International propagation of financial crises: The experience of 1888–93. In W. Engles *et al.* (eds.), *Wilfred Guth Festschrift, international capital movements, debt and monetary systems.* Mainz: Hase & Koehler Verlag.

Mitchell, B. R. (1975). *European historical statistics.* New York: Columbia University Press.

Schwarts, A. J. (1986). Real and pseudo-financial crises. In F. Capie and G. Wood (eds.), *Financial crises and the world banking system*. London: Macmillan.

Schwert, W. (1988). Business cycles, financial crises and stock volatility. Carnegie Rochester Conference on Public Policy.

Sprinkel, B. (1971). *Money and markets: A monetarist view.* Homewood, Illinois: Richard D. Irwin.

Tilly, R. (1973). Zeitreihen Zum Geldumlauf in Deutschland, 1870–1912. *J. für Nationalekonomie und Statistik, 87,* 360–63.

DISCUSSION

BANKING PANICS AND THE STOCK MARKET IN THE LATE 19TH CENTURY

Gary Gorton

Between the end of the Civil War and the founding of the Federal Reserve System, 1863–1914, the United States experienced seven banking panics. Five of these banking panics coincided with large sudden, declines in stock prices. Recessions typically followed. (See Gorton, 1988, and Sobel, 1968). Little is known about the dynamic relations between business cycles and financial crises, whether of the form of a banking panic or of a stock market crash. Less is known about how banking panics and stock price behavior are related. Yet, panics and crashes account for an enormous amount of government regulation of securities markets and of the banking system. Considering the potential regulatory impact of the events of last October 19th, the fragile state of the U.S. thrift industry, and the ongoing debate about re-regulation or deregulation of the U.S. commercial banking industry, questions about these issues are pressing indeed!

The authors of the two papers under discussion have undertaken the difficult task of elucidating the relations between business cycles, banking panics, and stock price behavior. Given the state of our current knowledge, the authors should be commended at the outset for their courage in undertaking this task. This kind of work is difficult, but very important if we are ever to give meaningful policy advice.

In analyzing the relations between business cycles, panics, and crashes the two papers are nicely complementary. Professor Kindleberger looks at the Panic of 1873 in great detail. Professors Wilson, Sylla, and Jones examine the entire National Banking era, 1863–1914, and a much longer period as well. Professor Kindleberger stresses the international dimension of the phenomenon, offers a wealth of detail to ascertain the proximate causes, and traces some international transmission mechanisms. Professors Wilson, Sylla, and Jones assess the behavior of volatility measures of stock prices, bond prices, and commercial paper.

Throughout, the two papers are sprinkled with terms like "panics," "crashes," "manias," and "bubbles," the meaning of which is not exactly clear. No definitions are given. These terms I take to be names we have given to the phenomena we would like to explain—phenomena which we take to be at odds with received theory or which are of special interest. However, since the task is to explain these phenomena it is not helpful to be casual about terminology.

Of the terms used, I know what constitutes a banking panic. A banking panic is an event in which depositors of banks demand such a large-scale transformation of deposits into currency that the banking system can only respond by suspending convertibility of deposits into currency, issuing clearinghouse loan certificates, or both. (See Sprague, 1910, and Gorton and Mullineaux, 1987). Banking panics are not mysterious events in the sense that the term has an ambiguous meaning. The difficulty is the theoretical one of explaining the causes and timing of panics. There are, however, competing theories which have been put forth. Diamond and Dybvig (1983) argue that panics are essentially random events which are manifestations of multiple equilibria. Smith (1988) claims that panics are due to regulation, while Gorton (1987) believes that panics are caused by an information asymmetry emanating from the organization of the clearing system, and Miron (1986) finds evidence that panics in the United States are caused by the seasonality of interest rates. Thus, we know a lot about banking panics compared to business cycles and stock price behavior.

The terms "bubbles," "manias," and "crashes" are all somewhat ambiguous. There are models of rational agents in which stock prices can deviate from their fundamentals, i.e., in which stock prices can be higher than the present discounted value of future dividends. Such a price deviation is a bubble. When the bubble ends it is said to crash. Loosely, a "mania" appears to refer to the period before the crash when the bubble is growing. Models of bubbles are mostly infinite horizon models in which the bubble cannot restart if it has crashed (e.g., Diba and Grossman, 1988). It is difficult to analyze the extreme episodes of stock price crashes using such infinite horizon models. Allen and Gorton (1988) present a finite horizon model with rational agents in which bubbles can occur. All other explanations depend on some form of irrationality which is usually not explained. The difficulty for empirical work is that few of the models have testable restrictions. Nevertheless there are restrictions if agents are to be thought of as rational.

An important difficulty with both papers is that they search for, attempt to explain, and test hypotheses about phenomena for which there are no clear meanings. While part of this confusion is due to the fact that we simply do not know much about events like crashes and panics, much of the confusion is due to the authors' casual use and abuse of the terms.

Before turning to the papers it is important to set their results against the background of some stylized facts about the relations between panics, business cycles, and the behavior of stock prices. While there is probably no consensus about the following observations, they represent the results of recent research.

(1) Stock price volatility is higher during recessions. (Schwert, 1988a).

(2) Industrial production volatility is higher during recessions. (Schwert, 1988a).

(3) The term *structure* is related to the state of the business cycle. Variance of expected future consumption growth is higher during recessions than during expansions. (Stambaugh, 1988).

(4) Stock volatility is related to panics, increasing after panics. (Schwert, 1988b).

(5) Panics occurred at business cycle peaks when a recession predictor spiked. (Gorton, 1988).

(6) Panics accurately forecast positive covariation between losses on deposits and marginal rates of substitution in consumption. (Gorton, 1988).

Panics thus occur in anticipation of recessions. During recessions the volatilities of many series, real and financial, are higher. In particular, the volatility of stocks is higher. Business cycles are asymmetric: recessions are shorter than expansions on average, and economic time series behave differently in expansions that in recessions. (See Hamilton, 1987). However, the volatilities of money, inflation, industrial production, and business failures are all higher during wars, but stock volatility is not high during wars (see Schwert, 1988a). Therefore, the volatility of stock prices is related to recessions but not as simply as a rational expectations/efficient markets approach might suggest—since time-varying volatility (conditional heteroskedasticity) should provide information about future macroeconomic behavior. What we lack is any explanation of how these stylized facts are related. These two chapters aim to shed some light on the relationships.

Professor Kindleberger focuses on the Panic of 1873. This episode dramatically illustrates the troublesome nexus of issues. On September 20, 1873, the stock market crashed. Western Union, for example, fell from 75 to 54 1/2. A banking panic ensued. There were similar, apparently related events in Europe's capitals. In the United States banks suspended convertibility and the Stock Exchange Board of Governors took the then unprecedented act of closing the exchange "for an indefinite period." The crash and the panic were roughly coincident in the United States. The National Bureau of Economic Research has dated the peak of the business cycle as October 1873 and the subsequent trough as March 1879. The question is: What can we learn from the events of 1873?

In analyzing the Panic of 1873 Professor Kindleberger focuses on a model he first proposed in an earlier book, *Manias, Panics and Crashes* (1978). The gist of the model is: (i) there is an exogenous shock which changes investment opportunities, leading to an "investment boom"; (ii) there may occur "overshooting"; (iii) expectations of continued price rises weaken and a period of distress follows; (iv) a crash or panic then follows. Basically, Professor Kindleberger does not distinguish between a recession, a panic, and a crash. All three events occur at the end of his business cycle. Most of his current paper is then devoted to identifying and discussing the exogenous shock or displacement that then subsequently resulted in the events of 1873. *Thirteen* candidate displacements are listed ranging from the end of the Civil War in the United States to the Chicago fire of 1871 to the relaxation of German banking laws.

It is difficult to figure out exactly what Professor Kindleberger's model means. It is certainly vague and untestable. The paper is not helpful in fleshing out its implications. Most of the paper is concerned with detailing the candidates for the initial shock. Everything is a candidate. Without a coherent theory it seems to be difficult to isolate any triggering mechanism. We are led on an abridged trip through some European history. The impression one comes away with is that Professor Kindleberger's model shares the same defect as the efficient markets model he would like to supersede, namely, it does not say much about what news is important and exactly why.

Professor Kindleberger stresses the fact that many of the recessions which had panics, which includes virtually all the major downturns, were international in character. This fact has been largely overlooked and I cannot cite a stylized fact concerning the international nature of these phenomena. Professor Kindleberger is correct to complain about this. Unfortunately, this international comparison is not done here in a useful way. Not all countries have had banking panics, though most have had large declines in stock prices. Not all banking panics have been accompanied by large declines in the stock market. Thus, there is a rich historical experience to analyze. It would be interesting to know the common characteristics of countries that had banking panics and no stock market crashes, and the common characteristics of countries without banking panics, and so on.

Professors Wilson, Sylla, and Jones calculate the volatility of stocks, bonds, and commercial paper. They also find an association between panics and stock volatility. In particular, banking panics tended to coincide with large declines in stock prices.

The first step is to compute monthly volatility measures of the time series. This task is nontrivial since for each month there is one observation. There are alternative ways of approaching this problem and the authors discuss the complications in a lengthy technical appendix. Three measures are compared in the appendix of their paper.

A major focus of their paper is to test one of the alleged links between banking panics and stock market declines. This hypothesis asserts that the net balance of trade between cities and the country favored cities. Country bank liabilities tended to end up in cities. Country banks, therefore, held clearing balances at city banks. Moreover, they were induced to do this because they were paid interest on those balances by city banks. City banks, in turn, lent money in the call loan market which financed stock purchases. It is alleged that unusual seasonal demands for currency by country banks could cause city banks to be forced to call loans, producing a stock market decline. The last step has never been convincingly articulated. If the stock market declines, then stock holders will default on their loans. Somehow this causes a banking panic. Thus, the two events would be roughly coincident. [See Griffiss (1925), Haney, Logan and Gavens (1932), Hedges (1938), Owens and Hardy (1930), and Woodlock (1908).]

This hypothesis is hard to understand but it has some testable implications. It implies, for example, that seasonal movements in interest rates should induce seasonal movements in stock prices. However, during the nineteenth century, stock prices show no seasonal variations. Seasonal variations in call loan rates existed, but there is no significant positive covariation of call loan rates and stock prices. In fact, the variation in the *volume* of stock sales rises when call loan rates are highest! (See Owens and Hardy, 1930). Thus, there is reason to doubt the already vague hypothesized channel of causation. However, it is the only known hypothesis that implies that stock volatility *is caused by panics* not vice versa.

A very loose alternative hypothesis is specified by Wilson, Sylla, and Jones. The alternative goes as follows. Suppose a stock "bubble" financed by the call loan market existed. When the bubble crashes, banks would fail and a panic would occur. In this case the stock volatility would precede the panic. This story is also hard to understand. Not only is the appearance of the bubble unexplained, but even granting a bubble, it is not clear why the bubble crashing should cause a panic. Even if some stock holders were to default on their bank loans, a more detailed scenario would be needed to generate a panic.

To discriminate between these two "theories" Wilson, Sylla, and Jones examine causally whether stock volatility increased sharply prior to the panic and find that it did not. This is not tested in any formal way which would be easy enough to do. Thus, we are left without having learned much about panics. For example, it's not clear whether changes in the currency-deposit ratio Granger-cause stock volatility, but not vice versa, or whether there is something "special" about a particular threshold of the panic. The authors simply conclude that "neither of the two hypotheses relating banking panics to stock market crashes is fully supported by the volatility evidence...."

A real contribution of the chapter is to examine other series that, to my knowledge, have not been studied before, namely, the bond and commercial paper price series. Most of the volatility in bond prices occurred in the last decade. Also, most of the commercial paper volatility occurred before the Civil War. Overall, both stock and bond markets were *less,* not more, volatile before 1914. This seems to have some strong implications for the noneffectiveness of certain regulations. These seem to me to be important new stylized facts.

Let me stress, in closing, that these authors have taken on tough tasks. Professor Kindleberger demonstrates the value of taking noneconometric historical evidence seriously. Professors Wilson, Sylla, and Jones add to our stock of stylized facts on the relations between panics and stock volatility.

REFERENCES

Allen, F., and Gorton, G. (1988). Finite rational bubbles. The Wharton School, University of Pennsylvania working paper.

Diamond, D., and Dybvig, P. (1983). Bank runs, deposit insurance, and liquidity. *Journal of Political Economy, 91,* 401–19.

Diba, B., and Grossman, H. (1988). Rational inflationary bubbles. *Journal of Monetary Economics, 21 (1),* 35–46.

Gorton, G. (1987). The Endogeneity of central banking. The Wharton School, University of Pennsylvania working paper.

Gorton, G. (1988). Banking panics and business cycles. *Oxford Economic Papers,* forthcoming.

Gorton, G., and Mullineaux, D. (1987). The joint production of confidence: Endogenous regulation and 19th century commercial bank clearinghouses. *Journal of Money, Credit, and Banking, 19 (4).*

Griffiss, B. (1925). *The New York call money market.* New York: The Ronald Press Company.

Hamilton, J. (1987). A new approach to the economic analysis of nonstationary time series and the business cycle. University of Virginia working paper.

Haney, L. H., Logan, L. S., and Gavens, H. S. (1932). *Brokers' loans: A study of the relation between speculative credits and the stock market, business, and banking.* New York: Harper and Brothers.

Hedges, J. E. (1938). *Commercial banking and the stock market before 1863.* Baltimore: Johns Hopkins University Press.

Kindleberger, C. (1978). *Manias, panics, and crashes: A history of financial crises.* New York: Basic Books.

Miron, J. (1986). Financial panics, the seasonality of the nominal interest rate, and the founding of the Fed. *American Economic Review, 76,* 125–40.

Owens, R. N., and Hardy, C. O. (1930). *Interest rates and stock speculation.* Washington, DC: The Brookings Institution.

Schwert, G. W. (1988a). Why does stock market volatility change over time? University of Rochester working paper No. GPB87–11.

Schwert, G. W. (1988b). Business cycles, financial crises and stock volatility. University of Rochester working paper.

Smith, B. (1988). Bank panics, suspensions, and geography: Some notes on the "contagion of fear" in banking. University of Western Ontario working paper.

Sobel, R. (1968). *Panic of Wall Street: A history of America's financial disasters*. London: Macmillan.

Sprague, O.M.W. (1910). *History of crises under the national banking system*. National Monetary Commission, Senate Doc. No. 538 (61st Congress, 2d session).

Stambaugh, R. (1988). The information in forward rates: Implications for models of the term structure. *Journal of Financial Economics, 21*, 41–70.

Woodlock, T. (1908). The stock exchange and the money market. In *The currency problem and the present financial situation*. New York: Columbia University Press, pp. 19–40.

PART 3

THE GREAT CRASHES OF 1929 AND 1987

CHAPTER 5

WHEN THE TICKER RAN LATE: THE STOCK MARKET BOOM AND CRASH OF 1929

Eugene N. White[*]

The spectacular rise and collapse of the stock market in the 1920s is one of the premier examples of an asset bubble. In spite of its fame, it has received very little analytical attention, even in the wake of the 1987 market crash. The stock market of the 1920s offers a natural comparison with the market of the 1980s. Both boom periods involved major changes in the structure of industry and widespread financial innovation. However, explanations of the recent collapse have focused on relations between financial markets and immediate economic conditions. The central question of whether volatile movements in asset prices reflect changes in fundamentals or speculative bubbles has been side-stepped. Fortunately, this issue stands at the forefront of any analysis of the crash of 1929, thus providing a stimulating comparison for the 1980s.

The characteristics of the stock market's boom and bust are described in this paper, which scrutinizes the numerous explanations for events offered by contemporaries and historians. The most convincing explanation of stock price movements is that they were driven by a speculative

---

*The author wishes to thank Hugh Rockoff and Anna Schwartz for helpful comments.

bubble where fundamentals played, at most, an initiating role. Rather than let the boom run out of steam, the Federal Reserve attempted to slow its advance. Tighter monetary policy did not directly halt rising stock prices; instead it helped to push the economy into a recession. The market responded to the downturn and the bubble burst, sending an additional shock to the weakening economy.

Although the conclusions reached reject many factors proposed to explain the behavior of the stock market, they concur, in part, with the conventional analysis of 1928–29. This cogent story must be examined first as it presents the basic hypotheses about why the market experienced a dizzying ascent followed by a resounding collapse.

THE CONVENTIONAL WISDOM

The preeminent description of the boom and crash is still to be found in Galbraith's classic book.[1] The explanation of events offered by Galbraith emphasizes the irrational element, the hysteria of the public first eager to participate and profit in the bull market and then panicked into selling when prices began to drop. He argues that the stock market bubble was formed during the long period of sustained economic growth of the twenties when unemployment was low and the price level stable. This produced a climate of rarely equalled faith in economic expansion and eliminated any caution leftover from the First World War or the post-war recession.

Unmindful of any moral from the collapse of the Florida land boom, investors were drawn to the stock market, which began to rise rapidly in early 1928. The conviction that stock prices would climb steadily changed investors' behavior. Those who had followed a buy-and-hold strategy began to speculate. People who had never bought stock before were drawn into the market. Thus, in Galbraith's rich prose, the market's rise depended on "the vested interest in euphoria [that] leads men and women, individuals and institutions to believe that all will be better off, that they are meant to be richer and to dismiss as intellectually deficient what is in conflict with that conviction."[2]   Consumed by the "pure speculative instinct," each investor presumed he could ride the market up and get out before it collapsed, unaware of the fallacy of composition that this reasoning entailed.[3]

In this dominant explanation of the boom, the rise in stock prices was fueled by an expansion of credit in the form of brokers' loans that encouraged investors to become dangerously leveraged. In addition, increased public credulity also allowed widespread financial swindles. The market reached its zenith in early September, after which confidence began to erode. Both Galbraith and Kindleberger are vague about the causes of the halt in the market, focusing instead on the inevitability of the bubble's collapse. The vertical price drops on Black Thursday, October 24, and Black Tuesday, October 29, forced margin calls and distress sales of stocks, forcing a further plunge in prices. When the stock ticker ran late as prices fell, investors panicked and sold their holdings. In the following weeks and months, the market erratically bounced downwards, propelled by and perhaps propelling the depression.[4]

While the dramatic tale of the market's boom and bust has been told with skill and color, there remain many unanswered questions. Even critics of the market acknowledge that the economic growth in the 1920s should have raised stock prices substantially. However, we have only a scant notion of how much fundamentals contributed to the bull market and the true extent of the "speculative mania." Similarly, all descriptions are vague about when the speculative boom began and what might have triggered the change in investor behavior. Easy credit in the form of loans to brokers is partly blamed for encouraging people to speculate, but the growth of this easy credit seems strange at a time when the Federal Reserve was pursuing a tight monetary policy. Standard histories can readily supply dramatic accounts of the crash, but it is more difficult to identify the relative importance of external events and endogenously changing expectations in provoking the collapse. To address these questions, it is proper to begin with an overview of the background of economic growth, industrial change, and financial innovation that characterized the 1920s and set the stage for the stock market boom.

THE "NEW ERA" AND THE NEW STOCK MARKET

After the disruptions of World War I and the sharp postwar boom and recession, the 1920s appeared to contemporary analysts, as it does to economic historians today, as a remarkable period of prosperity and growth.

From 1922 to 1929, GNP grew at an annual rate of 4.7 percent and unemployment averaged 3.7 percent.[5] Even within this period, 1929 stands out with growth reaching 6.8 percent and unemployment dropping to 3.2 percent. The engine for this prosperity was the emergence of large-scale commercial and industrial enterprises that took advantage of new continuous process technologies. Coordination by the emerging system of modern management produced more efficient vertically integrated enterprises that captured economies of scale and scope.[6]

The needs of these new industrial and commercial enterprises for financing altered the face of American capital markets. These firms rapidly came to dominate the equities market. The stocks included in the Dow Jones Industrial Average reflected this change. Between September 1916 and September 1928, Anaconda Copper, Central Leather, National Lead, and Peoples' Gas were dropped while Allied Chemical, American Can, American Locomotive, American Telephone and Telegraph, American Tobacco, International Harvester, Mack Trucks, Paramount Famous Lasky, Sears Roebuck, the Texas Company, United Drug, Western Union, and Woolworth were added.[7]

The large new capital-intensive firms preferred to raise funds out of retained earnings and new stock issues. Fewer firms financed inventories with bank loans. Commercial loans as a percentage of total earning assets of national banks fell from 58 percent in 1920 to 37 percent in 1929.[8] This left commercial banks in a quandary. As their traditional business declined, they needed new sources of income. Although they purchased more bonds, they could not legally acquire equities for their portfolio. To increase their fee income, banks began to supply their customers with an increased array of financial services, including trusts, insurance, and securities trading.[9]

Commercial banks could not, however, directly trade in equities. To circumvent this legal restriction, they set up wholly owned security affiliates. This allowed them to freely enter all aspects of investment banking and the brokerage business. The number of these affiliates grew rapidly. In 1922 only 10 national banks had security affiliates, but by 1931 114 had affiliates.[10] Compared to the traditional brokerage houses and investment banks with their small, well-to-do clientele, commercial banks had a large new pool of potential clients in their depositors. They took advantage of this opportunity and attracted business by charging fees that were sometimes only one quarter of the New York brokerage commission.[11] As big distributors of stocks, banks were in a favorable position to enter the business of underwriting. By 1930, commercial banks' security affiliates had obtained roughly half the bond originations.[12] By moving into investment banking through their affiliates, commercial banks were able to continue servicing the needs of their corporate customers.

Many small investors might still have shied away from buying securities, not having sufficient capital to purchase a diversified portfolio of stocks. This need was satisfied by the investment trusts. Before 1921, only 40 investment trusts had been organized. In the next five years, another 139 were organized, and as the stock market moved upwards they proliferated. In 1927 140 were established, in 1928, 186, and in 1929, 265.[13] The most common form of trust early in the decade was the fixed trust where once a portfolio of securities was selected it remained unchanged. These tended to be conservative in operation, purchasing blue chip securities. In the last three years of the decade, management trusts became the preferred form of organization. Purchasers of shares in these investment trusts relied on the skills of the directors or trustees to manage the underlying portfolio of securities. These were sponsored by professional managers whose principle business was the investment trust and part-time managers who included investment consultants, investment banks, trust companies, and commercial banks and their affiliates.[14] It is difficult to summarize the great variety of investment trusts, but the most adventurous were those sponsored by investment bankers. Their trusts were often closely intertwined with the parent firm's operations, acting together in the purchase, distribution, and underwriting of issues. While this close association and the leveraging and pyramiding by some trusts led to grave abuses in the late 1920s, the investment trusts performed an important service as conduits for savings to industry, by making it easier for small investors to buy a portfolio of stocks.

The structure of American industry and commerce experienced a profound transformation in the 1920s. There is little disagreement that up until the middle of the decade the bullish stock market only reflected the general economic prosperity brought about by these changes. The accompanying rapid financial innovations have, however, been treated with suspicion because they gave the public easy access to the stock market. But these developments were largely driven by the financing needs of industry. Regulations barring banks from investing directly in industry diminished their traditional role as intermediaries, and they turned to assist the public in buying equities.

BEGINNINGS OF A BUBBLE: THE FAVORED STOCKS

Among historians, there is general agreement about when the "speculative mania" took hold of the market. Both Frederick Lewis Allen and Galbraith select March 1928 as the month when the market began its ascent.[15] The index of common stocks in Figure 1 captures this first upward tick.[16] Following through the months of April and May these broad aggregates increased 15 percent.

In his influential account of the stock market, Allen dates the boom as beginning on Monday, March 5. In aggregate there seems nothing extraordinary about this date. The Dow Jones Industrial Average rose a little over two points from the previous day, a large but not exceptional change. Volume increased rapidly from 1.3 million shares to 3.1 million, but larger volumes had been traded in January. Lewis' reason for selecting March 5 is the five point rise in General Motors' stock on a volume of 1.2 million shares. This was the beginning of the rise in General Motors' stock, which by the end of the week had increased 10 points. Other stocks shared this excellent week, most notably RCA, which rose almost 13 points.

Allen attributes the initial sharp rise in March to the purchases by big bullish speculators, notably W. C. Durant, Arthur Cutten, the Fisher Brothers, and John H. Raskob. Yet one could argue that these events were fully justified by economic developments. The economy had been in a recession until late 1927. When business picked up, the stock market responded. General Motors was attractive for sound reasons. Ford, still a private company, had shut down in 1927 to retool for the Model A, opening a great opportunity for its competitors. With its more advanced management and organization, GM was able to take advantage of this opportunity, increasing production and sales and seizing the leading position in the industry. When the company's annual report released in February revealed its success, GM's stock proved irresistible. Its management exuded confidence. On March 9 GM's Managers' Securities Company bought 200,000 shares at 150 for its executives.[17] At the end of the month, GM's president predicted a price rise from 180 to 225, and he promised to return to stockholders 60 percent of earnings.[18]

The other stock that dominated the New York Stock Exchange was RCA. The purveyor of a new technology, RCA had grown rapidly with sales of $5.8 million in 1925 and $7.4 million in 1926. In its annual report

FIGURE 1
Index of common stocks

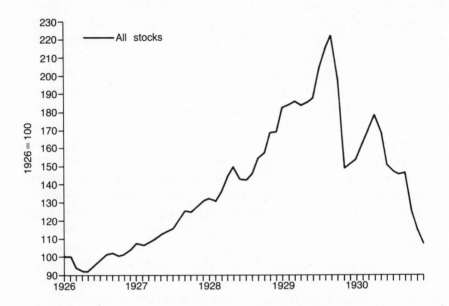

for 1927 released at the beginning of March 1928, the firm showed sales of $11.8 million. Its prospects looked excellent as the economy recovered. In addition, the firm was engaged in talks with its largest customer, Victor Talking Machine, and there were rumors of a merger. Although these fell through at the end of March, they had no effect on RCA's stock.[19] The chroniclers of the boom have devoted little attention to the attractions of RCA's stock, which were quite different from those of General Motors. While the latter was promising higher dividends, RCA had never paid a dividend, nor would it pay a dividend for many years to come. While purchasers of General Motors' stock could be said to acting on expectations of increased earnings, given the company's announced dividend policy, expectations of RCA's future dividends had to be extremely diffuse. Its stock would only be held in the short run or even medium run for capital gains.

   There were many other prominent companies traded on the exchanges that did not pay dividends and caught the public's attention. The stocks of the motion picture industry were favored by speculators. Among the studios, only Radio-Keith-Orpheum did not pay dividends, yet it was one of the most favored stocks with a high price-earnings ratio of 32 in 1929. The only other firm as popular as RKO was Warner Brothers, whose price-earnings ratio of 37 may have reflected its dividend yield, which was twice that of the next firm.[20] Other firms that did not pay dividends included the Aluminium Company of America and the United Aircraft and Transport Corporation. Like RCA, these firms used new, developing technologies.

The proportion of firms not paying dividends was very high among public utility holdings companies. These included the Commonwealth and Southern Corporation, Electric Bond and Share, and the North American Company. While some paid little or no dividends because they were recently formed, several had never paid dividends. The electric utility industry was undergoing a remarkable transformation in the 1920s where consolidation and expansion gave firms economies of scale in production and transmission. This was another frontier industry with potentially high but uncertain returns. Like the firms in manufacturing, these utilities' rapid growth, short histories, and lack of a dividend record made them easy favorites in a speculative wave. This is readily seen in Figure 2 which shows the movements in stock price indices for industrials, railroads, and public utilities. The boom in the stocks of public utilities far outstripped industrials, while the relatively stable, established railroads languished. Although previous writers have not concerned themselves with the prominence of public utilities, it was a major feature of the bull market reflecting the willingness of the public to buy shares in new industries.

The stocks that surged ahead in March remained favorites. When the market crashed on October 24, 1929, the stocks with the highest volumes on the New York Stock Exchange were General Motors and RCA.[21]

FUNDAMENTALS: DIVIDENDS AND EARNINGS

Although the bull market of the 1920s is widely regarded as a pure bubble, virtually all contemporary observers and historians are willing to concede that at least some fraction of the spectacular rise in the stock market may be attributed to real factors. At the height of the market in August of 1929 when many began to fear that there was excessive speculation, Charles Amos Dice, a Professor at Ohio State University, carefully argued that the new level of prices in the stock market was the product of economic fundamen-

FIGURE 2
Common stock indices, 1926–1930

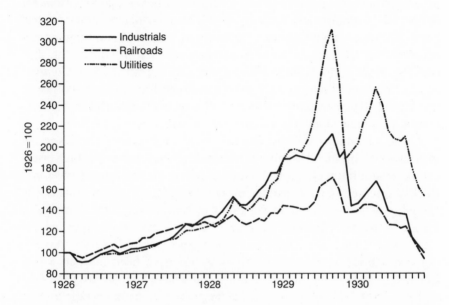

tals.[22] Even after the crash in December 1929, Irving Fisher of Yale retained his conviction that the rise in stock prices was justified and wrote, "My own impression has been and still is that the market went up principally because of sound, justified expectations of earnings, and only partly because of unreasoning and unintelligent mania for buying."[23] Although Galbraith has ridiculed the likes of Dice and Fisher, their views cannot be lightly dismissed.

Fisher's belief in the role of fundamentals was based on his observation of the same economic growth and transformation in the 1920s as described later by economic historians. He claimed that the prime reasons for the rise in earnings and for expecting higher future earnings were the systematic application of science and invention in industry and the acceptance of the new industrial management methods of Frederick Taylor and others that lowered unit costs. In addition to these developments, Dice noted the increased expenditure by firms on research and development and the application of the techniques of modern management that lowered unit costs as output rose.[24] Although he believed that it was necessary to guard against monopoly, Fisher saw the wave of mergers in industry and utilities as lowering production costs and raising profits. Combined with a stable price level and a cooperative labor movement, Fisher saw good reasons for the growth of earnings and stock prices. He claimed that these changes had borne fruit in the annual growth of earnings for industrial corporations of 9 percent from 1922 to 1927 and dividend payments of 6.8 percent, thus offering ample justification for the early phase of the bull market. Comparing the first nine months of 1928 and 1929, Fisher found a rise in corporate earnings of 20 percent and concluded, "This record is eloquent in justification of a heightened level of common stock prices during 1929."[25]

The convictions of Fisher and Dice have more recently found support in the work of Sirkin.[26] He believes that the high stock prices and high price-earnings ratios (an average of 24.3 for the highs of the individual Dow-Jones stocks) were a consequence of the expected rapid growth of earnings. The annual growth of earnings in the 1920s had been excellent. Earnings of stocks in the Dow-Jones Industrial Average grew at 14.1 percent for 1924–29 (1924 was a recession year) and 8.0 percent for 1925–29. Assuming that a price-earnings ratio of 15 would have been normal, Sirkin calculates what growth rate of earnings could have temporarily justified a higher ratio of 24.3. He finds that, for the peak price-earnings ratio to have been warranted, earnings would have had to grow at 9 percent for 10 years.[27] However, if the average price-earnings ratio of 21.6 for September 2, 1929— the high for the market—is used, earnings need only have grown at 6 percent for five years. Examining the individual stocks in the Dow-Jones, he finds that if earnings had grown at 9 percent for another five years, the price-earnings ratios of only one fifth of the stocks could not have been justified. Sirkin concludes that few stocks were wildly overvalued and that the "speculative orgy" was limited.

Sirkin's attack on the conventional story of excessively high stock prices rests on a few facts. His analysis simply uses the average growth rates for earnings, and he does not comment on why the public might have assumed the continuation of very high growth rates other than pure extrapolation. Sirkin offers no explanation for the very rapid rise or drop in prices, only evidence that in certain circumstances the peak prices might have been justified.

To examine this question more closely, it is useful to look at the behavior of earnings and dividends over a longer period. Figure 3 shows the annual earnings and dividends per share from 1871 to 1937.[28] The

FIGURE 3
Dividends and earnings, 1871–1937

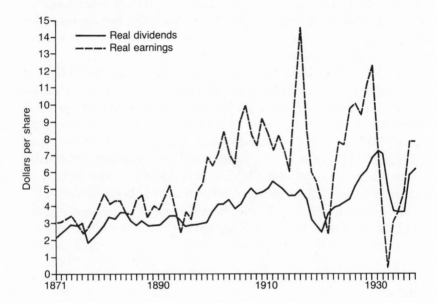

movement of these two series reflects the conventional view that managers are hesitant to increase dividends unless they perceive a permanent rise in earnings because they wish to avoid reducing dividends. The high earnings after the turn of the century brought about a gradual rise in dividends. The temporary jump in earnings during World War I left the dividend series unaffected as managers recognized its transitory character. The unexpected and sharp post-war recession forced dividends to be trimmed, but by 1922 they were on the rise again. It is easy to appreciate the business optimism of the 1920s in light of the rapid growth of earnings. Dividends also increased but not at the same rate as earnings.

The problem with Sirkin's argument can be seen in this diagram. If the expected earnings growth followed a path through the points for 1925 and 1929 (the second highest value), then stock prices during the boom appear largely justified in terms of fundamentals. Yet the choice of these dates is quite arbitrary. If 1927 and 1929 were chosen, the boom would appear wholly rational using Sirkin's analysis. On the other hand, an average for 1900–14 and 1929 could be selected, using the argument that earnings were returning to an earlier growth path. In this case, stock prices and price-earnings ratios would appear quite irrational.

While useful, this annual data hides the key developments of 1928–29, making impossible any careful judgment about the movement of fundamentals. To remedy this deficiency, I collected new data on quarterly dividend payments by firms in the 1929 Dow-Jones Industrial Index from 1922 to 1930.[29] An index of these dividends and the Dow-Jones Industrial Index is graphed in Figure 4. This figure reveals the remarkable change that overtook the stock market. From 1922 to 1927 dividends and prices moved together. In early 1928, prices rose and then soared above dividends.

The behavior of prices, dividends, and earnings seems to imply that managers did not share the public's enthusiasm. Investors might have bid up stock prices based on an extrapolation of a few years' rapid earnings

FIGURE 4
Stock price and dividend indices, 1922.1–1930.2

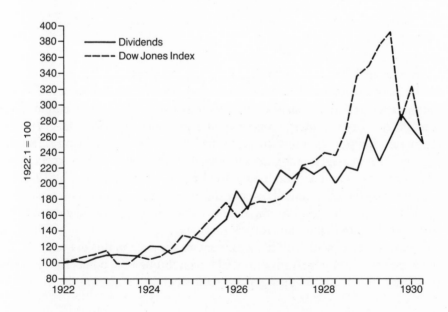

growth, but managers did not increase dividends as quickly. The determinants of dividend payments can be studied further by employing Marsh and Merton's model of dividend behavior for the aggregate stock market.[30] Presented in the appendix, this model captures the essential stylized facts that managers have a long-term target payout ratio and try only to increase dividends when permanent earnings rise to avoid cutting dividends later. The regression equation they estimated was:

$$\log[D_{t+1} / D_t] + (D_t / P_{t-1}) = a_0 + a_1\log[P_t + D_t / P_{t-1}]$$
$$+ a_2\log[D_t / P_{t-1}] + u_{t+1}$$

(1)

where D_t is the aggregate dividend (dollars per share) and P_t is the aggregate stock price at time t and u_t is the error term. Equation 1 implies that the changes in real dividends will be determined by the previous year's unexpected price-cum-dividend change and dividend yield. This model assumes that managers used the estimated value of the firm as revealed not just by earnings but all the market information contained in the price.[31] The coefficient a_1 represents the adjustment of dividends in response to an unanticipated change in permanent earnings, or more broadly the value of the firm. The absolute value of the second coefficient captures the speed of convergence of the payout ratio to its target.

This equation was first estimated using the Cowles data on stock prices and dividends for 1873 to 1927. The ordinary least squares estimates in Table 1 are similar to those reported by Marsh and Merton. When earnings were substituted for prices, the fit of the equation deteriorated drastically, as happened to Marsh and Merton. The first estimated equation was then used to forecast the dividends for the next three years. For the two years following 1928, the realized dividends and prices in earlier years were used in the forecast. The results show that this model overpredicts the dividends that were paid.

The second estimated equation in Table 1 employs the dividend and price data for Dow-Jones stocks. Quarterly dummy variables were added to capture the pronounced seasonal aspects of dividend payments. The ordinary least squares estimates were corrected for first order autocorrelation using the Cochrane-Orcutt method. As already mentioned, quarterly earnings were not available and industrial production was used as a proxy for the alternative specification. This again yielded a much poorer fit, so

TABLE 1
A Model of Dividend Determination for the Aggregate Stock Market

1873–1927

$$\log(D_{t+1} / D_t) + (D_t / P_{t-1}) = -1.049 + 0.561 \log[(P_t + D_t) / P_{t-1}]$$
$$(-4.63)(7.19)$$

$$-0.1701 \log(D_t / P_{t-1}) \tag{1}$$
$$(-2.57)$$

R2 = 0.491   F-Statistic = 27.01   D–W = 1.68

	Actual Dividend	Model Forecast	Percent Forecast Error
1928	5.97	6.45	+8.0
1929	6.62	7.70	+16.3
1930	6.38	7.63	+19.6

1922.2–1927.4

$$\log(D_{t+1} / D_t) + (D_t / P_{t-1}) = -1.046 + 0.40 \log[(P_t + D_t) / P_{t-1}]$$
$$(-1.55)(2.35) \tag{2}$$

$$0.212 \log(D_t / P_{t-1}) - 0.137D_1 - 0.056D_2 - 0.122D_3$$
$$(-2.26)(-2.36)(-1.76)(-2.26)$$

R2 = 0.633   F-Statistic = 6.75   *rho* = –0.497
$$(-2.03)$$

	Actual Dividend	Model Forecast	Percent Forecast Error
1928.1	0.815	0.915	+12.3
1928.2	0.737	0.811	+10.1
1928.3	0.813	0.812	–0.1
1928.4	0.797	0.857	+6.0
1929.1	0.963	1.024	+6.3
1929.2	0.842	1.006	+19.4
1929.3	0.950	1.004	+5.7
1929.4	1.060	1.038	+2.1
1930.1	0.993	1.107	+11.5
1930.2	0.926	1.037	+11.9

Note: The numbers in parentheses are *t*-statistics.

that only the original model of Marsh and Merton is reported. Like the annual forecasts, the quarterly projections also tend to overpredict dividends.

These results suggest that the boom was partly generated by the public's belief that dividends would be rising more rapidly than they actually did. The beginning of the bubble in the market may thus be traceable back to the jump in earnings that companies like General Motors experienced in early 1928. This created very optimistic expectations of future dividends. The overly optimistic forecasts helped to get the bull market started, but they do not explain the full rise in prices. Even if dividends had grown at the rate predicted, they would not have approached the increase in prices. Figure 5 shows this by graphing an index of forecasted dividends against the stock price and dividend indices of Figure 4. If the stock prices had only been based on this forecast of management's dividend decisions, there would have been no dramatic boom.

Many managers did not believe that the boom would continue and discounted the stock market's valuation in setting their dividends. Some executives were alarmed enough to warn the public. In 1928, A. P.

FIGURE 5
Stock price and dividend indices

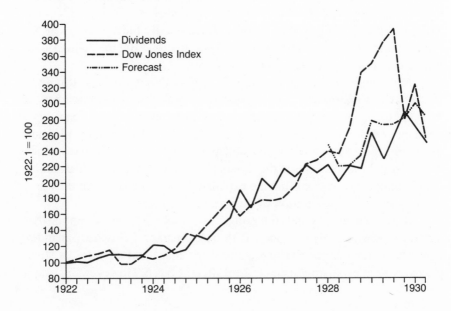

Giannini, head of Bancitaly (the future Bank of America), stated that the high price of his bank's stock was unwarranted, prompting a sharp drop. Canadian Marconi, another firm in the booming radio business, watched its stock leap from $3 to $28.50. When its chairman publicly doubted that Marconi's shares were being properly valued, their price fell 12 points. The market did not always heed executive warnings, and the price of Brooklyn Edison's shares continued their rise after the company complained that its stock was overvalued.[32]

A change in fundamentals may have initiated the boom, but fundamentals did not sustain it. The continued disappointment of unrealized dividends and public statements of some managers did not slow the rise in stock prices. This leaves the greater part of the boom to be explained. One favored candidate is easy credit.

DID CREDIT DRIVE THE STOCK MARKET BOOM?

Many contemporary observers and economic historians agree that the expansion of call loans or brokers' loans provided the means for speculative mania to gather speed. Galbraith sees the ability to purchase stock on margin as a great speculative lure. A buyer needed only to provide a fraction of the required funds, borrow the rest, and enjoy the full capital gain less the interest on the borrowed funds. Even Irving Fisher, who believed that the market was essentially sound, wrote: "Undoubtedly the contagion of the long bull market had encouraged unwise speculation. But the main trouble was that so much borrowed money was used."[33]

In the bull market, people were, in Galbraith's words, "swarming to buy stocks on margin."[34] He suggests that "even the most circumspect friend of the market would concede that the volume of broker's loans...is a good index of the volume of speculation."[35] Galbraith takes great pleasure in taunting the optimists during the bull market for dismissing the relevance of the rise in brokers' loans in the face of rising public clamor.[36] In a similar vein, Kindleberger argues that the expansion of stock market credit was a key element in the generation of the speculative mania.[37]

It is easy to understand Galbraith and Kindleberger's presumption that a credit expansion fueled the boom in the stock market. In Figure 6, an index of the New York Stock Exchange's brokers' loans and an index of stock prices are scarcely distinguishable until after the crash. However, this graph

FIGURE 6
The stock market and brokers' loans, 1926–1930

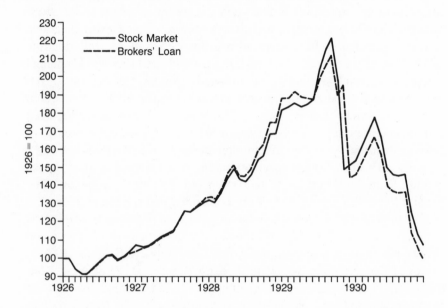

also suggests that there was not any alteration in the practices of brokers lending to their customers. Margin arrangements do not appear to have changed over the course of the boom. From 1926 until the crash in the market, brokers' loans as a percentage of the market value of all listed stocks was always between 8 and 10 percent.[38] Credit was not easy because brokers provided greater margins to their customers.

There are several obvious problems with the argument that easy credit helped drive the stock market boom. The first of these is that credit, in general, was not easy in the second half of the 1920s. Hamilton has shown that the Federal Reserve pursued a contractionary policy beginning in January of 1928, following gold outflows to France that occasioned that country's return to the gold standard.[39] Open market sales and a rise in the discount rate from 3-1/2 percent to 5 percent would have caused a drop in the monetary base of 12 percent in the first half of 1928, if there had been no offsetting increase in borrowings at the discount window. By most measures, money was tight during the whole course of the boom. In 1928 and 1929, high-powered money and the consumer price index fell and M1 grew only slightly in 1929.

The Federal Reserve's tight money policy during these years was, of course, a consequence of its fears about the flow of credit to the stock market. The Federal Reserve had always been concerned about excessive credit for speculation. Its founders were influenced by the real bills doctrine and had hoped the new central bank's discounting activities would channel credit away from "speculative" and towards "productive" activities. Although there was general agreement on this issue, the stock market boom created a severe split over policy.[40] The Federal Reserve Board believed that "direct pressure" could be used to restrict credit flowing to speculative activities without seriously affecting credit for productive purposes.

To curb stock market speculation, the Board wanted member banks making loans on securities to be denied rediscounting privileges. The Federal Reserve Bank of New York contended that the Federal Reserve could not refuse to discount eligible assets from its members and it was impossible to selectively control credit. It argued that speculation could only be reduced by raising the rediscount rate. Between February 1929 to August 1929, the directors of the Federal Reserve Bank of New York frequently voted to raise the discount rate, only to be turned down by the Board, which reaffirmed its policy of direct pressure. The New York Fed conformed and pressured its member banks but it did so without conviction.[41]

Looking at the rapid growth of brokers' loans in 1929, the Federal Reserve Board was understandably frustrated and angry with the lack of cooperation from its banks, notably New York. However, close inspection reveals that their policy enjoyed a limited, although ultimately pyrrhic success. There are two sources of information on brokers' loans. Every week, the Federal Reserve Bank of New York published a report on the brokers' loans made by its member banks in New York at the close of business on Wednesday.[42] The reports identified loans made by the member banks on their "own account," that is with their own funds, loans placed on a commission for out-of-town banks, and loans by non-banks or "others." The total brokers' loans and loans by sources for the date nearest the end of the month are depicted in Figure 7.[43] The New York Stock Exchange also compiled data from its members on the loans they had outstanding on the last day of each month.[44] This was a complete report of loans, but the loans were classified differently, coming from either New York banks and trust

FIGURE 7
New York City member banks' brokers' loans

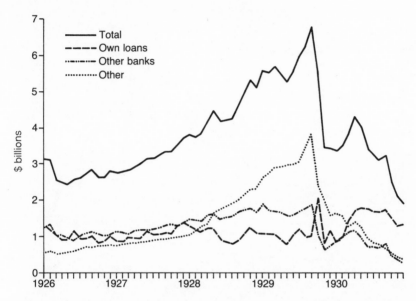

companies or from private bankers, brokers, foreign bank agencies and others.[45] A graph of the total and two sub-categories of loans is found in Figure 8.

Figure 7 reveals how the member banks in New York were cowed by the Federal Reserve Board's policy of direct pressure. Loans to brokers on member banks' own accounts reached a peak at the end of December 1927, and then declined to a lower level around which they fluctuated for the duration of the stock market boom. Loans made by these banks on account for out-of-town banks grew slowly during the boom. The rapid growth occurred in loans placed by the New York banks on account for non-banks as seen in Figure 7 and from private bankers, companies, and other sources as seen in Figure 8.

Dice identified some of the sources of these non-bank funds that were placed through banks or directly.[46] Large corporations' high earnings and big flotation of new issues flooded them with funds that they placed in the call market that proved more attractive with its high interest rates than bank deposits or Liberty bonds. He found that some investment trusts had used the funds pouring into their coffers to invest in the call market. Funds from

FIGURE 8
Sources of New York stock exchange members' loans

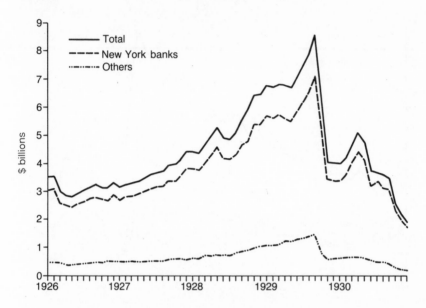

foreign banks, investors, and corporations from Europe and even Japan contributed to brokers' loans.

Criticizing the traditional measures of monetary stringency for failing to acknowledge innovations in the credit markets, Kindleberger blames the rising supply of brokers' loans from non-bank sources as responsible for fueling the stock market boom.[47] However, there is one very troubling fact for Kindleberger, Galbraith and others who have focused on the flow of funds to the stock market as a cause of the boom. This may be seen in Figure 9 that shows the movements in the discount rate, the commercial paper rate, and the call rate—the principal rate for brokers' loans.[48] After moving together with the other two rates for 1926 and 1927, the call rate increased sharply. Although the differential was not constant for the whole boom, it remained very large, suggesting that it was the rising tide of speculation that attracted funds, not any independent credit creation.

To examine this role of credit in the market boom, a simple model of the market for brokers' loans was estimated. The demand for brokers' loans, D_t, was assumed to depend on the call rate, $CALL_t$, the speculation in the market measured by the volume of trading on the New York exchange,

FIGURE 9
Interest rates, 1926–1930

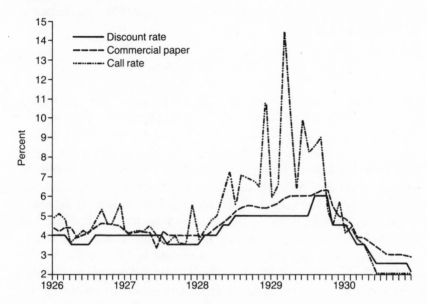

VOL_t, or an index of common stocks, $INDEX_t$, and new issues of common stock, $COMST_t$:[49]

$$D_t = a_0 + a_1 CALL_t + a_2 VOL_t + a_3 COMST_t + e_t \qquad (2)$$

The value of the new common stock issued is included as an explanatory variable because, contrary to Galbraith's contention that all brokers' loans were collateralized by securities purchased on margin, some loans were obtained by brokers to carry newly issued stock.[50] On September 11, 1929, the President of the Stock Exchange, E. H. H. Simmons, defended brokers' loans, emphasizing their importance in providing brokers' credit to hold new securities as they "season" and can be sold to the public.[51] Contemporary analysts like Dice recognized that brokers' loans included "collateral loans made to banking houses which bring out new issues for sale to customers. These loans are used to carry stocks and bonds until they are sold."[52] Brokers' loans thus supplied brokerage houses and investment banks with funds for a variety of purposes, not solely giving customers loans for stock purchases.

In the model, the supply of brokers' loans, S_t, was specified as a function of the call rate, the commercial paper rate, CPR_t, and either a dummy variable, $DUMMY_t$, or a trended dummy, $DUMTRE_t$, for the period of the stock market boom:

$$S_t = B_0 + B_1 CALL_t + B_2 CPR_t + B_3 DUMMY_t + v_t \qquad (4)$$

where $DUMMY_t = 1$ when t = March 1928 to September 1929, otherwise it was equal to zero, and $DUMTRE_t = 1, 2, 3, ...,$ for March 1928 to September 1929, otherwise it was equal to zero. The purpose for including a dummy variable is to ascertain whether there was an exogenous shift in the supply of funds into the market during the stock market boom as Galbraith and Kindleberger believe. Monthly data from 1926 to 1930 were used.

The two-stage least-squares estimates for four versions of the model of this market reported in Table 2 offer no support for the view that easy credit stimulated the stock market. The demand equation was corrected for autocorrelation using the Cochrane-Orcutt method, and the supply equation proved to be identified with the inclusion of a lagged dependent variable. The final equations were tested for the presence of autocorrelation using the asymptotically equivalent test for Durbin's h.[53] In the estimated demand equations, the variables for new issues and speculation on the stock market explained most of the variation in the demand for brokers' loans. However, it was impossible at even the 10 percent level to accept the hypothesis that the coefficient on the call rate was different from zero. This apparent indifference of the borrowers to the interest rate is in accord with the claim that they were transfixed by the potential for capital gains and paid little heed to the interest rate.

In the estimated supply equations, the coefficients on the call rate and the commercial paper rate had the expected signs. The lagged dependent variable contributed the most to explaining the variations in supply, reflecting lenders' incremental adjustments in their portfolios. The coefficients on the dummy variables, intended to capture any independent stimulus to lending during the boom, had negative signs. It was not possible to reject the hypothesis that the coefficients were different from zero at the 10 percent level. This suggests that there was no "pushing" of funds into the stock market. If anything, lenders retreated a bit, *ceteris paribus,* from lending on the bull market.

The weight of the evidence is that brokers' loans did not contribute to the stock market boom. What the boom did was to "pull in" funds by a major

TABLE 2
The Market for Brokers Loans (Two-stage Least-squares Estimates)

$$D_t = 2983.784 + 45.34\ CALL_t + 2.275\ COMST_t + 6.374\ VOL_t \tag{1a}$$
$$(3.03) \qquad (0.98) \qquad\quad (6.00) \qquad\qquad (2.28)$$

$R2 = 0.938 \qquad$ F-Statistic = 202.4 $\qquad rho = 0.942\ (15.83)$

$$S_t = 2432.595 + 715.389\ CALL_t - 1147.756\ CPR_t - 231.296\ DUMMY_t \tag{1b}$$
$$(1.83) \qquad\quad (2.00) \qquad\qquad (-1.65) \qquad\qquad (-0.40)$$
$$+\ 0.811 S_{t-1}$$
$$(5.02)$$

$R2 = 0.679 \qquad$ F-Statistic = 28.50

$$D_t = 3073.564 + 28.085\ CALL_t + 2.251\ COMST_t + 6.376\ VOL_t \tag{2a}$$
$$(0.67) \qquad\quad (0.62) \qquad\qquad (6.23) \qquad\qquad (2.32)$$

$R2 = 0.937 \qquad$ F-Statistic = 198.3 $\qquad rho = 0.985\ (17.09)$

$$S_t = 2295.809 + 935.534\ CALL_t - 1464.904\ CPR_t - 68.79\ DUMTRE_t \tag{2b}$$
$$(1.24) \qquad\quad (1.30) \qquad\qquad (-1.17) \qquad\qquad (-0.60)$$
$$+\ 0.957\ S_{t-1}$$
$$(2.78)$$

$R2 = 0.467 \qquad$ F-Statistic = 11.83

$$D_t = -2383.496 + 26.891\ CALL_t + 0.817\ COMST_t + 41.731\ INDEX_t \tag{3a}$$
$$(2.05) \qquad\quad (1.207) \qquad\qquad (3.87) \qquad\qquad (12.81)$$

$R2 = 0.985 \qquad$ F-Statistic = 867.37 $\qquad rho = 0.956\ (19.55)$

$$S_t = 2617.161 + 775.341\ CALL_t - 1257.928\ CPR_t - 300.727\ DUMMY_t \tag{3b}$$
$$(1.88) \qquad\quad (2.01) \qquad\qquad (-1.68) \qquad\qquad (-0.49)$$
$$+\ 0.819\ S_{t-1}$$
$$(4.70)$$

$R2 = 0.627 \qquad$ F-Statistic = 22.65

$$D_t = -2329.206 + 17.14\ CALL_t + 0.794\ COMST_t + 42.423\ INDEX_t \tag{4a}$$
$$(-2.83) \qquad\quad (0.73) \qquad\qquad (3.69) \qquad\qquad (12.85)$$

$R2 = 0.984 \qquad$ F-Statistic = 834.69 $\qquad rho = 0.951\ (20.09)$

$$S_t = 2063.094 + 795.067\ CALL_t - 1227.857\ CPR_t - 49.557\ DUMTRE_t \tag{4b}$$
$$(1.32) \qquad\quad (1.30) \qquad\qquad (-1.16) \qquad\qquad (-0.51)$$
$$+\ 0.912 S_{t-1}$$
$$(3.11)$$

$R2 = 0.611 \qquad$ F-Statistic = 21.22

Note: Numbers in parentheses are t-statistics.

reallocation of credit in the money and capital markets.[54]   Ivan Wright observed that as the call rate rose there was a sharp decline in commercial paper.   In September 1927 there was $600 million in commercial paper outstanding.   By the following September this declined to $430 million, and in the same month in 1929 it reached $265 million.[55] This development led commercial banks to provide more loans and discounts to firms that had previously relied on the commercial paper market, while their former lenders moved into the call market from which banks were discouraged by the Federal Reserve.[56] In the capital markets, there was a similar shift, as seen in Figure 10 that records the new issues of bonds, stocks, and foreign securities. The bull market made the issuance of American stocks to finance expansion or new companies very attractive. The growth in the new issues of domestic stock increased dramatically from $1,474 million in 1927 to $5,914 million in 1929. Meanwhile, issues of domestic bonds and notes declined from $3,183 million to $2,078 million and foreign securities fell even more spectacularly from $1,338 million to $673 million.

This evidence reaffirms the independent character of the stock market bubble, whose demand for funds and new issues forced major changes in

FIGURE 10
New securities issues, 1926–1930

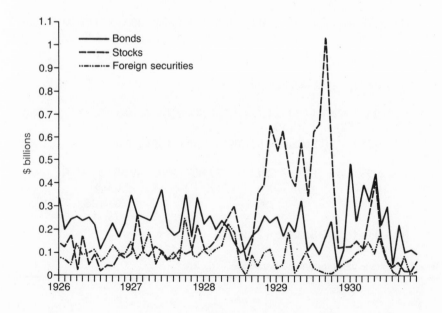

other financial markets. Although the Federal Reserve was not convinced, credit was tight and remained tight for the course of the boom in the stock market.

A BUBBLE IN THE STOCK MARKET?

If easy credit played no part in the boom and the role of rising earnings and dividends was restricted, the surge in stock prices requires an alternative explanation. The surviving candidate is that a bubble appeared in the stock market. While this seems an easy conclusion, the econometric identification of a bubble is elusive. There is a large literature that has debated the existence of bubbles in financial markets. This literature considers the possibility that the price of an asset may not reflect simply its market fundamentals, that is, information on its current and future returns.

Typically, this proposition is formalized by the current price of a share, P_t, being a representation of its expected future price, P_{t+1}, its future dividend, d_{t+1}, and a bubble component, u_{t+1}, discounted at a constant real rate of interest, r:

$$P_t = (1 + r)^{-1} E_t (P_{t+1} + ad_{t+1} + u_{t+1}) \qquad (5)$$

If $a = 1$ and $u_{t+1} = 0$, then there is no bubble and the expected rate of return is equal to the real rate of interest:

$$r = [E_t(P_{t+1}) - P_t + E_t(d_{t+1})] / P_t \qquad (6)$$

Deviations that move prices away from fundamentals but do not violate the arbitrage condition of efficient markets may produce rational bubbles.[57] The problem is that it appears impossible for the researcher to observe the bubble term as it is observed or constructed by market participants.

The typical strategy employed to search for bubbles is to test hypotheses for the absence of bubbles. Rejection of the hypothesis of no bubbles would thus offer positive evidence. The problem with any test is that while data on prices and dividends may be available, it is not easy to observe how new information on dividends is revealed to the market and how expectations about them are formed. Information becomes available infrequently and in a lumpy fashion that is not readily picked up by simple models.[58]

Robert Shiller first examined the claim that stock price volatility was too great to be explained by any changes in fundamentals.[59] Using annual data for stock prices and dividends for 1871–1979, he showed that stock price movements violated variance bounds tests. Stock price volatility was five to thirteen times higher than should be expected given uncertainty about future dividends.[60] This evidence suggested that bubbles may appear in the stock market. Shiller concluded that extraneous fads and fashions were important factors affecting stock prices and that social-psychology might be useful in explaining the movement of stock prices.[61]

Objections to Shiller's variance bounds tests were raised on the grounds that the small sample properties of his volatility tests were biased to find excessive volatility and dividends were less volatile and non-stationary because firms smoothed dividend payments.[62] Mankiw, Romer and Shapiro devised new tests that did not suffer from these problems.[63] They found some evidence for excess volatility, though not as striking as Shiller did.

The evidence has been contested by Kleidon who argued that once "nonstationarity" of prices was accounted for, variance bounds tests did not show excessive fluctuations in stock prices.[64] In the same vein, Diba and Grossman found that dividends and prices were nonstationary in levels but stationary in differences, suggesting that rational bubbles were not present.[65] Campbell and Shiller are not convinced and offer alternative evidence, including cointegration tests, supporting the case for excess volatility.[66]

This lack of consensus is quite striking. As already mentioned, it is difficult to distinguish between a speculative bubble and a system driven by fundamentals when the bubble term is unobservable.[67] Another problem with the empirical work is its dependence on annual data for stock prices and dividends. Thus, it effectively misses the 1928–29 boom that has been identified as a potential bubble.[68] Annual data also do not capture the lumpy pattern of dividends and earnings announcements.[69] Furthermore, the data employed are all aggregate. As accounts of 1929 show, it was not all stocks that were caught up in a wave of speculation. Railroad stocks were almost excluded from the boom, while utilities were the favorites of speculators. Bubbles may also have appeared in only some stocks' prices during certain periods. Testing with aggregate annual data is thus not appropriate for discovering bubbles.

In the absence of better data on dividends, price data alone may be used to search for bubbles. Gary Santoni performed a runs test using the daily Dow-Jones Industrial Index from January 3, 1928, to September 3, 1929, the period of the boom. He found that the observed number of continuous increases or decreases in the index was not different from what would be expected in a random sequence.[70] Daily data are not necessarily the natural unit of observation for finding a speculative bubble in prices. The appropriate time frame may be shorter or longer. Monthly data from January 1919 to September 1929 showed 30 runs while the mean for a random sequence of this length was 57 with a standard deviation of 4.9.[71] This suggests the presence of a bubble with long runs. The index rose continuously for seven months in 1927, four months each in 1928 and 1929.

This contradictory evidence is not surprising. Analysis that excludes fundamentals requires strong assumptions about the behavior of fundamentals. Price innovations are the sum of bubble and fundamental innovations. To make any judgment about bubble innovations requires assumptions about the fundamental innovations. Runs can arise only from a skewed distribution, thus only if fundamental innovations are assumed to be symmetric can runs be attributed to bubbles. Yet, there is no reason for the fundamental innovation to be symmetric even if the fundamental is symmetric. Runs tests thus have minimal power.[72]

While it is currently impossible to identify or measure a bubble with any statistical precision, the absence of any alternative explanation for the events of 1928–29 and certain qualitative evidence clearly point to the emergence of a bubble. Bubbles are most likely to appear where fundamentals are difficult to assess. Blanchard and Watson suggest that the gold market is a likely place to find bubbles. Gold is held either for industrial uses or as a precaution against major catastrophes. The latter are difficult to assess, leading investors sometimes to make decisions based on past returns not fundamentals.[73]

While Blanchard and Watson believe that bubbles are less likely to appear in blue-chip stocks, the stock market of the 1920s had characteristics favorable to the emergence of bubbles. Fundamentals were difficult to assess because of major changes in industry. In automobiles, there was an abrupt shift from the dominance of the proprietary Ford Motor Company to General Motors with its multidivisional system of modern management aimed at reaching all market segments. While investors had every reason to expect dividends to grow, they lacked the means to easily evaluate the future path of dividends. The same was also true for RCA. It was a highly successful firm in a new industry whose technology was rapidly changing. Not only were RCA's prospects uncertain but the absence of any payment of dividends left investors with little to judge fundamentals.

Experienced investors saw that expected earnings and dividends were rising. Owing to the new basis for prosperity their expectations became more diffuse and they may have used information other than fundamentals in trading stock. In general, investors' sophistication was weakened by the influx of many new people into the market. Regulation and the new demands of industrial finance had reduced the role of commercial banks as intermediaries between business and the saving public. Funds had to be channelled to firms directly. Banks and investment trusts responded by catering to people who had never invested in the stock market before. One of the most readily identifiable groups of new investors was women whom brokers catered to with special programs and even their own rooms to watch the ticker tape.[74] Women's magazines carried articles on how to buy stocks. One of the most famous articles was an interview in the *Ladies' Home Journal* with John J. Raskob, a leading bull, entitled "Everybody Ought to Be Rich."[75] While it is not easy to quantify these changes, they do provide qualitative evidence that the necessary conditions for the emergence of a stock market bubble were present.

The speculative urge that had propelled the market upwards began to falter in the autumn of 1929. The decline and then sudden plunge of the market has been well-chronicled, but the number and variety of explanations for the crash have left its causes unclear.

ORIGINS OF THE CRASH

The market reached its peak on September 3, 1929. The evaporation of bullish confidence is generally associated with the Babson Break of September 5—so named for Roger Babson who gave an extremely pessimistic address before the National Business Conference and predicted that a sharp recession was in the offing.[76] The market rallied after this shock but then gradually began to slide.

Among the students of 1929, there is a marked tendency to minimize the importance of any particular factor precipitating the crash. Its demise is treated as a nearly endogenous collapse of expectations. After discussing several often cited causes, Galbraith argues that the stock market's rise represented an "inherently unstable equilibrium" that could be "shattered by a spontaneous decision to get out."[77]   Anything could have caused investors to begin selling, and Galbraith states, "What first stirred these doubts we do not know, but neither is it very important to know." Kindleberger shares this same sense of inevitability and irrelevance of its cause.

The drop in the stock market is not, however, unworthy of study. Something convinced investors that their expectations of future price increases were no longer justified. The presence of a bubble will at some point leave prices to collapse, but this is not necessarily a result of a random shock to the market. Contemporary pundits offered many explanations, including the excessive issues of new stock, decisions by government regulators, the Smoot-Hawley tariff, foreign stock markets, and domestic credit. Each of these will be considered in turn.

NEWLY ISSUED STOCK

The rising stock market made it very attractive for companies to issue new stock. In 1927 $1,474 million of new preferred and common shares were issued. As the boom began this rose to $2,961 million in 1928 and reached $5,924 million in 1929. As in other bubbles, where speculation began with a nearly fixed supply of an asset, the rapid price rise eventually called forth significant additions to the total supply. As seen in Figure 10 this activity reached its peak during September 1929 when $1,029 million of shares were issued.

In a speech on November 11, 1929, to the American Acceptance Council, Fred I. Kent of Bankers' Trust Company suggested that this large addition of new securities overwhelmed the market and helped bring about the price drop. Yet, the last few months' additions were not very large in relation to the total value of stock. On September 1, 1929, the total value of the stocks listed on the New York exchange was $89.7 billion. Kent argued that the new issues were increasing faster than demand, measured by the increase in American domestic savings. He roughly calculated that in the first three quarters of 1929 $8.5 billion of securities of all kinds had been issued while investable savings had increased by only $5.5 billion.[78]

As the stock market boom had attracted funds formerly invested in other domestic assets and from abroad, it is difficult to put too much weight on this factor. The argument that the bubble burst principally because the growth of supply outpaced the growth of demand is difficult to accept as demand may have decreased because of other factors affecting expectations. However, the growing supply of an asset weakens a bubble's necessary condition that supply be inelastic; hence this must be considered to be, at least, a contributory factor.

THE BOSTON EDISON DECISION

Many utilities were among the high-flying stocks of 1929. Some pundits claimed that the Massachusetts Department of Public Utilities' refusal on Friday, October 11 to allow Boston Edison to split its stock four to one sent a threatening signal to the market. The regulators denied the request on the grounds that it would encourage further speculation and its price was already higher than could be justified by its earnings.[79] The authorities also began a rate inquiry on the grounds that if the stock price was four times par value, the company might be using its monopoly power to extract excessive profits from its customers.[80]

An examination of the movement of the Dow-Jones indices for industrials and utilities in the days immediately before or after the announcement shown no sign of anticipation or reaction to this decision. In the week of the announcement both industrials and utilities rose with the only declines, of under one percent, occurring on that day. It seems reasonable to expect that the decision would affect the regulated utilities more than industrials, but no pattern is evident. When the exchange closed on the following Monday, utilities were down one percent and industrials 0.6 percent. Tuesday they both dropped one percent. If this were truly a vital decision, there should have been a prompt large drop on Monday concentrated in utilities. Both industrials and utilities moved together and showed only small declines. While upsetting to the Boston Edison stockholders, this regulatory decision must be considered a minor, if not irrelevant, element in the crash of the market.

THE SMOOT-HAWLEY TARIFF

In most explanations of the Great Depression, the passage of the Smoot-Hawley tariff, which dramatically raised American tariffs, is regarded as a key factor in disrupting the international economy. Anticipation of the effects of the tariff has been blamed for causing the October crash.[81] Jude Wanniski gives sole responsibility for the market's collapse to the tariff.[82]

He claims that each successful step of the trade bill through Congress was accompanied by a pronounced drop in the market, culminating in the coincidence of a key Senate vote and Black Thursday. However, Wanniski is a too determined to show that every gyration in the market can be linked to a change in taxes or tariffs to the exclusion of other factors.

If the tariff was indeed a central factor in the crash, it should have especially hurt the export industries through decreased foreign demand by the operation of the foreign trade multipliers and foreign tariff retaliation. Nontradables and import-competing industries would not have sustained the same injury and possibly some of the latter may have benefitted. Comparing the change in the stock market indices of each of these groups during October offers a very simple test of this proposition.[83] All stocks declined 24.8 percent, with industrials falling 25.5 percent and utilities, 29.7 percent. The leading export was raw cotton which was not represented on the stock exchange. The next most important export was petroleum and petroleum products which fell 29.6 percent, automobiles and parts, 30.7 and 35.6 percent, and industrial and electrical machinery, 21.5 and 34.4 percent. Wheat (not represented on the exchange) was the fifth most important export followed by packinghouse products and iron and steel which dropped 7.5 percent and 22.1 percent.

The top three leading imports were raw materials not produced in the United States, silk, coffee, and rubber. The imports in succeeding importance were sugar, which fell 17.8 percent, and paper, 30.2 percent. Many remaining imports were raw materials but among the manufactures were woolens, falling 40.8 percent, and fertilizers, 32.3 percent. This small sample shows no apparent pattern, except for those items, both imports and exports, such as food where demand was inelastic. No import industries registered any apparent benefits from the tariff. Among nontradables, utilities tumbled as did industrials. Retail trade fell 28.1 percent, Mail Order Houses, 34.5 percent, and miscellaneous services, 29.5 percent. There is thus no evidence to support the view that the Smoot-Hawley tariff significantly contributed to the crash.

The assumption that the Smoot-Hawley tariff played a key role in beginning the Great Depression, which the market anticipated, has recently been challenged by Barry Eichengreen.[84] He finds that the direct and feedback effects of the tariffs on the American economy were small and its stimulus to new foreign tariffs slight. Eichengreen believes that the only way in which the tariff contributed to the depression was by increasing the

American balance of payments surplus, thereby putting additional strain on other countries' ability to adjust under the gold standard. Eichengreen's work suggests that the market had no reason even to consider the passage of the Smoot-Hawley tariff as singularly bad news.

FOREIGN STOCK MARKETS

One prominent factor cited as contributing to the October crash was the failure in Great Britain of the business and financial empire of Clarence Hatry on September 20, 1929. Beginning with coin-operated vending machines and ending with investment trusts, Hatry had built up a remarkable group of enterprises. When he was discovered to have financed some of this by forging stock certificates, the London stock market plummeted.[85] Pundits and some historians have claimed that the ripple effects of this collapse then depressed the New York market as panicked British investors began to sell their foreign stocks. Irving Fisher pointed out that there was strong circumstantial evidence for this liquidation and repatriation of funds. In a season when sterling was normally weak, its price rose from $4.85, near the American gold import point, on September 24 to above $4.88, at the American gold export point, on October 24.[86]

The strength of Fisher's argument rests largely on his stock price indices that show London prices fall sharply and in advance of New York's. However, this drop does not square with the monthly index published by *The Bankers' Magazine* that incorporated 278 issues.[87] This index is depicted in Figure 11 along with indices for the New York and Berlin exchanges.[88] For the month ending September 18, 1929, it rose 0.6 percent. By October 18, after Hatry and before the Wall Street plunge, the index had fallen 2.8 percent. This is far less than the drop depicted by Fisher and hardly alarming, given that a drop of 2.6 percent had occurred between June and July of 1929 followed by a recovery. *The Bankers' Magazine*'s index excluded the Hatry stocks, which were apparently included in Fisher's index. This highlights the fact that their fall was relatively isolated. Among the stocks in *The Bankers' Magazine* index that fell the most were American Railway stocks. These accounted for 43 percent of the 2.8 percent fall in the London market.

In its editorial comments, *The Bankers' Magazine* treats the collapse of the Hatry stocks as an isolated event and stated that in the month up to

October 18, "the main impulse from selling has come from the other side of the Atlantic."[89] British investors may have been selling their American stocks before the October crash, but they acted for the same reasons as American investors not because of a general collapse in Britain.

Foreign stock markets often moved independently of New York. As seen in Figure 11, the Berlin market had been falling since early 1928. This may have been partly a result of tighter credit policies of European central banks, discussed below. It may also have been prompted by the flight of American capital. As the pre-eminent creditor nation during the 1920s, the United States had lent heavily to Europe. This trans-Atlantic flow of funds slowed dramatically in 1928, when investors turned their sights on New York. Thus, it is not surprising to see the bond and stock prices sag in continental Europe, particularly Germany, which was heavily dependent on foreign capital. The weak stock prices on European markets before October 1929 were more a consequence of the stock market boom than a cause of its demise.

FIGURE 11
European stock markets

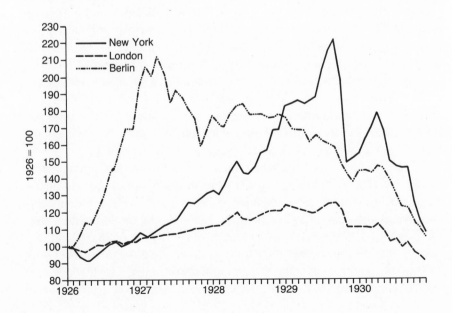

DOMESTIC CREDIT

The Federal Reserve's tight monetary policy was made even tighter by the stock market boom that drove up the demand for money and credit. High interest rates and the lure of the stock market attracted funds from Europe. The response by the Europeans was to pursue restrictive monetary policies in an effort to counter the pull of the New York market. Germany had the highest discount rate of all the major European economic powers, set at 7 percent in October 1927.[90] This was dropped to 6 1/2 percent in January of 1929, but the rise of the British rate from 4 1/2 percent to 5 1/2 percent in February caused a further tightening of credit conditions. In the face of balance of payments difficulties, the Germans were forced to raise the discount rate in April of 1929 to 7 1/2 percent.

After months of unsuccessful applications to the Board, the New York Federal Reserve Bank was finally allowed on August 9 to raise its discount rate from 5 percent to 6 percent.[91] Although the New York Bank hoped that this would restrain speculation, it brought no relief to other central banks which saw funds attracted to the now higher interest rates in the United States. The British saw a deterioration in their balance of payments, not only because of the short-term capital flows to the United States but also because the countries that had previously been able to raise new loans on the New York market were now crowded out by new stock issues. These nations were forced to draw down on their sterling balances in London. In August 1929, the Governor of the Bank of England warned the Treasury that Britain might be forced to abandon the gold standard. In September, the British discount rate was increased from 5 1/2 to 6 1/2 percent.[92]

In the United States, all interest rates showed a strong upward drift as credit tightened. Commercial paper rates rose slowly to their pre-crash peak of 6.25 percent. Similarly the interest rate on customers' loans charged by New York banks rose from 4.49 percent in October 1927 to 5.63 percent the following year and to a peak of 6.08 percent in October 1929.[93]

This general rise in interest rates did not have any immediately observable effects on brokers' loans—the ability of speculators to obtain credit. The comprehensive figures on New York Exchange members' borrowings was only collected monthly. In the last report before the crash, for October 1, 1929, total loans had reached a new peak of $8,549 million, having risen an impressive $667 million above the September level with little change in the bank and non-bank sources of funds. The less comprehensive figures from New York City member banks have four pre-crash observations: October 2, 9, 16, and 23. The total loans provided by these banks peaked on October 2 at $6,804 million, hovered and then dropped to $6,634 million on October 23. The major source of growth were loans placed "for others," that is, non-banks. These peaked on October 9 at $3,941 million, falling to $3,823 million on October 23. This decline of $118 million on the eve of the crash seems more to have been a result of a decline in the demand for loans than a decline in the supply, as the call loan rate hovered around 6 percent in the middle of October, far below its previous peaks. Nor does it seem to have provided a new signal to the market as these loans had larger temporary declines earlier in the boom.[94] As in the months during the boom, the credit markets and in particular the market for brokers' loans responded rather than drove the stock market's decline.

A CHANGE IN FUNDAMENTALS

The inadequacy of these explanations leads back to the question whether there was any change in expected dividends or earnings. The aggregate figures give no hint of new developments. The Cowles data shows earnings per share rising from $10.94 in 1928 to $11.86 in 1929 and dividends from $5.97 to $6.62. In Table 1, the quarterly dividends of the Dow-Jones Industrials show healthy increases in late 1929. They rose 12.8 percent in the third quarter and 11.6 percent in the fourth quarter. The first drop, of 6.3 percent, appears only in the first quarter of 1930. In the absence of any quarterly earnings figures, the Federal Reserve's index of industrial production may be examined as a proxy. The seasonally adjusted index, which had increased steadily since November 1927, revealed its first drop in July 1929 from 126 to 124.[95] It drifted down to 122 by the end of September. The Federal Reserve's other indices presented a mixed picture. While the volatile building contracts awarded slumped in August by 25.2 percent, factory employment, factory payrolls, and freight car loadings showed increases.

The peak of the business cycle has been dated from August 1929, but this would not have been necessarily apparent to anyone watching the Federal Reserve's indices.[96] The decline in all indices came only when the October figures were published after the crash. The growth of dividend payments and factory employment right up to the crash do not obviously suggest an imminent recession.

However, this mixed news was apparently all that was necessary to alter investors' expectations. The market had been slowly declining since early September. Unlike previous "pauses" during the boom, there was no good news to send the market higher. While still growing, dividends were not increasing at a rate that could have justified stock prices. Credit was tight, real interest rates in the U.S. and abroad were rising, and there was no indication that production would continue to surge ahead. Additional bad news could only have disappointed investors' hopes. No indicator of the economy showed any sharp departure from the past, but the timing of some signs of a slowing economy with declining stock prices proved enough to revise some stockholders' expectations.

The uncertain state of the economy brought about a downward drift of the market beginning in September and continuing through October. More and more analysts and brokerages offered less optimistic projections. In the week before the crash, October 14 to 18, noted bears such as Jesse Livermore and William Danforth became very active. Trouble was discernible as volume rose, brokerage firms were swamped, margin calls became more frequent, and the ticker began to run behind.[97] When prompt reporting of prices became impossible, investors lost track of their position in the market and began panic selling. In these circumstances, the exchange would sometimes issue "flash" bulletins of the prices of a few key stocks to indicate the market's trend. Such notices might induce panic just as well as they might halt it.

These developments were a prelude to Black Thursday and Black Tuesday. Brokers' offices were packed, but as the ticker fell behind it was impossible to keep customers informed, increasing uncertainty and contributing to the panic. The vertical price drops forced margin calls on impaired accounts and led many others to liquidate their holdings. Although the frenzied selling occasionally abated, the market could not be talked up by bankers and big investors' promises and large purchases of stock.

A more widespread financial crisis threatened as out-of-town banks and other lenders withdrew their loans to brokers. New York City banks stepped into the breach and quickly increased their loans, as seen in Figure 7. They were encouraged by the Federal Reserve Bank of New York, which made open market purchases and let its members know that they could borrow freely at the discount window. The New York banks took over brokers' loans as other lenders fled the market, and they did not press borrowers for immediate payment. The direct financial effects of the crash were thus confined to the stock market. The New York Fed's prompt action ensured that there were no panic increases in money market rates and no threat to the banks from defaults on security loans.[98]

CONCLUSION

The long wave of economic prosperity of the 1920s prepared the way for the stock market boom. Economic growth was a product of structural and technological changes in industry that altered the established patterns of production, distribution, and management. These brought the equities market of age and reduced the role of commercial banks as intermediaries between industry and the public. At the same time as people began to buy stock, the changes in industry made it harder to evaluate future earnings and dividends. This set the stage for a bubble where investors' expectations became more diffuse and their attention drifted away from fundamentals.

Irving Fisher and others have argued that the rise in stock prices was largely justified by the record growth of earnings. However, the increases in earnings and dividends were clearly outstripped by the astonishing rise in stock prices. A rapid recovery of earnings after the 1927 recession may well have initiated the boom. But the ascent of the stock market was not justified by any forecast of dividends—a fact that some managers recognized. Easy credit did not contribute to the boom, and monetary policy was tight for its duration. Brokers' loans grew because of the demand to buy stock, and the high call rate attracted funds from other money markets.

The rapid rise in stock prices appears to have been a speculative bubble. Unfortunately, even sixty years later, it is difficult, if not impossible, to identify any measure or variable that captures the degree of speculation in the market. This limits any econometric examination of the bubble, but the ample qualitative evidence reveals that the necessary conditions for the appearance of a bubble were present.

While conventional wisdom has held that the bubble was inherently unstable and prone to collapse, the October panic can be traced to several factors. In the late summer and early autumn of 1929, the supply of stocks began to increase, and there were large new issues. Fearful of financial and economic dislocations, the Federal Reserve tried to restrain speculation first by direct pressure and then by raising interest rates. These efforts had no discernible effect on the boom. It did, however, produce a general rise in interest rates that slowed the American economy and induced foreign central banks to raise their rates. Tighter credit then contributed to the beginning of a recession that was picked up in the mixed economic indicators of early August and September. These dispelled hopes that earnings would continue to grow at a rapid rate. As the economy faltered, wiser investors began leaving the market. When selling picked up speed, margin calls and delayed information from the ticker ensured a dramatic panic.

Intervention by the Federal Reserve Bank of New York in October prevented a collapse of the financial system. This was an appropriate response, but the same cannot be said for the Federal Reserve's earlier attempts to halt the boom. Instead of allowing the stock market bubble to run its course, the Federal Reserve's tighter monetary policy pushed the economy further into a recession, rendering it more vulnerable to the shock that came when the bubble finally burst.

APPENDIX

THE MARSH-MERTON MODEL OF
AGGREGATE DIVIDEND BEHAVIOR

Let $D(t)$ = dividends paid between $t-1$ and t
   $V(t)$ = instrinsic value of the firms
   $E(t)$ = permanent earnings per share
   $E(t)$ = $kV(t)$ and for managers $E^m(t) = kV^m(t)$

The dividend generating process depends on a distributed lag of the log of permanent earnings:

$$(1-f_1L)D(t) = a(t) + (g-h_1L)\log E^m(t-1) + n(t) \tag{A.1}$$

where L is the lag operator and $a(t)$ is a drift term. The dividend payment process is assumed to converge to a target ratio B as t goes to infinity:

$$\lim_{t \to \infty} \log [D(t) / E^m(t-1)] = B \tag{A.2}$$

Imposing (A.2) on (A.1), the short-run dynamics yield:

$$\log(D(t+1)) - \log(D(t)) = z(t) + g\{\log E^m(t) - \log E^m(t-1) - m(t-1)\}$$

$$+ j(B - \{\log D(t) - \log(E^m(t-1)\}) + n(t+1) \tag{A.3}$$

where $m(t-1)$ is the $t-1$ expectation of $\log E^m(t) - \log E^m(t-1)$, and $z(t)$ is $\log D(t) - \log D(t-1)$ if the target ratio has converged to B and the unexpected change in the log of permanent earnings is zero. Let the cum dividend stock price, $P_c(t) = E^m(t) / k$ and by market efficiency the market and managers will give the same intrinsic value to the firm so that $V(t) = P_c(t)$. The cum dividend stock price change can be decomposed into the ex-dividend price change and the dividend yield:

$$P_c(t) / P_c(t-1) = P(t) / P(t-1) + D(t) / P(t-1) \tag{A.4}$$

Substituting this in (A.3) produces:

$$\log[D(t+1) / D(t)] = [k - D(t) / P(t-1)]$$
$$+ g\{\log[P(t) + D(t) / P(t-1)]\} \tag{A.5}$$
$$+ j\{p - \log[D(t) / P(t-1)]\} + u(t+1)$$

where
   $p = B + \log k$

Rearranging the terms yields the regression equation:

$$\log[D(t+1) / D(t)] + [D(t) / P(t-1)] = a_0$$
$$+ a_1\log[P(t) + D(t) / P(t-1)] + a_2\log[D(t) / P(t+1)]$$
$$+ u(t+1)$$

where

$$a_1 = g,$$
$$a_2 = -j, \text{ and}$$
$$a_0 = (1-g)k + jp$$

NOTES

1. John Kenneth Galbraith (1954 and 1988), *The Great Crash 1929*, Boston: Houghton Mifflin Company.
2. Galbraith, pp. xii–xiii.
3. Charles P. Kindleberger (1978), *Manias, Panics and Crashes: A History of Financial Crises*, New York: Basic Books.
4. Milton Friedman and Anna J. Schwartz (1963), *A Monetary History of the United States, 1867–1960*, Princeton, New Jersey: Princeton University Press, pp. 305–08, 334–42. Christian D. Romer (June 1988), "The Great Crash and the Onset of the Great Depression," NBER working paper.
5. U.S. Department of Commerce (1975), *Historical Statistics of the United States, Colonial Times to 1970*, Washington, DC: Government Printing Office, Vol. I, pp. 135 and 226.
6. For a description of these developments, see Alfred D. Chandler, Jr. (1977), *The Visible Hand: The Managerial Revolution in American Business*, Cambridge, Massachusetts: Harvard University Press.
7. Richard Stillman (1986), *Dow Jones Industrial Average: History and Role in an Investment Strategy*, Homewood, Illinois: Dow Jones-Irwin.
8. Lauchlin Currie (August 1931), "The Decline of the Commercial Loan," *Quarterly Journal of Economics, 45*.
9. Eugene N. White (1984), "Banking Innovation in the 1920s: The Growth of National Banks' Financial Services," *Business and Economic History*, Vol. 13, pp. 92–104.
10. W. Nelson Peach (1941), *The Security Affiliates of National Banks*, Baltimore: Johns Hopkins Press, p. 75.
11. H. H. Preston and A. R. Finlay (1930), "Investment Affiliates Thrive," *American Bankers Association Journal, 24*, pp. 1027–28.

12. Eugene N. White (1986), "Before the Glass-Steagall Act: An Analysis of the Investment Banking Activities of National Banks," *Explorations in Economic History,* Vol. 23, pp. 36–37.
13. Vincent P. Carosso (1970), *Investment Banking in America: A History,* Cambridge, Massachusetts: Harvard University Press, p. 287.
14. Carosso, pp. 281–83.
15. Frederick Lewis Allen (1931 and 1975), *Only Yesterday: An Informal History of the Nineteen-Twenties,* New York: Harper and Row, pp. 293–298; and Galbraith, p. 12.
16. Board of Governors of the Federal Reserve System (1943), *Banking and Monetary Statistics, 1914–1941,* Washington, DC: Government Printing Office, pp. 480–81.
17. Allen, p. 295.
18. *Commercial and Financial Chronicle* (March 24, 1928), Vol. 26, p. 1988. Other automobile companies and suppliers ranked among the most heavily traded stocks and contributed to a lesser extent to the rise in the stock market indices.
19. *Commercial and Financial Chronicle* (March 24, 1928), Vol. 26, p. 1811; and (March 31, 1928), p. 1982.
20. Barrie A. Wigmore (1985), *The Crash and Its Aftermath,* Westport, Connecticut: Greenwood Press, pp. 62–63. The rest of the industry had high price-earnings ratios below 15.
21. Wigmore, p. 8.
22. Charles Amos Dice (1929), *New Levels in the Stock Market,* New York: McGraw-Hill.
23. Irving Fisher (1930), *The Stock Market Crash—and After,* New York: Macmillan, p. 53.
24. Dice, pp. 75–82.
25. Fisher, p. 69.
26. Gerald Sirkin (1975), "The Stock Market of 1929 Revisited: A Note," *Business History Review,* Vol. XLIX, No. 2.
27. Sirkin uses a model developed by Burton G. Malkiel (December 1963), "Equity Yields, Growth and the Structure of Share Prices," *American Economic Review,* Vol. 53, No. 5.
28. Alfred Cowles III and Associates (1938), *Common-Stock Indexes, 1871–1937,* Bloomington, Indiana: Principia Press, pp. 388–89, 420–21, series Da–1 and E–1.
29. *Moody's Manual of Investments: Industrial Securities,* New York, 1929–31.
30. Terry A. Marsh and Robert C. Merton (1987), "Dividend Behavior for the Aggregate Stock Market," *Journal of Business,* Vol. 60, No. 1, pp. 1–40.

31. If only the information from earnings was used by managers, then the first explanatory variables would be replaced by $\log[(E_{t+1} / E_t) + (D_t / P_{t-1})]$. By assuming that the stock market price is equal to its intrinsic price, Marsh and Merton implicitly assume there are no bubbles. This assumption should not pose a problem here as the estimations are for the pre-bubble period.

32. Robert T. Patterson (1965), *The Great Boom and Panic, 1921–1929,* Chicago: Henry Regnery Company, p. 31.

33. Fisher, p. 218. Writing in August of 1929, Dice believed that a break in the market would occur because brokers' loans as a percentage of the value of all stock listed on the New York Stock Exchange had risen to almost 9.5 percent, a number which was critical in his technical analysis.

34. Galbraith, p. 21.

35. Galbraith, p. 20.

36. Galbraith, pp. 68–69.

37. Kindleberger, pp. 52–53, 67. Also see Patterson, pp. 217–18.

38. New York Stock Exchange (1931), *Year Book, 1930–1931,* New York, pp. 123–25.

39. James D. Hamilton (1987), "Monetary Factors in the Great Depression," *Journal of Monetary Economics, 19,* pp. 145–53.

40. Friedman and Schwartz, pp. 251–66.

41. In a famous incident, after a break in stock prices in March 1929, Charles E. Mitchell, president of City National Bank, offered to lend $25 million to the call market in defiance of the Board. Galbraith (pp. 36–38) believes that Mitchell broke the Federal Reserve's will and revived the boom. However, Friedman and Schwartz (pp. 258–61) reveal that Mitchell had favored higher rates. Like other directors of the New York bank he disliked direct pressure. During the whole episode he was in close contact with George L. Harrison, president of the New York Federal Reserve Bank, suggesting there may have been connivance at undermining the Board's policy.

42. Dice, pp. 164–65.

43. Board of Governors of the Federal Reserve System (1943), *Banking and Monetary Statistics, 1914–1941,* Washington DC: Government Printing Office, pp. 497–500.

44. New York Stock Exchange *Year Book, 1930–1931,* pp. 108–19.

45. The figures from the New York Stock Exchange were somewhat higher. At the end of January 1929, brokers' loans from this source totaled $6,735 million with $5,664 million coming from New York banks and trust companies. According to the Federal Reserve Bank of New York, member banks gave $5,559 million of brokers' loans.

46. Dice, pp. 171–76.

47. Kindleberger, pp. 52–53, 63–74.

48. The call rate was for call loans, which were the bulk of brokers' loans. The rate for time loans followed the path of the call rate very closely in its movement away from other interest rates.

49. Unless otherwise indicated, all sources of data are from Board of Governors of the Federal Reserve, *Banking and Monetary Statistics*.

50. Galbraith, p. 20.

51. Fisher, pp. 221–22.

52. Dice, p. 165.

53. George G. Judge et al. (1980), *The Theory and Practice of Econometrics,* New York: John Wiley and Sons, pp. 219–20.

54. The stock market boom also had a powerful effect on the demand for money, via the demand for transactions balances to buy stocks. Field has shown that this caused money markets to tighten further as the boom progressed, misleading the Federal Reserve as to the actual effect of its policies [Alexander J. Field (1984), "Asset Exchanges and the Transactions Demand for Money, 1919–1929," *American Economic Review,* Vol. 71, No. 4].

55. *Banking and Monetary Statistics,* pp. 465–66.

56. Ivan Wright (April 1929), "Loans to Brokers and Dealers for Account of Others," *Journal of Business,* Vol. II, No. 2, pp. 123–25.

57. Behzad T. Diba and Herschel I. Grossman (June 1988), "Explosive Rational Bubbles in Stock Prices?" *American Economic Review,* Vol. 78, No. 3, pp. 520–30.

58. Olivier J. Blanchard and Mark W. Watson (1982), "Bubbles, Rational Expectations, and Financial Markets," in Paul Wachtel (ed.), *Crises in the Economic and Financial Structure,* Lexington, Massachusetts: D. C. Heath and Company, pp. 303–4.

59. Robert J. Shiller (June 1981), "Do Stock Prices Move Too Much to Be Justified by Subsequent Changes in Dividends?" *American Economic Review,* Vol. 71, No. 3, pp. 421–36.

60. Also see Blanchard and Watson (pp. 304–309), who find that relation between prices and dividends is weak providing further evidence for the existence of bubbles.

61. Robert J. Shiller (1984), "Stock Prices and Social Dynamics," *Brookings Papers on Economic Activity, 2,* pp. 457–510.

62. Marjorie A. Flavin (December 1983), "Excess Volatility in the Financial Markets: A Reassessment of the Empirical Evidence," *Journal of Political Economy,* Vol. 91, pp. 929–56.

63. N. Gregory Mankiw, David Romer, and Matthew D. Shapiro (July 1985), "An Unbiased Reexamination of Stock Market Volatility," *Journal of Finance,* Vol. 9, No. 3. pp. 677–89.

64. Allan W. Kleidon (1986), "Variance Bounds Tests and Stock Price Valuation Models," *Journal of Political Economy,* Vol. 94, No. 5, pp. 953–1001.

65. Diba and Grossman, pp. 520–30.
66. John Y. Campbell and Robert J. Shiller (October 1987), "Cointegration and Tests of Present Value Models," *Journal of Political Economy, 95,* pp. 1062–88; and (January 1988), "Stock Prices, Earnings and Expected Dividends," Princeton University Research Memorandum No. 334.
67. Hamilton warns against identifying the existence of a bubble because the dynamics of driving the fundamental variables have not been accurately specified [James D. Hamilton (October 1986), "On Testing for Self-Fulfilling Speculative Price Bubbles," *International Economic Review,* Vol. 27, No. 3, pp. 545–52).
68. One exception is Santoni's examination of 1928–29. He found that the log of the first differences of daily Dow Jones price data was stationary [Gary Santoni (November 1987), "The Great Bull Markets of 1924–1929 and 1982–1987: Speculative Bubbles or Economic Fundamentals?" *Federal Reserve Bank of St. Louis Review,* Vol. 69, No. 9, p. 27).
69. The autocorrelation coefficients for the quarterly data collected were examined, and Box-Pierce tests suggested that prices were nonstationary in levels but stationary in differences. However, dividends were nonstationary in both levels and differences.
70. Santoni, p. 27.
71. In this nonparametric test the number of runs is normally distributed with mean $(2xy / x+y) + 1$ and a standard deviation of $\{[2xy(2xy - x-y)] / [(x+y)^2 (x+y - 1)]\}^{1/2}$ where x is the number of rises in the index and y is the number of drops in the index. See Damodar N. Gujarati (1988), *Basic Econometrics,* New York: McGraw-Hill, pp. 372–73.
72. Blanchard and Watson (pp. 310–11) give other reasons for the weakness of these tests.
73. Blanchard and Watson, pp. 300–1.
74. Frances D. McMullen (November 1930), "Women and the Ticker Tape—A Year after the Crash," *The Women's Journal.* This article argued that women investors had fared no worse, if not better, than men.
75. Samuel Crowther (August 1929), "Everybody Ought to be Rich," *Ladies' Home Journal.*
76. This forecast brought Babson great fame. In September 1930, he attempted to duplicate his success, predicting that an economic recovery was at hand (Patterson, p. 89).
77. Galbraith, p. 91.
78. Fisher (pp. 48–49) believed that Kent had overestimated the increase in the total securities outstanding by including the securities issued by investment trusts and by merging companies.
79. Galbraith, p. 91; and Fisher, p. 37.

80. Patterson, p. 105.
81. Fisher, pp. 47–48; and Patterson, p. 188.
82. Jude Wanniski (1978), *The Way the World Works,* New York: Basic Books, pp. 125–140.
83. The leading import and export industries were identified using Department of Commerce (1929), *Commerce Yearbook,* Washington DC: Government Printing Office. The stock indices were those produced by Alfred Cowles.
84. Barry Eichengreen (August 1986), "The Political Economy of the Smoot-Hawley Tariff," NBER working paper No. 2001.
85. Galbraith, p. 90–91; and Patterson, pp. 92–93.
86. Fisher, pp. 31–33.
87. *The Bankers' Magazine* (June 1931), pp. 896–98.
88. The source for the Berlin exchange is the *Federal Reserve Bulletin* (May 1931), p. 283.
89. *The Bankers' Magazine* (November 1929), p. 694.
90. Stephen V.O. Clarke (1967), *Central Bank Cooperation, 1924–1931,* New York: Federal Reserve Bank of New York, pp. 147–50.
91. Friedman and Schwartz, p. 264.
92. Clarke, p. 150.
93. *Banking and Monetary Statistics,* p. 463.
94. Between May 15 and June 12, loans for the account of others fell by $131 million.
95. *Federal Reserve Bulletin* (May 1931), p. 257.
96. Friedman and Schwartz, p. 306. The unadjusted indices of manufacturing and industrial production recovered in August and September.
97. Patterson, pp. 112–15.
98. Friedman and Schwartz, pp. 305–6 and 334–39.

CHAPTER 6

BUBBLES OR FUNDAMENTALS: NEW EVIDENCE FROM THE GREAT BULL MARKETS

Gary J. Santoni
Gerald P. Dwyer, Jr.

"The binge is over. It couldn't go on forever—...all the glitz and glamour, the danger and thrill. It's over."

—Robert B. Reich,
The New York Times
October 22, 1987

The October 1987 crash in stock prices stripped roughly 26 percent from stock values in the United States. More disconcerting, however, were the speed of adjustment, the tumultuous trading activity in financial markets and the uncertainty that prevailed during the week of October 19. These aspects of the crash bore a surprising resemblance to previous financial panics that many thought were historical artifacts outmoded by modern regulatory and surveillance systems as well as advances in the financial sophistication of market participants. The crash shocked this complacency and has reawakened considerable interest in financial panics and their causes.

The search for an explanation of the recent crash has led to comparisons between the bull markets of 1924–29 and 1982–87 like the one shown in Figure 1. The chart shows closing levels of the Dow Jones Industrial Index on the last day of the month. The behavior of stock prices during the two periods is strikingly similar. Both bull markets began about the second quarter of the year; each lasted about 21 quarters; each hit its peak in the third quarter with the timing of the peaks separated by only a few days (September 3, 1929, and August 25, 1987); in each case, 54 days elapsed between the peak and the crash; and each crash slashed more than 20 percent from the stock market averages.

The popular explanations for both episodes also are quite similar (see Santoni, 1987). For the most part, these explanations attribute both bull markets and the subsequent panics to "excessive speculation" that pushed share prices well beyond the levels supported by the fundamentals (for example, Galbraith, 1955; Kindleburger, 1978, p. 17; and Aiyagari, 1988). According to this view, crashes are inevitable consequences of the speculations that precede them because the resulting price bubble must eventually burst. This idea is formally analyzed in Flood and Garber (1980 and 1982), Schiller (1981), Blanchard and Watson (1982), Diba and Grossman (1985,

FIGURE 1
The Great Bull Markets and Panics

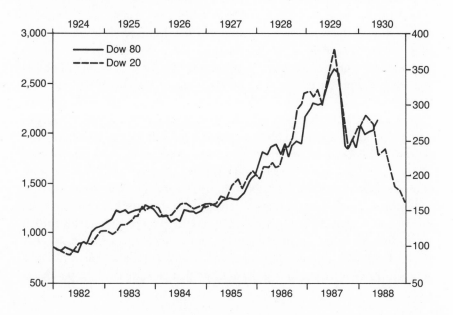

1986, and 1988), Hamilton (1986), West (1986), Singleton (1987), Campbell and Shiller (1987), and Aiyagari (1988).

The belief that speculative bubbles may cause a persistent deviation in stock prices from the price consistent with the fundamentals is important. At the time of the 1929 crash, it spawned legislative proposals that would curb credit for speculation, amend the National Banking and Federal Reserve acts, impose an excise tax on stock sales, and regulate the activities of stock exchanges and investment trusts.[1] Similar proposals have followed the panic of 1987.[2] Furthermore, stock price bubbles are important for economic stabilization policy because bubbles imply that plans to save and invest may be based on irrational criteria and subject to erratic change.[3]

This paper compares the implications of a theory of stock prices based on fundamentals to one that allows for bubbles and examines data from the 1920s and 1980s to determine which set of implications is supported by the evidence.

I. PRICE BUBBLES

A price bubble is a deviation in the price of an asset (gold, foreign currency, stock) from the price consistent with the fundamentals (Hamilton, 1986, and Diba and Grossman, 1988).[4] In one case, the notion of price bubbles is based on the proposition that stock prices are too variable to be explained by variation in the fundamentals (Shiller, 1981; Mankiw, Romer, and Shapiro, 1985). This analysis is not concerned with persistent one-sided errors in stock prices and, consequently, is not relevant for the notion of bubbles that allegedly produced the great bull markets of the late 1920s and mid-1980s.

An alternative theory of price bubbles, sometimes called the theory of rational bubbles, allows bubbles to possess the following characteristics[5]: (1) *Bubbles have some persistence* so that a forecast of stock prices based solely on the fundamentals is biased. This characteristic captures the spirit of the critique of the bull markets of the 1920s and 80s that "Neither assets or earnings, ..., warrant the market values of hundreds of stock issues."[6] (2) *Bubbles are explosive* in the sense that the observed price deviates further and further from the fundamentals price for as long as the bubble lasts. The reason for this is that no rational investor will purchase shares of stock unless its price is expected to grow at a rate that compensates the purchaser for the additional amount invested due to the bubble. (3) *Bubbles are not negative*. A negative bubble means that stock prices are less than implied by the fundamentals. The explosive characteristic of bubbles means that prices implode with some probability that stock prices will be negative in the future.[7] Negative stock prices, however, are impossible: they are inconsistent with the liability rules associated with common stock.

II. FUNDAMENTALS, BUBBLES, AND FOOLS

Assume that investors equate the expected holding period return on a stock to a constant expected real interest rate, r. Then, with the price measured at the start of the period just after the dividend is paid,

$$r = \frac{E_t p_{t+1} + E_t x_{t+1} - p_t}{p_t} \qquad (1)$$

where $E_t y_{t+1}$ is the expected value of y in period $t+1$ conditional on all information available in period t (which includes the price in period t, p_t, and the dividend in period t, x_t). This can be rewritten as:

$$p_t = \delta (E_t p_{t+1} + E_t x_{t+1}), \qquad (2)$$

where $\delta = (1+r)^{-1}$. This equation is the basis for both the model of the fundamentals and the model for bubbles.

Fundamentals and Bubbles

The fundamental price in period t, p_t^f, is the discounted present value of the expected future stream of dividends,[8]

$$p_t^f = \sum_{i=1}^{\infty} \delta^i E_{t+1} x_{t+1} \quad \text{if } \lim_{t \to \infty} \delta^1 E_t x_{t+1} = 0 \qquad (3)$$

If the growth rate of the dividend is constant, then (3) holds only if that growth rate is less than the real interest rate. The empirical content of the fundamental model of stock prices can be seen most clearly by comparing its implications with the implications of the price being partly determined by a bubble.

A simple theory of bubbles can approximate the notion that the Coolidge market was a price bubble that eventually burst. Assume that the actual stock price in period t deviates from the fundamental price by an amount B_t with probability $\pi > 0$ of continuing each period. This specification of a bubble follows Blanchard and Watson (1982), although other specifications are possible (Hamilton, 1986; Campbell and Shiller, 1987; and Diba and Grossman, 1988). A solution for the price that includes the bubble, p_t^b consistent with (2) is:

$$p_t^b = p_t^f + B_t , \tag{4a}$$

where

$$B_t = \begin{bmatrix} (1 + r)\pi^{-1} B_{t-1} & \text{with probability } \pi \\ 0 & \text{with probability } 1 - \pi \end{bmatrix} \tag{4b}$$

The term π^{-1} appears in the bubble part of the price because purchasers of the stock must be compensated for the possibility that the bubble will burst: a lower probability of the bubble continuing is associated with a higher rate of increase of the bubble part of the price if the bubble continues. As long as the bubble continues, the bubble part of the price grows at the rate:

$$g^b = r + (1 + r) \frac{(1 - \pi)}{\pi} . \tag{5}$$

Because $1-\pi$ and π are greater than zero, the bubble part of the price grows at a rate greater than the real interest rate. When the bubble bursts, the expected growth rate of this part of the price is zero. Zero expected growth is the equilibrium solution until another bubble begins.

Stock Prices and Dividends—Long-Run Implications

These two models of stock prices have different implications for the relationship between stock prices and dividends. Equation (3) for the fundamental price can be written as:

$$p_t^f = x_t \sum_{i=1}^{\infty} \delta^i + \sum_{i=1}^{\infty} \delta^i (E_t \, x_{t+1} - x_t) \qquad (6)$$

Suppose that the actual price, p_t , equals the fundamental price. If the price and the dividends each have one unit root (as turns out to be consistent with the data), then equation (6) implies that the price and dividend are cointegrated (Granger and Engle, 1987).[9] That is, the regression:

$$p_t = \alpha + \beta x_t + \epsilon_t \qquad (7)$$

has a residual that does not have a unit root. This follows from the stationarity of differences of x_t and the convergence of $\delta^i (E_t x_{t+1} - x_t)$ to zero as i goes to infinity.

Alternatively, if bubbles are an important component of the actual price, the stock price is not cointegrated with dividends.[10] By assumption, the bubble part of the price reflects the expected return on the bubble. When a bubble is on, the bubble part of the price increases with time. In addition, the bubble part of the price is independent of the dividend and therefore appears in the residual of (7). Hence, the estimated residuals in (7) increase with time, which implies that they are nonstationary. As a practical matter, the ability to discern this unit root in a finite sample depends on the proportion of periods with bubbles on, with crashes, and with no bubble.

Implications for Bubble Periods

The second test between the two models is based on implications for a period alleged to be characterized by a bubble. Over a short period when dividends reasonably can be assumed to grow at a constant rate, the fundamental model and the bubble model have different implications for the serial correlation of proportional changes of stock prices.

If the expected growth rate of dividends is constant, the fundamental model implies that proportional changes in the stock price are unpredictable. If dividends grow at a constant rate, g, and deviations of dividends from this constant rate are unpredictable, then

$$x_{t+1} = (1 + g) x_t + \eta_{t+1} \qquad E_t \, \eta_{t+1} = 0, \qquad (8)$$

where g is the growth rate of dividends and η_{t+1} is the unexpected part of dividend growth in period $t + 1$. Substitution of (8) into (3) and calculation of the proportional change in the fundamental price yields:

$$\frac{\Delta p^f_{t+1}}{p^f_t} = g + \frac{\eta_{t+1}}{p^f_t} \sum_{i=1}^{\infty} \delta^{\,i}(1 + g)^i \qquad (9)$$

If the standard deviation of the unexpected part of dividends relative to the price, η_{t+1}/p^f_t, is homoskedastic, proportional changes in the price have an autocorrelation function that is zero for all lags.

On the other hand, if there is a bubble, proportional changes in the price are serially correlated. If the dividend grows at a constant rate, the proportional change in price including the bubble obtained from (4a) is:

$$\frac{\Delta p^b_{t+1}}{p^b_t} = \frac{\Delta p^f_{t+1}}{p^f_t} \frac{p^f_t}{p^b_t} + \frac{\Delta B_{t+1}}{p^b_t}. \qquad (10)$$

Let g^f denote the proportionate rate of increase of the fundamental price in equation (9). Using this definition and rearranging, gives:

$$\frac{\Delta p^b_{t+1}}{p^b_t} = g^f - g^f \frac{B_t}{p^b_t} + \frac{\Delta B_{t+1}}{p^b_t}. \qquad (11)$$

The result of using (4b) and (5) to replace ΔB_{t+1} and rearrangement is

$$\frac{\Delta p^b_{t+1}}{p^b_t} = g^f + (g^b - g^f) \frac{B_t}{p^b_t}. \qquad (12)$$

Using (4a), we find that:

$$\frac{\Delta p^b_{t+1}}{p^b_t} = g^f + (g^b - g^f) \; \frac{1}{1 + p^f_t / B_t}. \tag{13}$$

The proportional change in the stock price equals the proportional change in the fundamental price plus a term due to the bubble. The first part of the term due to the bubble is $g^b - g^f$, which has a strictly positive expected value because $g^b > r$ and the expected value of g^f is $g < r$. The second part is not stationary in finite time. Let period 0 be any period when the bubble is on. Then the ratio of the fundamental price to the bubble part of the price in later periods when the bubble is on is

$$\frac{p^f_t}{B_t} = \frac{(1 + g^f)^t}{(1 + g^b)^t} \; \frac{p^f_0}{B_0} \tag{14}$$

where p^f_0 / B_0 is constant for all $t > 0$. Because the expected value of g^f is less than g^b, this ratio is a decreasing function of time. This indicates that, for any finite period when a bubble is on, the proportional change in price is an increasing function of time. As a result, the proportional change in price is serially correlated in general. As time goes to infinity, the ratio goes to zero because the bubble part of the price eventually dominates the actual price. Some idea of the order of magnitude of a bubble's effect on the autocorrelation function can be gained from Santoni (1987) and Diba and Grossman (1987).

Greater Fools

In addition to the economic theory of rational bubbles, a more popular notion, known as the "greater fool theory," generates similar implications for the behavior of stock prices. According to this theory, people regard the fundamentals as irrelevant. Rather, they buy stock on the belief that some (bigger?) fool will buy the shares from them at a higher price in the future. People maintain this belief because they think "that market values will rise—as they did yesterday or last week—and a profit can be made

(Galbraith, 1955, p. 23)."[11]   Once the speculation begins, stock prices continue rising because people, seeing the rise in the previous period, demand additional shares in the belief that prices will rise further and this pushes prices still higher.

The greater fool theory is based on the presumption that there are times when past movements in stock prices matter. According to this theory, during the "fooling" periods, there should be positive correlation in the sequence of price changes and long runs of positive changes that exceed the median change for the sample period.

Both the greater fool theory and the theory of rational bubbles discussed in this paper imply that stock prices behave similarly.

III. WHAT CAUSES A BUBBLE?

Attributing the advances in stock prices during the 1920s and 80s to bubbles is not very satisfying, particularly since the cause of the bubbles is never precisely identified. In some explanations, the bubble simply arises without explanation (the theory of rational bubbles).[12] In others, it is attributed to "intense optimism," "manias," "vulgar grasping for gain," etc. This confronts the investigator with the impossible task of identifying periods when investors are particularly optimistic, vulgar, or irrational. Attributing crashes to bursting bubbles adds little to our understanding of why crashes occur or how to prevent similar occurrences in the future.

IV. FUNDAMENTALS VERSUS BUBBLES: SOME
EVIDENCE

Testing stock prices for the presence of bubbles would be easy if direct observation of the fundamentals were possible. Although these data are not available to investigators, it may still be possible to test stock prices for bubbles. As shown above, evidence that stock prices and dividends are cointegrated is consistent with the claim that stock prices are largely determined by fundamentals.[13] Furthermore, evidence that percentage changes in stock prices are uncorrelated during the Coolidge and Reagan bull markets is inconsistent with the notion that bubbles were important components of stock prices during these episodes.

Cointegration of Stock Prices and Dividends

Engle and Granger (1987) define two series (say, real stock prices, P_t, and dividends, X_t) to be cointegrated if both series are integrated of order d and a linear combination of these (say, $Z_t = P_t - \lambda X_t$) is integrated of order zero.[14] If this holds, Engle and Granger (1987, p. 253) explain that the constant λ is such that the bulk of the long-run components of P_t and X_t cancel out so that the series do "not drift too far apart" as implied by the fact that "their difference is I(0)."[15]

A finding that real stock prices and dividends are cointegrated suggests that the series do not diverge much, at least in the long run, as would be the case if a bubble were driving a larger and larger wedge between observed prices and dividends.

This is tested against January levels of the Standard and Poor's 500 index for 1883 to 1987 and the 12-month total of dividends per share (as of the fourth quarter) adjusted to the index for 1926 to 1987. These series were spliced to the Cowles Commission index of all stocks and per share dividend payments.[16] The resulting series are annual observations from 1871 to 1987. Each series is deflated by the annual level of the implicit price deflator for GNP. The data are similar but not identical to the data employed by Shiller (1981), Campbell and Shiller (1987), and Diba and Grossman (1988).

Figure 2 plots the data. The two series track each other fairly well, especially during the 1920s. Furthermore, note that dividends were relatively high in comparison to prices in the 1980s. The popular notion that stock prices were inflated during these two periods is puzzling given the Figure 2 comparison.

As a first step in testing for cointegration, the properties of the time series of real stock prices and dividends are examined to determine whether they can reasonably be characterized as integrated of order 1, I(1). Table 1 shows the sample autocorrelations of the levels and first differences of real stock prices and dividends. As indicated, the autocorrelations for the levels damp out very slowly as the lag is increased, indicating that the means of the series are nonstationary. The autocorrelations of the first differences, however, decline fairly quickly, suggesting that these series are stationary. Tables 2 and 3 report the results of Dickey/Fuller and augmented Dickey/Fuller (1981) tests for one and two unit roots for each of the series. Like the Table 1 results, those in Tables 2 and 3 suggest that real stock prices and dividends are both I(1).

FIGURE 2
Real Stock Prices and Dividends: 1872–1987

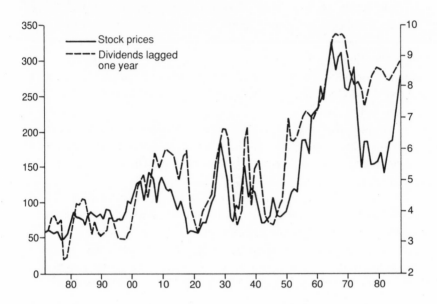

TABLE 1
Autocorrelations of Real Stock Prices, Dividends, and Their First Differences

	Variable			
Lags	P_t	X_t	ΔP_t	ΔX_t
1	.93	.94	.07	.17
2	.86	.87	−.24	−.17
3	.82	.81	.13	−.10
4	.77	.76	.15	−.08
6	.66	.67	−.09	−.04
8	.56	60	.01	−.14
10	.45	.58	.01	.19
12	.35	.53	−.16	−.13
14	.29	.49	−.06	.16
16	.21	.40	−.08	−.15
18	.17	.34	−.09	−.10

TABLE 2
Dickey/Fuller (1981) Tests[a]

	Variable			
Parameter[b]	P_t	X_t	ΔP_t	ΔX_t
C	4.06	.38	−.13	.00
	(.82)[c]	(2.12)	(.03)	(.03)
Υ	.18	.01	.03	.00
	(1.97)	(2.70)	(.47)	(.33)
ρ	.90	.85	.07	.16
	(20.60)	(16.85)	(.69)	(1.71)
ϕ_3	2.85	4.57	45.29	38.85

[a]Regressions are of the form $Z_t = C + \Upsilon t + \rho Z_{t-1} + U_t$. Sample size is 111 (1877–1987).

[b]The statistic ϕ_3 tests the null that $(\Upsilon, \rho) = (0, 1)$ against the alternative that $(\Upsilon, \rho) \neq (0, 1)$. Reject if $\phi_3 > 6.49$ for a test of size .05.

[c] t-scores are in parentheses.

TABLE 3
Augmented Dickey/Fuller (1981) Tests[a]

	Variable			
Parameter[b]	P_t	X_t	ΔP_t	ΔX_t
C	4.62	.44	-.05	.01
	(.97)[c]	(2.37)	(.01)	(.08)
Υ	.22	.01	.03	.00
	(2.33)	(2.81)	(.46)	(.43)
ρ	.87	.82	.08	-.22
	(18.85)	(13.98)	(.33)	(1.01)
β_1	.18	.27	.04	.40
	(1.78)	(2.79)	(.18)	(2.12)
β_2	-.16	-.11	-.20	.19
	(1.62)	(1.05)	(1.11)	(1.17)
β_3	.22	.05	-.04	.16
	(2.28)	(.54)	(.25)	(1.24)
β_4	.14	-.01	.04	.07
	(1.35)	(.14)	(.38)	(.73)
ϕ_3	4.01	4.77	8.62	16.35

[a]Regressions are of the form $Z_t = C + \Upsilon t + \rho Z_{t-1} + \Sigma^4 \beta_1 \Delta Z_{t-1} + U_t$. Sample size is 111 (1877–1987).

[b]The statistic ϕ_3 tests the null that $(\Upsilon, \rho) = (0, 1)$ against the alternative that $(\Upsilon, \rho) \neq (0, 1)$. Reject if $\phi_3 > 6.49$ for a test of size .05.

[c] t-scores are in parentheses.

The estimate of the cointegrating regression is given in Table 4.[17] Engle and Granger (1987) discuss three statistics that are relevant in testing the null hypothesis that the two series are not cointegrated. The first test statistic, ξ_1, is simply the cointegrating regression Durbin-Watson statistic. Since the calculated Durbin-Watson given in Table 4 exceeds the critical value for ξ_1 of .386, the null hypothesis is rejected at the 5 percent level. The remaining two statistics, ξ_2 and ξ_3, are Dickey/Fuller and augmented Dickey/Fuller tests for stationarity of the residuals of the cointegrating regression. The results of these tests are given in Table 5. Since the calculated test statistics exceed their critical values in both cases, these tests reject the null hypothesis that real stock prices and dividends are not cointegrated. These results are inconsistent with the presence of a rational bubble in stock prices since a bubble would produce nonstationary residuals in the cointegrating regression.

The above estimates differ slightly from those obtained by Campbell and Shiller (1987). While they draw the same general conclusion regarding the presence of a rational bubble, their Engle/Granger tests produced mixed results (Campbell and Shiller, 1987, p. 1077).[18] Their calculation of ξ_3 narrowly fails to reject the null hypothesis at the 10 percent level.

TABLE 4
Cointegrating Regression of Real Stock Prices and Dividends

Theoretical Model

$$P_t = \frac{(1 + g)}{(r - g)} \; X_{t-1} = \beta X_{t-1}$$

Estimate[a]

$$P_t = -36.15 + 30.39 X_{t-1} + U_t$$
$$\quad\quad (3.90)^b \;\; (17.78)$$

$R^2 = .74$

$DW = .66$

$\beta = 30.39$

$r = (I + g) / \beta + g$

[a] Sample size is 116 observations (1872–1987).

[b] *t*-statistics in parentheses.

TABLE 5
Tests for Stationarity of the Residuals of the Cointegrating Regression[a]

Dickey / Fuller

$$\Delta U_t = -.32U_{t-1}$$
$$(4.57)^b$$

$$\xi_2 = 4.57$$

Augmented Dickey / Fuller

$$\Delta U_t = -.29U_{t-1} + .05\Delta U_{t-1} - .23\Delta U_{t-2} + .10\Delta U_{t-3} + .04\Delta U_{t-4}$$
$$(3.21)\qquad (.48)\qquad (2.08)\qquad (1.02)\qquad (.38)$$

$$\xi_3 = 3.21$$

[a]The null hypothesis that the two series are not cointegrated is rejected at the 5 percent level if ξ_2 and ξ_3 exceed their critical values of 3.37 and 3.17. Sample size is 111 observations of the dependent variable (1877–1987).

[b] *t*-statistics in parentheses.

A further difference exists between Campbell and Shiller's interpretation of β and the one presented here. In this paper, $\beta = (1+g)/(r-g)$. Campbell and Shiller interpret β as the inverse of the real discount rate since their model assumes that the expected growth rate in real dividends is zero. Furthermore, given their estimate of β (=31.092), they calculate an implied discount rate of 3.2 percent. This is an estimate of the *real* discount rate given their assumption concerning expected dividend growth. They compare this estimate to the sample *nominal* return of 8.2 percent. The two rates of return differ markedly for two reasons. First, real and nominal returns are not comparable if the price level is changing. Second, Hendry (1986, p. 206) argues that β, given by the cointegrating regression, is a biased estimate of the true β, and the bias can be substantial. This is of some importance because Campbell and Shiller use the different estimates of β to check on the robustness of their methods (p. 1077) and conclude that the evidence for cointegration is weak because their tests fail to reject the unit root null for $SL_t(= P_t - BX_{t-1})$ when $\beta = 1/.082$. For what it is worth, the sample real return is 6.1 percent so the discrepancy is reduced considerably by simply comparing the discount rates on a consistent basis.

The test results presented in Tables 1–5 are evidence against a rational bubble in stock prices. In contrast to the theory of bubbles that implies stock prices that drift away from the price consistent with the flow of dividends, the results indicate that price shocks dampen out over time, suggesting that stock prices return to an equilibrium level which is some constant multiple of dividends.

The above tests concern the long-run behavior of real stock prices and dividends. The short-run behavior of stock prices during the Coolidge and Reagan Bull Markets are next examined for the presence of bubbles.

The Great Bull Markets

If bubbles are not present, the theoretical analysis suggests that percentage changes in stock prices are not correlated and the sequence of changes does not exhibit long runs that are greater or less than the sample median. Conversely, if stock prices are driven by the type of bubble discussed above, percentage changes in the index are positively correlated and the data should exhibit long runs.

The following examines the behavior of stock prices during two periods from each bull market. Daily closing levels of the Dow are used from the beginning of January 1928 (January 1986) through the market's peak on September 3, 1929 (August 25, 1987). The data are first differences of the log of the Dow's daily closing level and are approximately equal to the daily percentage change in the index. Each sample contains more than 400 observations. Stock prices advanced very rapidly during these periods. If bubbles were present, they should be apparent in these data.

In addition to these data, month-end closing levels of the Dow were examined from January 1924 (January 1982) through the peak in September 1929 (August 1987). These data are first differences of the log of the Dow's month-end closing level and are approximately equal to the monthly percentage change in the index. Each sample contains about 70 observations. These data cover the entire period of both bull markets.

Difference or Trend Stationary?

Table 6 gives the results of Dickey/Fuller (1981) tests for unit roots. Panel A uses daily data from the later phase of the Coolidge Bull Market. Panel

TABLE 6
Dickey / Fuller Tests: Daily Data[a]

Panel A: January 4, 1928–September 3, 1929

Unrestricted Model

$$LP_t = .086 + (.050E\text{-}3)t - (.035E\text{-}7)t^2 + .973LP_{t-1} \qquad RSS = .059012$$

$$\quad\;\; (1.22)^b \quad\;\; (.64) \qquad\quad (.13) \qquad\quad (97.39)$$

Restricted Model

$$\Delta LP_t = .0013 \qquad\qquad\qquad\qquad\qquad\qquad RSS = .060024$$

$$\quad\;\; (2.58)$$

$$\phi_3 \quad = 4.24$$

Panel B: January 2, 1986–August 25, 1987

Unrestricted Model

$$LP_t = .033 - (.017E\text{-}2)t + (.087E\text{-}6)t^2 + .972LP_{t-1} \qquad RSS = .039097$$

$$\quad\;\; (2.72) \quad\;\; (1.85) \qquad\;\; (2.11) \qquad\quad (85.95)$$

Restricted Model:

$$\Delta LP_t = .0014 \qquad\qquad\qquad\qquad\qquad\qquad RSS = .039846$$

$$\quad\;\; (2.83)$$

$$\phi_3 \quad = 3.99$$

[a]The null hypothesis is that $(\Upsilon_1, \Upsilon_2, \rho) = (0, 0, 1)$ in the regression $LP_t = C + \Upsilon_1 t + \Upsilon_2 t^2 + \rho LP_{t-1}$ against the alternative that $(\Upsilon_1, \Upsilon_2, \rho) \neq (0, 0, 1)$. The null is rejected in favor of the alternative if $\phi_3 > 6.25$.

[b] *t*-scores in parentheses.

B reports a similar test for the last stage of the Reagan Bull Market. Equations (13) and (14) imply that both the log of the level as well as percentage changes in price are positively related to time so the unrestricted model includes both time and time squared (the time variables are treated as only one restriction in calculating the test statistic). These tests fail to reject the null hypothesis that the log of stock prices is difference stationary, which is inconsistent with the notion that stock prices were driven by self-sustaining bubbles during the great bull markets of the 1920s and 1980s.

The constant term is positive and significant in the restricted model for both sets of data. Today, the upward drift in stock prices during these two bull markets is obvious. At the time, however, the upward drift is not something that investors could have bet on with any confidence.

Were Stock Prices a Random Walk?

Table 7 presents the results of a Box-Pierce test based on the estimated autocorrelations of percentage changes in the Dow Jones Industrial Index. This test is designed to determine whether there is significant autocorrelation in the data, that is, whether current changes in the index are related to past changes.

Table 7 shows test results for the two periods of daily data discussed above. None of the test statistics indicates significant correlation at conventional confidence levels. These data suggest that stock prices followed a random walk and are inconsistent with the bubble hypothesis.

Table 8 performs the same test for the month-end data. The results are qualitatively identical to those shown in Table 7.

Runs Test

A run is the number of sequential observations that are greater or less than the sample median (the middle value of the sample). If a series of observations exhibits too few runs relative to what is expected for independent observations, the data are positively correlated or drawn from different populations.

TABLE 7
Autocorrelation Coefficients and Box-Pierce Statistics: Daily Data

	January 3, 1928–September 3, 1929[a]			*January 1982–August 1987*[a]	
To Lag	*Auto- Correlation Coefficient*	*Box- Pierce Statistic*	*To Lag*	*Auto- Correlation Coefficient*	*Box- Pierce Statistic*
1	.0196	.18	1	.0553	1.28
2	−.0325	.70	2	−.0140	1.36
3	−.0494	1.91	3	−.0095	1.40
6	.0200	10.41	6	−.0151	4.66
12	.0069	16.43	12	−.0076	7.86
18	−.0521	21.65	18	−.0044	13.14
24	.0213	29.58	24	.0024	14.24

[a]First differences of logs of Dow Industrial Index.

TABLE 8
Autocorrelation Coefficients and Box-Pierce Statistics: Month-End Data

	January 1924–September 1929[a]			January 1982–August 1987[a]	
To Lag	Auto- Correlation Coefficient	Box- Pierce Statistic	To Lag	Auto- Correlation Coefficient	Box- Pierce Statistic
1	−.019	.81	1	−.102	.70
2	.013	.82	2	.155	2.31
3	−.189	3.25	3	.058	2.54
6	.017	3.42	6	−.137	7.10
12	.104	6.49	12	−.034	8.00
18	−.080	9.22	18	−.083	8.58
24	−.036	21.03	24	.149	11.54

[a]First differences of logs of Dow Industrial Index.

Table 9 presents the results of a runs test for the bull markets of the 1920s and 1980s. The third column of the table shows the number of runs observed for the daily and month-end data (percentage changes in the Dow Jones Industrial Index) during the various periods of rapidly increasing stock prices. Column 4 gives the number of runs expected for a series of independent observations, and column 5 gives the variance of this series. Since the observed number of runs is not much different than expected, the hypothesis that percentage changes in the Dow Index behaved randomly during the sample periods is not rejected by these data. This evidence on the behavior of stock prices during the 1920s and 1980s also is inconsistent with the notion that stock prices were driven by the types of speculative bubbles discussed in this paper.

V. CONCLUSION

Many people attribute the stock market crashes of 1929 and 1987 to bursting speculative bubbles.   The perception that stock prices may be driven by bubbles presents economic policymakers with an important problem be-

TABLE 9
Runs Test

Sample Period	Number of Observations	Observed Number of Runs	Expected Number of Runs[a]	Variance[b]
	Daily Data			
January 3, 1928–				
September 3, 1929	495	233	248.0	123.50
January 2, 1986–				
August 25, 1987	417	220	209.0	104.00
	Month-End Data			
January 1924–				
September 1929	68	38	34.5	16.75
January 1982–				
August 1987	67	34	34.0	16.50

[a]Expected number of runs = (Number of observations + 1) / 2.
[b]Variance = (Number of observations − 1) / 4.

cause such bubbles suggest that plans to save and invest may be based on irrational criteria and subject to erratic behavior.

This paper has examined long-run data on stock prices and dividends and concludes that the two series are cointegrated. Shocks to stock prices damp out over time. This is evidence against the presence of a bubble which suggests that such a shock causes the price and dividend series to drift apart over time. Other data around the time of the Coolidge and Reagan bull markets provide additional evidence contrary to the notion that the crashes were the result of bursting speculative bubbles. The log of stock prices appears to be difference stationary, and no evidence was found that changes in stock prices were autocorrelated or that the data contained long runs. Rather, the data suggest that stock prices followed a random walk which is consistent with a theory that assumes stock prices are largely determined by fundamental factors.

NOTES

1. *New York Times* (October 25, 1929).
2. See the Report of the Presidential Task Force on Market Mechanisms (January 1988), United States Commodity Futures Trading Commission (January 1988), and United States General Accounting Office (January 1988).
3. Keynes (1935, p. 159). Keynes discusses erratic shifts in the investment schedule caused by changes in the "state of confidence," "waves of optimistic and pessimistic sentiment," "anti-social fetish for liquidity," "the dark forces of time and ignorance" (pp. 153–55) and "speculation" (p. 161). He argues that a "...boom which is destined to end in a slump...is a situation in which over optimism triumphs over a rate of interest which, in a cooler light, would be seen to be excessive" (p. 322). See, as well, Gordon (1952), p. 378.
4. For discussions of the fundamentals, see Shiller's (1981) model of stock price determination or Brealey (1983, pp. 67–72), and Brealey and Meyers (1984, pp. 43–58).
5. See Flood and Garber (1980 and 1982), Blanchard and Watson (1982), Aiyagari (1988), Diba and Grossman (1985, 1986 and 1988), Hamilton (1986), and Campbell and Shiller (1987).
6. *New York Times* (October 25, 1929).
7. See Diba and Grossman (1985 and 1986) and Blanchard and Watson (1982).
8. If the limit of the present value of expected dividends sufficiently far into the future were not zero, there would be no forward solution to equation (2) such as (3).
9. See Campbell and Shiller (1987) and Diba and Grossman (1988).
10. Diba and Grossman (1988) present a related analysis.
11. Malkiel (1981, pp. 31–49) presents a similar discussion.
12. Brunner and Meltzer (1987) note that "Some further reflections on bubbles and sunspot equilibria should make us doubt their contribution to a useful reconciliation of analysis with critical observations. The bubble term refers neither directly nor indirectly to any observable entities. It is fundamentally inconsistent with any rational exploitation of information invoked by the same analysis (p. 2)." See, as well, Singleton (1987, pp. 28–30); Sirkin (1975); Schwartz (1981, p. 25), and Hamilton (1986).
13. This does not suggest that the failure of stock prices to exhibit this property necessarily implies the existence of a bubble. See Diba and Grossman (1988).
14. See, as well, Hendry (1986, p. 202).
15. See, as well, Campbell and Shiller (1987, pp. 1070–71).

16. Both price and dividend series are spliced at 1938 using the coefficients of regressions that relate each series for the data that overlap. In the case of stock prices, the series overlap from 1883–1938, while the series for dividends overlap from 1926–38. The data are from the Cowles Commission, Common-Stock Indexes 1871–1937 (Principia Press, Inc., 1939), pp. 66–67 and pp. 388–89; Standard and Poor's, Security Price Index Record (Standard and Poors Corporation, 1986), p. 110 and pp. 118–21. (The series were updated to 1987.) The implicit price deflator is from Milton Friedman and Anna J. Schwartz, Monetary Trends in the United States and United Kingdom (NBER, 1982), table 4.8. The series was updated to 1987 using the implicit price deflator reported in the Economic Report of the President.
17. Although the theoretical model contains no constant term, one was included in the estimated regression. The estimated constant is negative, and the t-score is 3.77. Little can be made of this, however, since the statistic is not distributed t.
18. Diba and Grossman (1988) draw the same general conclusion.

REFERENCES

Aiyagai, S. R. (Winter 1988). Economic fluctuations without shocks to fundamentals; or, does the stock market dance to its own music? Federal Reserve Bank of Minneapolis Quarterly Review, pp. 8–24.

Blanchard, O. J., and Watson, M. W. (1982). Bubbles, rational expectations and financial markets. In Paul Wachtel (ed.), Crises in economic and financial structure. Lexington, Massachusetts: Lexington Books, pp. 295–315.

Brealey, R. A. (1983). An introduction to risk and return from common stocks. Boston: The M.I.T. Press.

Brealey, R. A., and Meyers, S. (1984). Principles of corporate finance. New York: McGraw-Hill.

Brunner, K., and Meltzer, A. H. (Spring 1987). Bubbles and other essays. Carnegie-Rochester Conference Series on Public Policy, pp. 1–8.

Campbell, J. Y. and Shiller, R. J. (October 1987). Cointegration and tests of present value models. Journal of Political Economy, pp. 1062–88.

Diba, B. T., and Grossman, H. I. (June 1988). Explosive rational bubbles in stock prices? American Economic Review, pp. 520–30.

Diba, B. T., and Grossman, H. I. (1986). On the inception of rational bubbles in stock prices. National Bureau of Economic Research working paper No. 1990.

Diba. B. T., and Grossman, H. I. (1985). Rational bubbles in stock prices? National Bureau of Economic Research working paper No. 1779.

Dickey, D. A., and Fuller, W. A. (July 1981). Likelihood ratio statistics for autoregressive time series with a unit root. *Econometrica,* pp. 1057–72.

Flood, R. P., and Garber, P. M. (1982). Bubbles, runs and gold monetization. In Paul Wachtel (ed.), *Crises in economic and financial structure.* Lexington, Massachusetts: Lexington Books, pp. 275–93.

Flood, R. P., and Garber, P. M. (August 1980). Market fundamentals versus price-level bubbles: The first tests. *Journal of Political Economy,* pp. 745–80.

Galbraith, J. K. (1955). *The great crash.* New York: Houghton Mifflin.

Gordon, R. A. (1952). *Business fluctuations.* New York: Harper Brothers.

Hamilton, J. D. (October 1986). On testing for self-fulfilling speculative price bubbles. *International Economic Review,* pp. 545–52.

Hendry, D. F. (1986). Econometric modelling with cointegrated variables: An overview. *Oxford Bulletin of Economics and Statistics, 48: 3,* pp. 201–12.

Keynes, J. M. (1935). *The general theory of employment, interest and money.* New York: Harcourt, Brace and Company.

Kindleburger, C. P. (1978). *Manias, panics and crashes.* New York: Basic Books.

Malkiel, B. G. (1981). *A random walk down Wall Street.* New York: W. W. Norton and Company.

Mankiw, N. G., Romer, D., and Shapiro, M. D. (July 1985). An unbiased reexamination of stock market volatility. *Journal of Finance,* pp. 677–87.

Report of the Presidential task force on market mechanisms. (January 1988). Washington, DC: U.S. Government Printing Office.

Roepke, W. (1936). *Crises and cycles.* London: William Hodge and Company, Ltd., pp. 51–52.

Santoni, G. J. (November 1987). The great bull markets 1924–29 and 1982–87: Speculative bubbles or economic fundamentals. *Federal Reserve Bank of St. Louis Review, 69,* pp. 16–29.

Schwartz, A. J. (1981). Understanding 1929–33. In Karl Brunner (ed.), *The great depression revisited.* New York: Martinus Nijhoff, pp. 5–48.

Shiller, R. J. (June 1981). Do stock prices move too much to be justified by subsequent changes in the fundamentals? *American Economic Review,* pp. 421–36.

Singleton, K. (Spring 1987). Speculation and the volatility of foreign currency exchange rates. *Carnegie-Rochester Conference Series on Public Policy,* pp. 9–55.

Sirkin, J. (Summer 1975). The stock market of 1929 revisited: A note. *Business History Review,* pp. 223–31.

Sparling, E. (1930). *Mystery men of Wall Street.* New York: Blue Ribbon Books.

United States Commodity Futures Trading Commission (January 1988). *Final report of stock index futures and cash market activity during October 1987.* Washington, DC: U.S. Government Printing Office.

United States General Accounting Office (January 1988). *Financial markets: Preliminary observations on the October 1987 crash.* Washington, DC: U.S. Government Printing Office.

West, K. D. (July 1986). Dividend innovations and stock price volatility. Princeton, New Jersey: Princeton University working paper No. 113.

Willis, P. H. (February 1930). Who caused the panic of 1929? *North American Review,* p. 183.

CHAPTER 7

COMMENTS ON THE MARKET CRASH: SIX MONTHS AFTER

Hayne Leland
Mark Rubinstein*

Six months after the market crash of October 1987, we are still sifting through the debris searching for its cause. The most likely antecedent, very significant new news, is difficult to find. Most of the negative news often cited, such as the rising federal budget and balance of payments deficits, should have been well digested by the market before October 19. With hindsight, it now appears that, unlike the October 1929 crash, the 1987 crash did not presage a general economic decline.

However, one piece of news, the prior behavior of the market itself, was new. In the second week before the crash, the S&P500 index had fallen 5.2 percent This decline accelerated in the week preceding the crash when the index fell 9.2 percent culminating with one of the largest one-day declines on record (and the largest in terms of Dow Jones Industrial Average points) of 5.2 percent on Friday, October 16. The market had suddenly exhibited a jump in volatility. This was mirrored in the volatilities implied by the market prices of S&P500 index options, which increased from 22 percent per annum on October 15 to 30 percent at the close on October 16. Over the weekend, many investors were absorbing the fact that market

*The authors are professors at the Graduate School of Business, University of California at Berkeley, and consultants to the investment management firm, Leland O'Brien Rubinstein Associates.

volatility had at least temporarily increased. Under these conditions, the nervousness of some small investors surfaced in the form of mutual fund redemptions. If you had called one large mutual fund, which offers a telephone transfer service, you would have found the telephones busy at 11:00 p.m. Saturday night. With foreign markets, which begin trading prior to the NYSE, opening down early Monday morning (–2.5 percent in Japan and –10 percent in London), the stage was set for something dramatic.

Unprecedented order imbalances in several large stocks delayed openings on Monday in some cases for as much as two hours. The S&P500 December futures contract, a much more sensitive barometer of the market under these conditions than the S&P500 index itself, gapped open down 6.5 percent. By that measure the market had already declined by more than on any date since the 1929 crash and the day was just starting. As the 19th wore on, investors witnessed symptoms of market failure and were frightened by rumors that the NYSE would close. They also worried that other investors had come to believe the market was overvalued. Fear fed upon fear as investors en masse rushed to sell their stocks. By the end of the day, the S&P futures contract closed down 29 percent and the S&P index closed down 20 percent on NYSE volume of 604 million shares valued at over $20 billion. This is a story that belongs as a new chapter in Charles Mackay's *Extraordinary Popular Delusions and the Madness of Crowds*.

But is that what happened? Perhaps, as the Brady Commission report argues, what would have been a relatively minor decline was turned into a rout by the orders of just a few large traders, many of whom were portfolio insurers. These traders use computerized strategies which dictate buying after the market rises and selling after the market declines. The extreme version of this argument maintains that portfolio insurance first pushed the market up because the "insured" investors were willing to buy more stock since they had planned for systematic sales in market declines.[1] In other words, they could afford to take greater risks in rising markets because portfolio insurance offered a disciplined way of avoiding risk in declines. This additional demand in the year prior to the crash accounted for a good part of the 1000 point rise in the Dow Jones Industrial Average.[2]

Then, as the market went into decline, the insurers began to unwind their positions, forcing the market in reverse. But this time the amount of capital devoted to portfolio insurance strategies had reached a critical mass of about $60–$80 billion, enough for portfolio insurance sales to fuel themselves. With the sudden fall in the market during the last half hour of trading on October 16, many insurers found themselves with an overhang of unfilled sell orders going into Monday. In addition, several smart institutional traders knew about this overhang and tried to exit the market early Monday before the insurers could complete their trades.[3] The conjunction of these sell orders arriving nearly simultaneously in the market created the unprecedented opening gap. As the insurers sold and market prices fell, the computer programs of other insurers then triggered further sales causing further declines, which in turn caused the first group of insurers to sell even more stock, etc. This in turn generated other sell orders from the same sources and the market experienced the computer-driven meltdown, just a few months earlier predicted by the Chairman of the New York Stock Exchange.

An extension of this point of view takes account of the most significant change in U.S. stock markets in the 1980s: Many large investors (not just portfolio insurers) now trade very large blocks of stock or index futures on short notice while the net liquid assets of floor traders has not kept pace. In large part, the willingness to make large trades is due to reductions in the cost of trading following the May 1, 1975, switch from fixed to negotiated commissions. Here are some interesting statistics. The 1986 annual share trading volume on the NYSE had grown sevenfold since 1975. The 1987 share turnover on the NYSE had reached 73 percent, 3 times greater than in 1975, and block trades represented 50 percent of traded shares, about 3 times greater than their share in 1975. In addition, the introduction of index futures in 1982 and index options in 1983, as well as new technology-based methods of programmed trading, has increased the ease with which portfolios of stocks can be traded as a group. On the other hand, during this period, the net liquid assets of NYSE specialists, as a percent of the dollar value of NYSE trading volume, had fallen by 1986 to one third of its 1977 level.[4] In this new environment, it becomes easier for exchanges to become overwhelmed with orders on one side of the market.

As plausible as these two theories of the crash sound — one based on a market panic and the other based on large trader transactions — as we search through the wreckage, we come across other evidence that is difficult to reconcile. Here is a brief list: the crash was international in scope; the U.S. stock market continues to experience a significant increase in volatility, even at a six month remove; and bid-ask spreads in the stock market remain much greater than before the crash. Most jarring, the U.S. market remained within 1.3 percent of its Black Monday close one week after the crash and has still, as this is written six months later on April 18, 1988, not significantly rebounded. If the crash were caused by either of our two explanations, many economists would have expected more of a correction back to pre-crash conditions by now.

In a recent UCLA working paper entitled, "Portfolio Insurance and Financial Market Equilibrium," by Michael Brennan and Eduardo Schwartz, the authors start with a "standard" financial market equilibrium model, inject portfolio insurance investors, and ask, given realistic parameter estimates, how much market volatility would be affected. The standard model is a single-period pure exchange economy with continuous trading during the period but consumption only at the beginning and end. Prices are determined by a representative rational risk averse investor with an additive utility function in current and future consumption who assumes his decisions have no influence on prices. After subtracting current consumption, expectations about end of period aggregate wealth evolve according to geometric Brownian motion according to a known drift and variance. A representative portfolio insurer is added to this structure and treated as a "pure automaton" who blindly follows a portfolio strategy, known to the other market participants, which yields an insured position on the market portfolio.

Brennan and Schwartz show that for levels of portfolio insurance as high as 5 percent of total market capitalization, while portfolio insurance trades do increase market volatility, the additional volatility is negligible. The actual amount of assets under systematic portfolio insurance at the end of the second quarter of 1987 was between $60 and $80 billion dollars, which compares to a total U.S. equity market capitalization of $3.6 trillion, or about 2 percent. Compared to total market capitalization, including corporate bonds, non-corporate real estate, and other assets, this percentage would be less than .5 percent. That portfolio insurance or even large trades from other investors could create a single-day 20 percent equity market decline in the absence of significant negative news, even without the other surrounding related events we have mentioned, is wildly at variance with the predictions of standard financial models of equilibrium. To be specific, in the absence of significant news, sales by portfolio insurers should be matched by purchases by other investors who are willing to bear more risk to take advantage of the higher expected returns from somewhat reduced prices. On October 19, it is estimated that portfolio insurance trades in S&P 500 index futures and NYSE stocks amounted to only $6 billion out of a total of $42 billion. In contrast, in the standard model, few other investors would have been selling along with the portfolio insurers. Had this happened, October 19th would have probably been just an ordinary day in stock market history.

If we are to believe the market panic theory or the Brady Commission's theory that the crash was primarily caused by a few large traders, we must strongly reject the standard model. That model is based on three important assumptions: (1) rational investor expectations, (2) continuously functioning markets, and (3) continual optimization by all investors.

With rational expectations, in which all investors are fully aware of the strategies followed by portfolio insurers, smart institutional traders could not have expected to profit from front-running. Contrary to rational expectations, investors may have overreacted because they were uncertain about the amount of trading that would be generated by portfolio insurance. Or they may have interpreted the portfolio insurance trades as information-based, when instead these trades were merely reactive to changes in market prices.

Instead of continuously functioning markets, large sales created an imbalance between supply and demand which led to temporary stock-by-stock closures. This made investors fear that the market mechanism would fail, entailing bankruptcies, clearing firm failures, and a total market closure. Understandably, panic could have ensued.

Finally, and most important, contrary to our models, most "investors" have other things on their minds besides the securities markets. Most investors have better things to do; they work during the day and spend time with their families in the evening. Most investors don't know what stocks are worth, tacitly leaving this valuation up to a small set of professional investors. But only a subset of these stand ready to make active investment decisions. All this means that for the purpose of explaining stock price movements, the stock market should be treated as much smaller than the $3.6 trillion quoted earlier.

The visible breakdown of these three assumptions on October 19th may also help explain the related events surrounding the crash. The U.S. market did not rebound because there may be only a few truly "value-based" investors who are willing to put their money down. Most investors are on the sidelines, implicitly confessing incompetence when it comes to security valuation, themselves confused about whether the crash could reflect a fundamental weakness in the economy. To the extent stocks take value from their perceived liquidity and to the extent the events of the week of October 19th revealed that the market was not as liquid as people believed, stocks are not worth as much today as they were prior to the crash. With thinner markets and with heightened uncertainty stemming from concern over rational expectations and the viability of market mechanisms, price volatility and bid-ask spreads have remained much higher than prior to the crash.

While it is difficult to distinguish between the market panic or large trader theories (and they are hardly mutually exclusive), we believe the evidence favors emphasis of the former. The crash of 1987 was not the first. Many non-equity markets, as well as the U.S. stock market itself on previous occasions and all major foreign stock markets during October, have crashed without investors following systematic portfolio insurance. In many of those cases, a cascade of stop-loss orders, an informal type of portfolio insurance, was a contributing factor. To place systematic portfolio insurance in perspective, on October 19, portfolio insurance sales represented only .2 percent of total U.S. stock market capitalization. Could sales of 1 in every 500 shares lead to a decline of 20 percent in the market? This would imply a demand elasticity of .01 — virtually zero — for a market often claimed to be one of the most liquid in the world.

Acceptance of the market panic or large trader theories has important implications for both market regulation and the standard model. The sources of breakdown in the standard model each point clearly in the direction of corresponding regulatory mechanisms. Problems deriving from irrational expectations suggest improvements such as formalized "sunshine" trading which permit investors to distinguish between information-motivated and informationless trades.[5] The potential of discontinuously functioning markets suggests supplementing our current market-making systems with more frequent single-price auctions with open limit order books. Inertia by most investors holding stocks suggests mechanisms which enlarge the scope of the market to involve greater numbers of investors by improving coordination between underlying and derivative markets and increasing global market integration. Unfortunately, regulatory discussion has centered around "circuit breakers" which are largely at cross-purposes with these objectives.

The standard model must itself be seriously flawed. Even if we can only detect its failure during rare events like October 19th, these events make us suspect the model even during normal times. In addition, enough money changes hands during these rare events that they become much more important in the long-run than their frequency alone would indicate. We need to build models of financial equilibrium which are more sensitive to real life trading mechanisms, which account more realistically for the formation of expectations, and which recognize that, at any one time, there is a limited pool of investors available with the ability to evaluate stocks and take appropriate action in the market.

NOTES

1. "The rapid rise in the popularity of portfolio insurance strategies also contributed to the market's rise. Pension fund managers adopting these strategies typically increased the funds' risk exposure by investing more heavily in common stock during this rising market. The rationale was that portfolio insurance would cushion the impact of a market break by allowing them to shift quickly out of stocks."—*Report of the Presidential Task Force on Market Mechanisms,* January 1988, page 9.

2. Even if one believes that portolio insurance was a major factor in the precipitous decline of the stock market, we believe it is stretching the imagination too far to extend this theory to explain the market rise in the year preceding the crash. To put the Brady Commission claim in perspective, consider that only $60 to $80 billion was being applied to systematic portfolio insurance strategies. Of this, at most $10 billion at the market peak in August 1987 represents additional commitment to stock by insurers over and above what they would have invested if they had followed their original asset allocation approaches. Indeed, many insurers were implicitly less invested in equities than they otherwise would have been because many simply added a futures insurance umbrella while leaving their cash market asset allocation unchanged. In addition, many insurers had restarted their policies (thus reducing their commitment to stocks) during the market rise to "lock in" gains. All in all, the additional investment in equities due to portfolio insurance at the peak of the market must have been less than 1/3 of 1 percent of total market capitalization. It is very difficult to believe that such a small amount of buying power, based as it was on a passive informationless strategy, could push the DJIA up over a period of a year even 50 points, let alone the total actual increase of about 1,000 points.

3. "The activities of a small number of aggressive trading-oriented institutions ... posed the prospect of further selling pressure on Monday. These traders could well understand the strategies of the portfolio insurers and mutual funds. They could anticipate the selling those institutions would have to do in reaction to the market's decline. They could see those institutions falling behind in their selling programs. The situation presented an opportunity for these traders to sell in anticipation of the forced selling by portfolio insurers and mutual funds, with the prospect of repurchasing at lower prices."—*Report of the Presidential Task Force on Market Mechanisms,* January 1988, page 29.

4. For example, the specialist in IBM has capital of $20 million, representing less than .2 percent of IBM's total stock value of $13 billion. This is well in excess of the revised post-crash requirements imposed by the NYSE which would only require, in the case of IBM, a holding of .014 percent.

5. In a sunshine trade, an investor attempts to preannounce his trading intentions (his identity, order size, and timing) several hours prior to the actual trade hoping to deepen the market during the time his trade takes place. Presumably, only non-information based orders would be filled in this way. To formalize this, an exchange would allow posting of sunshine trades on bulletin boards or computer screens on the exchange floor and notice of sunshine trading intentions would be carried via computer to broker-dealers around the world.

DISCUSSION

COMMENTS ON WHEN THE TICKER RAN LATE: THE STOCK MARKET BOOM AND CRASH OF 1929

*Robert J. Shiller**

I think that White's paper is right on target on its account of the crash. His account is a little unconventional in places, but to good effect. He cites, for example, the well-known work of Frederick Lewis Allen for evidence of the true causes of the crash. Now Allen was a very good popular writer whose amusing book *Only Yesterday* has been read by millions. But Allen was also given to a little exaggeration, was not an economist, and virtually never cited any quantitative evidence. (I remember that in one place in *Only Yesterday* he took as evidence the percent of people who were seen with papers open to the financial page in a subway, but that's about the extent of it.) But Allen's perceptions about the crash may be important if we take the view that what goes on in people's minds is important for the crash. The amusing accounts in Allen's work of dinner table conversations or of eager investors around the time of the crash may tell us more about the causes of the crash than many statistical studies. Galbraith's book also provides much

---

*Professor of Economics, Cowles Foundation, Yale University.

evidence (though not hard evidence) on the enthusiasm that preceded and panic that surrounded the crash.

My own survey questionnaire work of investors at the time of the crash of 1987, which asked investors for their thoughts at the time of the crash, shows evidence of a psychological phenomenon that was in some ways similar to the story presented by Allen and Galbraith. The crash of 1987 appears to be associated with a sudden concentration of investors, attention, a large amount of anxiety, a sense that one ought to do *something,* a search among investors for intuition and gut feelings for what to do, and an effort to be reasonable and calm. Despite efforts to stay calm, the actions of investors nevertheless generated behavior that served to get other investors upset, in a snowball fashion. It occurs to me that a good analogy might be an argument with one's spouse. After the argument, one also often asks, "What started this anyway?"

Yet White is correct that evidence for speculative fever is not *prima facie* evidence that a speculative fervor caused the runup of prices in the late 1920s. He is right that we cannot "identify any measure or variable that measures the degree of speculation in the market." We could never be completely convincing on this score, since we economists just do not know how to compute what the rational price of the market *should* be.

There is no well-defined theory as to how fundamentals *ought* to affect the stock market. The statistical literature on the excess volatility of stock prices continues without any final resolution, because the issues involved are inherently difficult. Many of the tests that were formerly thought convincing are viewed as inconclusive with further study.* If it turns out that the final conclusion in this literature is that markets are not efficient, how can we call the average investor in 1929 distinctly irrational, who could not have known the statistical niceties we now appreciate.

White's points are well taken that there were eminent economists who felt that stock prices were not overpriced in the late 1920s. Irving Fisher had the reputation as perhaps the greatest economist that America had yet produced. His arguments that the market was not overpriced were very carefully reasoned. In his book published two months after the crash (and

---

*For example, the runs tests that White described were found by Shiller and Perron (1986) to have very little power when high frequency data (say, the daily data quoted by White) but perhaps more power when less frequent data (say, the monthly data quoted by White) are used.

hence no doubt mostly written *before* the crash) he presented arguments that were very much more sophisticated than the run of the bland statements by other authorities that the market was, in their opinion, overpriced. Irving Fisher certainly understood how to compute present values; he had published pioneering work in the field as early as 1896. White's discussion of the Sirkin paper shows the fundamental ambiguity. To me, looking at the long time series of earnings suggests intuitively that we would not extrapolate the earnings growth of the 1920s past 1929, but Irving Fisher's argument was precisely there is no reason to look at history before the 1920s.

We just cannot call people irrational or crazy who bought Irving Fisher's sophisticated argument. But what is striking about investors is not their position at any moment, but their willingness to change from one position to another so strongly. These changes of opinions seem to come about without any news.

If we are talking about Black Monday, October 28, 1929, we need news that broke on that morning or over the preceding weekend. Of all the news stories that White discusses, only the Smoot-Hawley Tariff news really fell on the morning of October 28. The notion that the Smoot-Hawley Tariff might be the ultimate cause of the stock market crash in 1929 was first suggested by Allan Meltzer (1976). The problem with this story is that the advent of this tariff does not coincide precisely with the crash. Jude Wanniski tried to claim that the important news about this tariff came just before the crash. The precipitating event just before the crash October 28 was a story that appeared in *The New York Times* on that morning, which was picked up by the Associated Press and the United News the following day, and given front-page treatment around the country on the morning of October 29 (the second day of the two-day drop). This story reported that on Saturday, September 26, a Senator Reed said that the Smoot-Hawley Bill, in committee in Congress, was "dead." This provoked denials by Senators Smoot and Borah. The *Times* quoted Senator Smoot as saying, "If that is Senator Reed's opinion, I suppose he has a right to it. But it isn't the view of the Finance Committee." Senator Borah said, "My opinion is that the tariff bill is not going to die." It's hard to tell whether this news story should be read as optimistic for the passage of the bill, and indeed, while the *Times* wrote the story as if the news was optimistic, other newspapers wrote the story as if it were pessimistic. It's hard to claim that the story is important, since newspapers had written many stories about the outlook for the tariff bill. Anyway, it can be argued that the Smoot-Hawley tariff was just not important, in a country where exports were only 7 percent of GNP in 1929. Dornbusch and Fischer (1986) pointed out that the Fordney-McCumber Tariff of 1922 increased tariff rates as much as did the Smoot-Hawley, with no disastrous consequences.

In the crash of October 19, 1987, there was also very little news on that morning. The only possibly substantive news breaking then was the news of the bombing of the Iranian oil platform. In my questionnaire survey of individual and institutional investors then, I found that indeed people did not report that this or any other news story was on their minds. What was on their minds was the price drop on the morning of October 19. The second biggest news story on their minds was the price drops of the preceding week.

The estimates of the Marsh-Merton model of dividend setting behavior for the period 1873 to 1927 look remarkably similar to the equation that Marsh and Merton estimated over the sample 1928 to 1980—a sample that does not overlap at all. This result might be construed as favorable to the Marsh-Merton theory. However, I think that the estimates of the Marsh-Merton equation may not reflect what Marsh and Merton theorize, and they may be essentially spurious. John Campbell and I showed that coefficients roughly like those estimated here might be expected under the assumption just that price and dividend move together, with price contaminated also by a little extra noise. Since with Marsh and Merton (and I assume with White as well) price is end of year price but dividend is total for year, when we assume that instantaneous price is driven by instantaneous dividend, simple calculations of the effect of time aggregation of dividends under a Wiener process assumption for dividends, coefficients like those estimated can be derived.

The simultaneous equations model whose estimates are presented in Table 2 appears to be moderately successful, judging from the signs and magnitudes of the coefficients. The supply of brokers' loans depends positively on the call rate and negatively on a competing rate, the commercial paper rate, as one would expect. The demand for brokers' loans depends positively on the speculation measures. However, there is a problem: the call rate has a positive coefficient in the demand equation—a wrong sign.

I have some doubts about the specification of this simultaneous equations model. I see no reason why the dummy variables—DUMMY or DUMTRE—should not enter the demand equation as well as the supply.

These dummy variables might well proxy for speculative demand better than the measures used in the demand equation as it is shown. The supply equation has a dependent variable with a growth trend to it (the supply of brokers' loans) but no right-hand-side variable has a secular trend to it. This may not be a serious problem with such a short sample. However, there is an asymmetry here—a lagged dependent variable enters the supply equation (whose estimated coefficient is very large, near one)—but not the demand equation. Apparently the exclusion of the lagged dependent variable from the demand equation helps to identify it—but why should the lagged dependent variable be excluded?

REFERENCES

Campbell, J. Y., and Shiller, R. J. (April 1988). Interpreting cointegrated models. Cambridge, Massachusetts: NBER working paper No. 2568. (Forthcoming, *Journal of Economic Dynamics and Control*, 1989).

Dornbusch, R., and Fischer, S. (1986). The open economy: Implications for monetary and fiscal policy. In R. J. Gordon (ed.), *The American business cycle: Continuity and change*. National Bureau of Economic Research and University of Chicago Press, pp. 459–501.

Fisher, I. (1986). Appreciation and interest. *Publications of the American Economic Association*, pp. 23–29, 88–92.

Meltzer, A. H. (November 1976). Monetary and other explanations of the start of the great depression. *Journal of Monetary Economics, 2*, 455–71.

Shiller, R. J. (November 1987). Investor behavior in the October 1987 stock market crash: Survey evidence. Cambridge, Massachusetts: NMER working paper. (Forthcoming, R. J. Shiller, *Market volatility*).

Shiller, R. J., and Perron, P. (1985). Testing the random walk hypothesis: Power versus frequency of observation. *Economic Letters, 18*, pp. 38–86.

DISCUSSION

COMMENT ON BUBBLES OR FUNDAMENTALS?

Peter C. Warman

One year after the 1987 crash, the question still remains for even the most ardent proponents of efficient markets theory: Why did stock prices rise so quickly only to collapse? Were movements in stock prices the result of some wild speculative excess or was there some basic change in the economy that prompted the crash? These are precisely the same questions asked about the stock market of 1929. Unfortunately, economic historians disagree about what caused 1929 and offer no guide for understanding 1987. G. J. Santoni, Jr., and Gerald P. Dwyer have subjected stock price and dividend data to a battery of statistical tests that seem to show that the two great bull markets of the twentieth century were simply the product of changing fundamentals. Santoni and Dwyer's tests are an important first step toward improving our understanding of 1929 and 1987, but their findings are not as conclusive as may seem at first glance.

To detect the presence of bubbles, Santoni and Dwyer apply new tests for cointegration of annual dividends and stock prices. Their results are very similar to those of Campbell and Shiller (1987) and Diba and Grossman (1988). While these other studies find no evidence for rational bubbles, their test results are somewhat mixed. However, Diba and Grossman concluded that the mixed results most likely reflect the low power of the tests rather than the presence of rational bubbles. All three studies thus conclude that the preponderance of evidence is that there are no rational bubbles present in the data they have examined. For most economists, this is a satisfying conclusion. It would be very disturbing if there were bubbles present over long periods of time. Instead, prices seem to follow fundamentals in the long run.

However, historical accounts of bubbles do not claim that bubbles are anything but short-term phenomena. The elegant econometric tests thus do not square with the popular notion of a bubble, and annual data may not be the best means for detecting the presence of speculative manias. In the absence of a dividend series that is more frequent than annual, additional tests for bubbles must rely solely on price data. The problem with these tests, like the cointegration tests, is their low power and sensitivity to the span and frequency of data.

One test that Santoni and Dwyer employ is a runs test on daily and monthly data. They find that the number of runs is not statistically different from the expected number of runs in a random series. Again this seems like very convincing evidence, but Shiller and Perron (1985) have shown that the power of test of the random walk hypothesis is not directly related to the number of observations. They held the span of the data (measured in years, whether the observations were annual, monthly, or daily) fixed and varied the frequency of observations. Shiller and Perron found that increasing the frequency of observation with a fixed span destroyed the power of the runs tests and that the ability to reject a false null hypothesis depended more on the span of the data than on the number of observations. The daily data used by Santoni and Dwyer spans less than two years and thus their test may fall prey to this problem. Using monthly data, Santoni and Dwyer increase the span of the data but reduce the number of observations. This change does not necessarily increase the power of the test.

Although the power of other random walk tests has not been studied, some simple comparisons suggest that problems similar to those encountered with the runs tests may arise. Santoni and Dwyer employ a Box-Pierce test based on the estimated autocorrelations of the first differences of the logs of the Dow Jones Industrial Index for the same daily and monthly periods examined with the runs test. They find an absence of any significant autocorrelation; that is, current prices do not appear to be related to past changes. In a simple exercise, I have replicated the Box-Pierce test on Santoni and Dwyer's chosen interval for 1928–29 in Table 1. Additionally, I have examined two periods before and after their selected interval. The

TABLE 1
Box-Pierce statistics[a]: Daily data

First interval
January 2, 1926–December 31,
1927 (600 trading days)

To Lag	Box-Pierce Statistic[b]
1	80.65
2	81.00
3	81.10
6	81.61
12	83.15
18	89.64
24	95.84

Second interval
January 3, 1928–September 3, 1929[c]
(495 trading days)

To Lag	Box-Pierce Statistic[b]
1	0.18
2	0.66
3	1.91
6	10.32
12	16.20
18	21.28
24	28.74

Third interval
September 4, 1929–December 31,
1930 (389 trading days)

To Lag	Box-Pierce Statistic[b]
1	0.66[d]
3	20.12
3	21.13
6	44.10
12	68.50
18	76.30
24	86.77

Uniting first and second intervals
January 2, 1926–September 3,
1929 (1,095 trading days)

To Lag	Box-Pierce Statistic[b]
1	80.23
2	80.94
3	81.44
6	84.59
12	87.67
18	95.64
24	103.76

Uniting all three intervals
January 2, 1926–December 31, 1930
(1,484 trading days)

To Lag	Box-Pierce Statistic[b]
1	22.03
2	40.04
3	40.45
6	66.40
12	87.38
18	99.08
24	107.34

[a] First differences of logs of Dow Jones Industrial Index.

[b] Statistically significant at the 5 percent level.

[c] Santoni-Dwyer interval.

[d] Not statistically significant at the 5 percent level.

Box-Pierce test does not detect autocorrelation in the 20-month Santoni-Dwyer period. However, the two other periods curiously show significant autocorrelation. In an earlier paper, Santoni (1987) noted the presence of autocorrelation in the post-crash period but dismissed its importance on the grounds that bubbles cannot be negative. Yet, the appearance of autocorrelation in my prior period is more troubling as it was a time when it seems unlikely that there was a bubble. To study how autocorrelation changes when the span is increased, I have performed Box-Pierce tests for two longer periods—January 2, 1926, to September 3, 1929, and January 2, 1926, to December 31, 1930. These longer periods both display significant autocorrelation. My replications of Santoni and Dwyer's monthly Box-Pierce tests do not discover any autocorrelation, but a longer interlude between observations decreases the likelihood of detecting autocorrelation.

These problems with testing for the presence of speculative bubbles suggest that it may be desirable to qualify Santoni and Dwyer's categorical conclusions. The preponderance of the statistical evidence argues that stock prices follow the dictates of fundamentals over the long run. It may very well be that for most of the bull markets of 1929 and 1987, stock prices rose in response to improved earnings and dividends. However, with the present state of econometric testing, it is not possible to rule out that part of the boom may have been generated by a speculative mania rather than fundamentals.

REFERENCES

Campbell, J., and Shiller, R. (October 1987). Cointegration and tests of present value models. *Journal of Political Economy, 95,* 1062–88.

Diba, B. T., and Grossman, H. I. (June 1988). Explosive rational bubbles in stock prices? *American Economic Review, 78,* 520–30.

Santoni, G. J. (November 1987). The great bull markets 1924–29 and 1982–87: Speculative bubbles or economic fundamentals? *Federal Reserve Bank of St. Louis Review, 69,* pp. 16–29.

Shiller, R. J., and Perron, P. (1985). Testing the random walk hypothesis: Power versus frequency of observation. *Economic Letters, 18,* 381–86.

DISCUSSION

THE CRASH OF 1987 AND THE CRASH OF 1946*

Merton H. Miller

The many references at this conference to the Crash of 1987 and portfolio insurance must make Mark Rubinstein, as one of the co-inventors of that strategy, feel like Harriet Beecher Stowe, the author of *Uncle Tom's Cabin,* who was invited by President Lincoln to the White House, and introduced by him as "the little lady who brought on this great war."

Lincoln was surely exaggerating and so are those who credit the liquidity illusion spawned by portfolio insurance with fueling the remarkable rise of 30 percent in U.S. equity values between the end of December 1986 and the peak reached in August 1987. The added demand for equities by the insured was too small to account plausibly for a boom of that order, as Rubinstein points out (and, as was noted also in at least one of the post-crash reports, to wit, the Report of the Chicago Mercantile Exchange's Committee of Inquiry of which I served as chairman). In the period just before and surrounding the fateful day of the 19th, portfolio insurers were indeed among the conspicuous sellers, but none of the many post-crash reports has successfully isolated their contribution either to specific price movements at given times or to the cumulative price change over the interval. Far too much attention has been devoted, in my opinion, especially

---

*Comment on "Comments on the Market Crash: Six Months After," Chapter 7.

by the Brady Commission, to these painful and so far fruitless attempts to relate the sequence of price changes on the 19th and 20th to the activities of particular transactors, as if patient investigation of the wreckage would somehow lead us to the economic equivalent of a failing O-ring. These well-intentioned post-mortems serve only to reinforce in the minds of our legislators the delusion that once the "cause" of a crash has been found, appropriate regulatory remedies can prevent further recurrences.

The remarkable persistence in our country's politics of this "accident reconstruction syndrome" struck me with great force recently when I had occasion to look into the contemporaneous accounts of an earlier crash. I refer to the Crash of September 3, 1946—not one of the more storied episodes in U.S. financial history perhaps, but at –4.4 percent (equivalent currently to a drop of 120 points in Dow) a noteworthy enough event to call for an official investigation that had some striking parallels to the more recent one.

The study of the crash of September 3, 1946, was undertaken not by a specially appointed task force, like the Brady Commission, but by the staff of the U.S. Securities and Exchange Commission, then a regulatory agency at the height of its prestige—the jewel in the crown of the New Deal reforms. The report by the Commission's Trading and Exchange Division, published almost a year later, was shorter (only 68 pages of text) than the 1987 crash report by the SEC Division of Market Regulation, and much duller (with over a hundred pages of detailed cross-classifications of transactions); but at least the authors of the August 1947 report were open-minded. The staff approached the task with no preconceptions as to who or what the villains might be. As in 1929 and 1987, no major bad-news economic or political event could be singled out as the precipitating cause, though, as in 1987 after the August peak, a certain souring of the atmosphere seems to have accompanied the downward drift in prices in the weeks before the crash. To pinpoint cause or causes of the selling wave, therefore, the Commission staff supplemented its own voluminous records on the day's transactions with a detailed interview study of most large transactors and a sample of smaller public customers who bought or sold securities on the 3rd. [The Brady Commission, in similar circumstances, went even further sending a detailed questionnaire not just to market participants but to "other interested parties" (Appendix V)].]

In the staff interviews after the 1946 crash, two specific reasons for selling on the 3rd were given with great frequency. The second most frequently cited reason, accounting for about 28 percent of the shares sold by the 50 largest sellers and about 17 percent of those by other sellers involved a trading strategy in which the sell orders were triggered by a known mechanical rule or formula. Obviously that rule could not have been portfolio insurance; it hadn't been invented yet. A fairly primitive proto-type of portfolio insurance had long been followed, of course, through stop-loss orders and the Commission staff was fully aware of their destabilizing potential. But stop-loss orders appeared to have been involved in only 9 to 10 percent of all transactions. In the crash of 1987, by comparison, portfolio insurance selling played a somewhat larger role on the 19th, but still amounted to at most 20–25 percent of the total volume of the day, though the fact that selling by others was thus four to five times as large as that by the portfolio insurers may not be readily apparent from the many censorious references to portfolio insurance in the accounts of the 1987 crash by both the Brady Commission and the SEC's Division of Market Regulation.

Nor was the destabilizing selling on September 3, 1946, induced by margin calls. The cascade-producing potential of such calls had been and in many quarters still are regarded as the major accelerant in the October 1929 crash, though subsequent research has substantially downgraded their probable role. The folk-view of speculative margin buying as the major culprit in the 1929 episode was strong enough, however, in the early 1930s to have led Congress to take margin-setting authority away from the private-sector securities exchanges in 1934 and assign it to the Federal Reserve Board. Although the Board had kept margin requirements between 40 and 75 percent through the 1930s and the war years, it had set the initial margin rate at 100 percent in January 1946 so that by September 3, there was no margin to be called.

Nor could the selling frenzy be laid at the door of bear-raiders, hammering down prices with self-reinforcing waves of short-selling. That barn door, too, had been locked by the institution of the uptick rule in 1937.

With so many of the usual suspects eliminated, what then was the formula-based strategy cited by so many sellers on the fateful day? Amazingly enough, it was the Dow Theory! That theory, of course, has long since lost its vogue with investors, though we are daily reminded of its once prominent role by references, especially in *The Wall Street Journal* (Dow Jones and Co. publishers) to the Dow-Jones Industrial Average. That average and its companions, the Dow-Jones Transportation Average and the Dow-Jones Utility Average, were the key indicators in what Wall Street argot designates as a "technical" (and we might prefer to call an informationless) trading system. A "bear market," calling for immediate sales by followers of the rule, was signalled whenever all three Dow Jones Averages had broken through their "resistance levels"—essentially their recent previous lows. Just such a conjunction of the averages apparently had occurred by the close on Friday, August 29, the last previous trading day; and the Dow Theory true believers (plus the non-believers who knew of the true believers) had the long Labor Day weekend to stew over their moves for the Monday open.

But if the Friday close led the Dow Theorists to produce the same kind of order imbalance on the next trading day's opening that the close on Friday, October 16 supposedly led the portfolio insurers to produce on October 19th, what accounts for all the subsequent selling? The Dow Theory, it will be recalled, was only the second most cited reason. The reason for selling most frequently mentioned in the 1947 SEC tabulation was that prices were falling and other people were selling! That, of course, was precisely what Bob Shiller found 40 years later in his now famous questionnaire on the 1987 crash; and I suspect he would have found the same had he distributed his questionnaire in October 1929 or any other crash in market prices accompanied by heavy trading volume.

Nor is it really helpful to interpret as hopelessly irrational those frantic attempts by some sellers to get out before prices fall even further. As in a bank run, such efforts may make perfect sense even for those who know that much of the selling by others is informationless, if they have reason to believe, or even to suspect, that they can execute their own sale before price drops to, or below, the level needed to accommodate the reduced demand to hold equities. Efforts by market makers to slow the fall in prices, combined with the inevitable stale bids on the limit order books, may serve only to intensify their belief that they can be among the fortunate early leavers. As markets go, the NYSE is particularly vulnerable to this perversity, precisely because it has so successfully sold its clientele on the price continuity that its vaunted "specialists" are supposed to provide. And, indeed they do, on any ordinary day when they face very minor asynchronizations between the random arrivals of buyers and sellers. But when faced with order imbalance of massive proportions, their attempts to lean against the storm may actually be counterproductive.

The sight of panicky sellers ritually acting out the fallacy of composition on live TV is far from edifying, but hardly serious enough by itself to warrant major regulatory changes that might well impair the efficiency of the market on the vastly more numerous non-crash days. One minor restructuring, however, for which I believe a case can be made is instituting the kind of coordinated, inter-market circuit breakers hammered out recently by the CME and NYSE after long negotiation, and which are extensions of procedures they had jointly developed earlier for expiration-day imbalances. The case for such arrangements rests not on any social worker-like concern for protecting panicky sellers from their own folly, but on the recognition that continuous double-auction market systems, and especially those like the NYSE with designated market stabilizers, are not the best possible market structures in all circumstances. Under conditions of large, known imbalances, particularly those induced by portfolio insurance, futures expirations, or similar informationless trades, temporary call-auction procedures might be preferred, and with good reason, by most market participants. My Japanese friends assure me that they understand better than we do this need to be able to switch between market types when extraordinary imbalances suddenly arise, and that one reason is why their capital markets are less susceptible to panicky runs than ours. I suspect we may soon have a chance to put that proposition to the test.

PART 4

ARE THERE ANY LESSONS FROM HISTORY?

ROUNDTABLE DISCUSSION

ARE THERE ANY LESSIONS FROM HISTORY?

Eugene N. White

Like Halley's comet, the October 1987 crash was an event that not everyone may witness in his or her lifetime. Except for the rare few who could remember 1929, it was a plunge that had no parallel since the Great Depression. Furthermore, it erased the general presumption that the New Deal's institutions and regulations were sufficient to guarantee the orderly operation of the securities markets. If it was the job of the Securities and Exchange Commission and the Federal Reserve System to prevent a crash, then they obviously failed and some new forms of regulation may be necessary to restore order and stability to Wall Street.

The pundits and several investigations have already identified new investment strategies, derivative financial instruments, and the internationalization of markets as key factors in the crash. Their findings emphasize the unique characteristics of the 1987 crash. However, in the rush to impose new regulations on the financial markets, it is instructive to look back at previous crashes. Given the infrequency with which stock market booms and busts occur, historical comparison is one of the few approaches that can provide insights into the common factors responsible for these phenomena and serve as a guide for policy makers.

Reformers have typically fixed upon the failure of some market or market mechanism for creating a boom and setting up a crash. The most likely candidates are new arrivals whose appearance at the time of the boom makes them suspect.   After tulip prices collapsed, authorities in the Netherlands attacked the recently developed futures markets as responsible for the "tulipmania." This may appear silly from our vantage point, yet the futures market in tulips was new, and its appearance coincided with the spectacular rise in tulip prices.   After the 1929 crash, Congress found villains among the investment banking affiliates of commercial banks and the investment trusts.   The recently developed practices of programmed trading and portfolio insurance have received a good deal of the blame for the 1987 crash. These may be limited or outlawed, yet they represented only a small fraction of the market. Their cardinal sin seems to have been their newness.

None of the earlier reform efforts was obviously successful. Asset bubbles and crashes were not eliminated. The problem with these well-intentioned reforms was that they were not designed to tackle the underlying causes of bubbles but were, instead, formulated in reaction to some unique features of each episode.   One means to identify the common characteristics and causes of bubbles is by historical comparison.   The papers in this volume show that the stock market crash of 1987 was not a singular event and put it into its proper perspective.

Surveying the bubbles from the seventeenth century to the present, the principal factor that leads to the emergence of a bubble is that the underlying fundamentals of the assets in question, be they stocks or tulips, cease to be well identified. This may be the result of some innovation, technological change, or change in structure of the economy. These developments make predictions of future earnings more difficult, that is, expectations of future dividends become more diffuse.

In the Netherlands in the early seventeenth century, the arrival of the tulip from the Near East brought a new asset to Dutch markets. However, the process by which new varieties were created was imperfectly understood. The ability and speed with which rare varieties could be multiplied was not yet well-known to the general public and perhaps even to the market specialists. The appearance of a new variety represented an opportunity for substantial gain for investors but the magnitude of that gain was unclear. The increased but uncertain attractiveness of the asset drew in the public and bid up prices. Professor Garber has shown that stories of the tulipmania are overblown and there are sound economic reasons for the movement of tulip prices.   Nevertheless, while fundamentals were central to events, some price fluctuations are not easily explained.

The South Sea Company's planned conversion of government debt from a mass of highly illiquid annuities into more modern securities promised to benefit the British government, its creditors, and the company. The problem with this vast project was that the exact gains from more liquid assets and the privileges conferred on the South Sea Company were extraordinarily difficult to measure. The public thus easily erred in judging the profitability of the enterprise, failing to recognize that the company had promised more than it could deliver to all interested parties.

The long-term transformation of the American economy in the nineteenth century created similar enormous but difficult to evaluate opportunities for profit. It is not surprising then that in 1873 a crisis occurred in railroad securities. The railroads, which had previously provided integrated systems for local or at best regional transportation, were being forged into a nationwide network. There appeared to be profits available for anyone willing to invest in railroad securities, but it was impossible for investors to have a very precise idea about what the future earnings or dividend payments of the railroad would be. It was a change that was outside anyone's experience.

The boom and bust of the 1920s offer the clearest parallels with the events of the 1980s. The economy of the 1920s underwent major structural changes. New industries using new technologies became the leading sectors, and the system of industrial finance was wholly changed. Confidence in prosperity based on these new industries was not misplaced, but there was no past experience to evaluate the profitability of emergent companies, such as General Motors or RCA. Parallel to the unification of the railroads in the 19th century, utilities in the 1920s were combining to create regional and national networks. This was another immense advance, but one whose success was hard to measure. Speculation was centered in these securities whose fundamentals were not well defined.

Although we do not have the benefit of several decades or centuries of hindsight, the changes occurring in the American economy of the 1980s bear a strong resemblance to the changes of the 1920s. There has been a structural change in many industries, and new ones have come into prominence. Furthermore, the method of financing business has changed, although the reasons for this development are still somewhat opaque. Given these developments, it was probably difficult to evaluate the fundamentals of stocks in new industries or ones in the process of change. The uncertain profit opportunities were a boon to speculation.

Another feature of asset bubbles is the appearance of new, apparently inexperienced investors. Attracted by the new and, perhaps, rich opportunities, they flock to the markets. Their less than fully informed participation appears to help drive up prices above what is warranted by fundamentals.

During the tulipmania, Garber notes that the middle classes and even monied workers began to speculate in the market for tulips, which previously had been the province of specialists. In their enthusiasm to participate, new investors seem incredibly incautious. During the South Sea Bubble, annuitants swarmed to exchange their government securities for South Sea stock. They entered their names in the company's registers but did not trouble themselves to read the preamble which allowed the clerks to determine the terms of exchange. In 1873, new German investors played a prominent role. They busily acquired new, untested foreign securities for their portfolios.

In the 1920s the shift in business financing from short-term commercial bank loans to bonds and stocks meant that instead of commercial banks who had considerable experience in evaluating firms, the general investing public became the chief creditors of corporations. Americans who had never owned stocks before were now buying. Given the increased difficulty of evaluating fundamentals and the general optimism from the decade of prosperity, it is not surprising that prices were pushed above fundamentals. Similarly in the 1980s, new financial instruments and markets drew in new investors from both at home and abroad.

One feature of stock market crashes that has deeply worried market participants and regulators is the extreme volatility associated with the collapse of prices. The general fear is that this volatility may be a cause of crashes. This turbulent behavior has been attributed to the activities of large traders or new markets. However, as Jones, Sylla, and Wilson have shown for the whole history of American securities markets, volatility does not appear to be a cause of stock market crashes. The timing for the rise in volatility is wrong for it to be a contributing factor. Before any stock market crash, be it in the 19th century, 1929, or 1987, volatility does not appear to be abnormal. Volatility only rises after the crash.

The reasons for this seem fairly straightfoward. When prices fall, they do not immediately reach a level consistent with fundamentals. Optimistic expectations have evaporated, but expectations remain diffuse, highly sensitive to good and bad economic reports. Additionally, many of the investers who had recently entered the market have exited and the markets have become noticeably thinner. However, eventually the securities markets settle down as expectations about fundamentals become more focused and the public adjusts to new economic conditions.

The one exception that proves the rule about post-crash volatility is 1929. After the October 1929 plunge in the stock market, volatility rose and then increased to even higher levels. This behavior was a response to the deepening depression of 1930–33. Volatility continued to climb because of the increasing uncertainty about economic conditions. The economy was deteriorating in a way which was outside of anyone's experience.

Volatility after 1987 rose but has now fallen back to near pre-crash levels. Although pundits and regulators have been greatly concerned with the high level of volatility, a historical perspective shows it to be a consequence rather than a cause of the plunge in the stock market.

While recent financial developments cannot be held accountable for the crash and increased volatility, it is true that many of the market mechanisms do not perform well. But this is also a common feature of other crashes. In a crash, prices drop so rapidly that the mechanisms for disseminating information about current prices are overwhelmed. This is, of course, one of the features of a crash that understandably angers the public.

During the last stages of the South Sea bubble the means for transferring stock were not operating well, as the transfer books were closed to enable payment of the dividend. In the nineteenth century during American stock market crises, the ticker tape always ran late. In spite of the efforts to improve the ticker's performance, it was impossible to ensure that it would run fast enough during the next financial crisis. This was dramatically true in October 1929 and in October 1987.

Investors in all these episodes could not know with any precision at what prices their orders would be executed. In addition, the lack of current quotes created anxiety about the actual prices. Possessed only of late information that prices had dropped significantly, it is not surprising that panic selling occurred. When prices begin to move back towards fundamentals, the drop might not be so frightening, if the mechanisms for disseminating price information did not break down. However, given the continued growth in the size of financial markets, there is good reason to doubt that when the next bubble collapses price information will be kept current.

The broadly similar characteristics of the various booms and crashes explored in this conference suggest that they are not unique events. If they are similar, is there a pattern that will permit the identification of a boom before it a crashes and allow some corrective action to be taken?

The key, here, is what is the cause of a bubble. What I have argued is that bubbles arise when the underlying fundamentals become more diffuse and difficult to predict. This may happen for several reasons. The tulipmania appears to have been the result of a lack of good information on how these flowers reproduce. The South Sea bubble was the consequence of uncertain gains from increased liquidity of government securities coupled with officially condoned manipulation.

Closer in time the American stock market booms seem to have been the product of technological change and major sectoral shifts in the economy. An attempt to prevent a boom, either by imposing regulations on some market participants or markets, targets only the characteristics of the last boom and is misdirected. Worse yet, efforts to contain a boom may backfire spectacularly. The attempts by the Federal Reserve in the 1920s to dampen speculation in the stock market deterred it from the mission of maintaining price and income stability. So distracted did the Federal Reserve become that its tight money policy, aimed at the stock market, contributed to the onset of the depression. In hindsight, there should have been no reason for the Federal Reserve to worry, for when there was no central bank in the nineteenth century, stock market crashes happened but they were not necessarily followed by recessions.

If stock market bubbles are, for the most part, a reflection and reaction to underlying changes in the economy, then the correct policy is simply to let them run their course, however distressing this may be to individual investors. Any attempt to prevent bubbles and ensuing crashes requires an undesirable effort to rein in the technological and industrial transformations that are central to long-run economic growth.

ROUNDTABLE DISCUSSION

HISTORICAL PERSPECTIVE AND PROPOSED CHANGES

Franklin R. Edwards

We have been treated today in enlightening and intellectually stimulating historical analyses of prior speculative price bubbles (or manias). We are not, however, any closer to identifying and agreeing on the key factors responsible for the 1987 stock market crash.

The broad historical perspective taken by participants in this conference suggests that we may be focusing too narrowly in our effort to identify what happened in 1987. Speculative bubbles and subsequent market collapses have occurred often in the past, in the context of many different institutional structures. Efforts to understand these episodes rely heavily on distant hindsight to identify key events of the day. When market collapses are viewed in this perspective, a particular institutional or structure defect is seldom seen as playing a major role. As time passes the importance attached to structural details pales against the significance of other economic and political events.

What will the 1987 stock market crash look like to scholars 50 years hence? Will they point to the critical role of portfolio insurance, or to index arbitrage, or to the existence of equity futures and options markets? It seems doubtful. If today's conference is any indication, tomorrow's scholars will center their attention on why stock prices rose so much in 1986–87, and on the importance of government deficits, trade imbalances, and other fundamental economic factors. Today's preoccupation with institutional particularities as explanations of the October 1987 crash will recede into the background.

In the meantime, we are faced with the question of whether to change the current institutional structure in response to criticisms stemming from the 1987 crash. These criticisms and the associated policy proposals fall into two categories: proposals to curb trading that is perceived as harmful (speculative trading, large institutional trading, index arbitrage, and so forth); and proposals to shore up the present market-making system so that it is not as vulnerable to the type of trading that is prevalent today.

Examples of the first category are proposals to raise margins and to impose inhibiting taxes on short-term trading, presumably to reduce destabilizing speculative trading. Proposals that fall into the system-preserving category are circuit-breakers, "sunshine" trading, and limits on index arbitrage and other large, concentrated institutional trading. The latter seek to enhance market liquidity by protecting market-makers from having to provide "immediacy" in the face of large order imbalances.

I have analyzed many of these proposals elsewhere and have reached two general conclusions. First, neither economic theory nor statistical evidence provide support for proposals directed at curbing so-called "speculative" trading. There is no reason to believe that any of the proposed interventions can efffectively limit harmful speculative trading, and their potential for harming markets is significant. Second, proposals to shore up the present market-making system are both myopic and counterproductive. The evidence is reasonably clear that in the not-too-distant future we may need to alter the present market structure in several ways. Trading must be placed on a global footing, and large institutional traders will have to be given greater flexibility and alternatives to facilitate trading with each other. Rather than attempting to preserve the systems already in place, we should be thinking of ways to adapt these systems to new international and trading realities, and to the kinds of customers and trading we will have in the future.

Finally, an aspect of the recent stock market crash which was not explored at today's conference is its broad international scope. Markets in every country of the world collapsed in unison in October, despite the existence of quite different institutional structures among countries. In particular, outside of the United States there were no significant stock index futures markets, no portfolio insurance trading, and virtually no stock index arbitrage trading. Yet, markets in all countries collapsed. Is this evidence that institutional factors unique to the United States could not have been responsible for the crash, or does it demonstrate that effects in U.S. markets are immediately transmitted to all markets around the world? If it is the latter, a new dimension of market collapses may be upon us, the ramifications of which deserve careful attention by scholars, practitioners, and regulators.

The recent crash has raised our consciousness about many aspects of both our economy and our financial system. Much has been learned and many changes have been made. This conference visibly reminds us that it is utopian to think that we can legislate or regulate crashes and panics out of existence. No one cares more about the sanctity of markets than those who rely on them every day for their livelihood. In the complex markets we have today, well-intentioned regulatory intervention can result in unforeseen detrimental effects. Unless the evil is obvious and the remedy clear, caution should guide our action.

ROUNDTABLE DISCUSSION

1929 AND 1987—PARALLELS AND CONTRASTS

Barry J. Eichengreen

With the passage of a year, the parallels between the Great Crash of 1929 and the Great Correction of 1987 are more striking than ever. In what follows I will note several of those parallels before focusing on one very important difference.

Both episodes underscore the futility of seeking to identify a single cause of a stock market crash. In both cases the most popular explanation was also the most tautological: that prices fell because they had reached unsustainably high levels immediately before.

At a deeper level, whatever set off either collapse must have been international in scope. In 1929, due to England's Hatry bankruptcy and increasingly high European interest rates, foreign markets had already begun to show signs of weakness in advance of the Wall Street crash. In 1987 foreign markets broke in advance of New York. In neither case is it plausible that the explanation for these events rests entirely with developments in the United States.

In both instances the difficulty of identifying a cause led to a search for scapegoats. Unprecedentedly large institutional traders (investment trusts in 1929, mutual funds in 1987) were blamed for destabilizing the market. Certain classes of investors (short sellers like Jesse Livermore in 1929, program traders in 1987) were accused of singlehandedly undermining the market, without any acknowledgment that they accounted for only a small fraction of transactions.

Whatever the disturbance that sparked the price decline, mechanical trading strategies well may have served as the accelerant. Here on cannot but be impressed by the analogy between margin trading and portfolio insurance. In 1929, even a moderate decline in prices dictated margin calls for investors who had purchased shares on credit. Forced liquidation of the holdings of margin traders led to a further imbalance between buyers and sellers and to a further decline in prices. Other traders scrambled to get out first, setting off a self-reinforcing spiral.

The analogy with portfolio insurance is apparent. Portfolio insurers tend to sell in a declining market to cut losses. Knowing that, other traders will try to beat them by getting out first. By exacerbating the market decline, their actions automatically induce more sales by portfolio insurers, which provoke more anticipatory sales by other traders. The relevance of portfolio insurance, then, may lie not in the volume of transactions in which insurers engage but in the incentives it creates for other traders to react in certain ways.

Academic research has not resolved the question of whether this kind of behavior can bring about more than a small increase in the volatility of asset prices in an otherwise efficient market. According to some studies, incomplete information is required for there to be a large increase in market volatility due to the actions of a small minority of portfolio insurers. (A small volume of sales by portfolio insurers may lead to a dramatic reaction by other traders if, for example, the latter suspect rightly or wrongly that portfolio insurers have superior access to information, or even when they do not know the source of the sales but take them as a signal that new information not available to them has been received by other traders.) For those skeptical of the efficiency of financial markets, this debate is beside the point. But whatever one's view, it is dangerously misleading to refer interchangeably to "larger trader" and "portfolio insurance" theories of the crash.

Both crashes lay bare the difficulty of making a market. Brokers normally take for granted their ability to match buyers with sellers. Buyers and sellers take for granted the accuracy and timeliness of information. But in both 1929 and 1987 the fragility of these relationships was revealed. Buyers and sellers had no idea of current transaction prices for extended periods of time. Shareholders continued to place orders on the basis of outdated information. There were substantial intervals where no buyers could be found to pair with sellers. However efficient the market under normal conditions, both episodes illustrate its susceptibility to breakdown under exceptional circumstances.

In both 1929 and 1987 there was an attempt to paper over these difficulties through organized support. In 1929, in a failed effort to restore confidence, Richard Whitney purchased key securities on behalf of a syndicate of bankers. In 1987 a number of leading corporations repurchased large blocks of their own shares. However reassuring such intervention, both episodes reveal the futility of a few large traders attempting to swim against the tide.

Given the extent of the parallels, the contrasting economic aftermaths of the two crises are all the more remarkable. One popular explanation for the stability of the economy in the last 12 months is that the October 1987 crash wiped out what was no more than a transitory gain in wealth. Although the crash destroyed as much as $1 trillion in stock market wealth, the Dow Jones Industrial Average ended 1987 more or less where it began the year. If speculators knew they were riding a bubble, they had little reason to raise their spending during the boom or reduce it following the crash. And given the stability of consumer spending, investors had little reason to alter their plans.

As an explanation for the contrast between 1930 and 1988, this argument is difficult to sustain. Many of the gains of the 1920s bull market were equally transitory. Between April 1928 and September 1929, the Dow rose by nearly 50 percent. Perhaps consumers failed to recognize the transitory nature of the rise. But only analysts with a taste for paradox can comfortably argue that consumers were rational enough to recognize the market's irrationality—and by implication their own collective irrationality—in 1987 but not in 1929.

Perhaps the difference lies with the Federal Reserve, whose rapid response last October has been the subject of universal acclaim. Pumping up the monetary base at an annual rate of 40 percent in the two weeks just after the crash was decisive action. What is less well known is that in the month immediately following the 1929 crash, Federal Reserve credit rose even more rapidly than in 1987, largely as a result of aggressive intervention on the part of the Federal Reserve Bank of New York. This is not to deny the Federal Reverse's subsequent failure to maintain monetary stability during the Great Depression. But with expansionary open market operations continuing into 1930, the contrast between Federal Reserve policy in the immediate aftermath of the two crises can be overdrawn.

Probably the crucial difference between the two episodes was the state of the economy immediately preceding the crash. In the first nine months of 1987, spending was strong. In October 1929, in contrast, a full-blown recession was already under way. Indicators of economic activity had been falling since the summer of that year. Hence the 1929 crash reinforced other signals. With unemployment rising, the consumer already had reason for caution. With sales declining, investment was already depressed. The crash therefore served to reinforce managers' inclination to cancel investment plans. In 1987, in contrast, the stock market and other indicators emitted conflicting signals. Although households still had reason to retrench, with the leading indicators pointing in divergent directions, consumers hedged their bets. After dropping in October, personal consumption recovered quickly. The relatively strong economy could easily absorb such a short-lived dip in household spending.

The lesson to be drawn from the 1987 crash, then, is not that the stock market is irrelevant to economic activity. Rather, it is that a financial panic can have a much more devastating impact on a declining economy than on an expanding one. Historically, panics have followed the beginning of economic downturns at least as often as they have preceded them. If the order of events is reversed the next time around, there will be good reason to worry about the impact of the crash.

ROUNDTABLE DISCUSSION

THE ACHILLES HEEL OF THE FINANCIAL SECTOR: A COMMENT ON THE CRASH

William L. Silber

Whether gyrations in stock prices are rational or not is a much more enticing question than whether people will ultimately pay for the securities they buy. Nevertheless, the second problem is the one that threatened the integrity of the financial system during October 1987, not the first. It is not well documented that on October 20 a number of clearing firms associated with the nation's futures exchanges were threatened with bankruptcy.[1] Moreover, there were many who were concerned that securities purchased on the 19th would not be settled properly five days later. Were it not for courageous action by the Federal Reserve in its capacity as lender of last resort, financial obligations that most market participants take for granted would have gone unfulfilled. If that had occurred, the implicit trust that underlies most financial transactions would have disappeared and the financial sector as we know it would have ceased to function.

Although the clearing systems used for settling financial transactions have been discussed in the various reports on the October crash,[2] few have made it the focal point of attention.[3] In fact, clearinghouses and clearing systems have always been at the center of financial panics in the past and are likely to be similarly situated in the future. In the old days,[4] bank clearinghouses issued clearinghouse loan certificates that often succeeded in stemming the spread of financial panic. Bank clearinghouses could accomplish this objective because they played a central role in the payments system. But the clearinghouses associated with futures markets, stock markets, and options markets do not have that characteristic. They must rely on others, most notably the Federal Reserve System, to come to the rescue.

Will the Federal Reserve always be there to insure that payments are made as promised? Although that may be part of the Fed's mandate, there are times when the Federal Reserve may be distracted by competing goals, such as promoting exchange rate stability or fighting inflationary sentiment. Although such distracting concerns fell by the wayside in October 1987, it is quite possible that this will not always be the case.

More importantly, there may be occasions when the Federal Reserve's role of lender of last resort will be insufficient to guarantee payments as promised. Foreign participation in U.S. financial markets has expanded to the point that may require not just a domestic lender of last resort, but an international lender of last resort. Foreigners are likely to demand payments not just in dollars, but in their own currencies. Although the Fed can accommodate the need for dollars without restriction, it cannot do the same for *marks* and *yen.* That requires either an international lender of last resort or close coordination among the central banks in the industrialized world. The late Henry Wallach, a wise central banker and first-rate economist, suggested as early as 1976 that such action would be necessary as the globalization of commerce increased.[5] At this point it seems that the internationalization of financial transactions, along with the increased volatility of securities prices, will require significant concerted action to prevent the next crash from turning into a life-threatening disaster for the financial system.

NOTES

1. See James Stewart and Daniel Hertzberg, "How the Stock Market Almost Disintegrated After the Crash," *The Wall Street Journal,* November 20, 1987.
2. See, for example, *Report of the Presidential Task Force on Market Mechanisms,* January 1988.
3. For an exception, see W. Silber, "Sources of Financial Fragility," *Investment Management Review,* January/February 1988.
4. See Jack Wilson, Richard Sylla, and Charles Jones, Chapter 4, this volume.
5. See Henry Wallach, "Central Banks as Regulators and Lenders of Last Resort in an International Context," in *Key Issues in International Banking,* Federal Reserve Bank of Boston, 1977.

INDEX